Legacies of Lynching

Legacies of Lynching

RACIAL VIOLENCE AND MEMORY

Jonathan Markovitz

 University of Minnesota Press || Minneapolis | London

A previous version of chapter 3 was published as "Collective Memory, Credibility Structures, and the Case of Tawana Brawley," *Discourse* 22, no. 1 (2000): 31–52.

Published by the University of Minnesota Press
111 Third Avenue South, Suite 290
Minneapolis, MN 55401-2520
http://www.upress.umn.edu

Library of Congress Cataloging-in-Publication Data

Markovitz, Jonathan.
    Legacies of lynching : racial violence and memory / Jonathan Markovitz.
        p.   cm.
    Includes bibliographical references and index.
    ISBN 0-8166-3994-9 (hard : alk. paper) — ISBN 0-8166-3995-7 (pbk. : alk. paper)
        1. Lynching—United States.   2. United States—Race relations.
    3. African Americans—Violence against.   I. Title.
    HV6464.M37 2004
    364.1'34—dc22
                                                                    2004001457

Printed in the United States of America on acid-free paper

The University of Minnesota is an equal-opportunity educator and employer.

12 11 10 09 08 07 06 05 04   10 9 8 7 6 5 4 3 2 1

F OR MY PARENTS

Contents

ix   Acknowledgments

xv   Introduction: On Memory and Meaning

1   1. Antilynching and the Struggle for Meaning

33   2. Cinematic Lynchings

69   3. Lynching as Lens: Contemporary Racialized Violence

111   4. The Hill–Thomas Hearings and the Meaning of a "High-Tech Lynching"

137   Conclusion: Not Just Memory

149   Notes

203   Works Cited

217   Index

Acknowledgments

When I started this project in the early 1990s, I never could have imagined the directions it would take me or how much of my life I would devote to it. I would never have completed the book if not for the friendship and support of people too numerous to name. I can't thank everyone who has helped me, but some people deserve special consideration.

This book grew out of my dissertation at the University of California, San Diego, and I would like to acknowledge the support and assistance of my doctoral committee. As the chair of my committee, Bennetta Jules-Rosette could always be counted on for rigorous criticism and guidance, and she has followed the project closely from its inception. Her research group on the Study of Art, Culture, and Knowledge provides a crucial interdisciplinary forum at UCSD for scholars to receive feedback on their work at formative stages, and my work has benefited immeasurably through participation in this group. Steven Epstein was a careful reader of my work from its earliest stages and provided detailed comments for every chapter; the book is considerably stronger as a result. Stephen Cornell provided important feedback and encouraged me not only to consider the explicitly political stakes in struggles over collective memory but also to address the importance of the relationship between collective memory and identity formation. Rosaura Sánchez helped me to more fully examine what it meant to take the lynching metaphor out of its original context and to understand what made it possible for Clarence Thomas to gain political mileage by referring to himself as a lynching victim while facing the spotlights of the media rather than the angry glares of the mob. George Lipsitz was a careful reader and offered suggestions and guidance that allowed me to address the limited malleability of metaphors and the possibilities for reconstructing collective memory. Judith Halberstam was on my committee in the project's earliest stages, and she forced me to question my initial understandings of the Hill–Thomas hearings in useful ways. Marita Sturken was not a formal member of my committee, but she provided invaluable assistance helping me to think about collective memory.

My research informs my teaching, and my writing has benefited from the opportunity to discuss my work with students in a variety of courses in the sociology department and the Muir College Writing Program at UCSD. I thank Jo Rudolph, Dee-Dee Higgins, and the rest of the staff of the sociology department for helping me navigate the UCSD bureaucracy. In the Muir College Writing Program, Barbara Tomlinson helped me to learn about teaching as a craft, while Cindy Dupray has always been available to discuss teaching issues and has become a valued friend.

I first became interested in sociology as an undergraduate at Brandeis University. Professors Gordie Fellman, Maurie Stein, Morrie Schwartz, and Jacqui Alexander helped me decide that I wanted to become a sociologist. Their work and teaching informs my own in many ways.

I relied on the support of a network of friends to complete this book. I'd like to thank Lisa Askenazy, Julie Berman, David Cutler, Bart Garry, Alexandra Halkias, Douglas Krassnoff, Miles Liss, Susan Markens, Marni Port, Kevin Reardon, and David Weinstein for long conversations, escapes, laughter, and commiseration. Alexandra Halkias and David Weinstein were important editors, gave crucial assistance for thinking through the complexities of the issues that I wanted to address, and encouraged me to keep moving whenever I reached an impasse.

Christie Photinos has been a constant source of intellectual and emotional support over the past five years. I have lost track of the number of times that she has edited portions of the manuscript. I might have completed the book without her, but it would have been a considerably more difficult and solitary process.

I had the opportunity to develop parts of this book as a fellow in a

National Endowment for the Humanities (NEH) Institute on Black Film Studies organized by Gladstone Yearwood and Mark Reid at the University of Central Florida during the summer of 1999. The institute brought together a wonderful and warm group of scholars in an environment unlike any other I have been exposed to in academia. United in our efforts to survive the extreme temperatures of an Orlando August (ranging from the sweltering heat on the summer streets to the arctic chill of the air-conditioned screening room on the UCF campus), every single participant worked to make the experience as intellectually stimulating and fulfilling as possible. My thanks to Gladstone and Mark for organizing the institute and to all of the participants, but especially to Kimberly Brown, Anne Carroll, Phyllis Jackson, Paula Massood, and John Williams.

Carrie Mullen, my editor, has been steadfast in her commitment to this project for the past several years. Her efforts to protect the manuscript and to usher me through the publication process with a minimum of frustration have been greatly appreciated. The rest of the editorial staff at the University of Minnesota Press, including Robin Moir, Anna Pakarinen, and Jason Weidemann, have also worked to make the process as straightforward as possible. Kathy Delfosse's copyediting was thorough, graceful, and highly valued. I am extremely grateful to S. Craig Watkins, W. Fitzhugh Brundage, and Valerie Smith for their generous, rigorous, and insightful reviews of earlier versions of the manuscript, and to Carrie Mullen and the rest of the editorial staff for tracking down such wonderful reviewers. Fitz Brundage, whose work provides much of the historical foundation for my own, has remained extremely supportive of the project. He put me in contact with Jane Gaines, who offered important and much-appreciated feedback on my film chapter. I also thank Raphael Allen and the outside reviewer from Duke University Press, both of whom were enthusiastic supporters of the book when I first started to consider publication.

I have presented parts of this book at a variety of academic conferences, including annual meetings of the American Sociological Association and the Pacific Sociological Association and, most important, at the first national conference on lynching in America, "Lynching and Racial Violence in America: Histories and Legacies," which was held in Atlanta in the fall of 2002. The organizers, panelists, and audience members at all of these conferences offered invaluable feedback, while the participants in the lynching and racial violence conference made me think of myself and this project as belonging to an academic community in ways I had not considered before.

I try to acknowledge my intellectual debts as thoroughly as possible in the pages that follow, but I would like to single out a handful of writers whose importance to my own understanding of race, gender, and representation cannot be adequately expressed in a note. These include Teshome Gabriel, Jacqueline Goldsby, Jacquelyn Dowd Hall, Stuart Hall, Trudier Harris, bell hooks, Iwona Irwin-Zarecka, Emma Coleman Jordan, Michael Omi, Patricia Williams, and Howard Winant. Ida B. Wells set the standard for lynching scholarship more than a century ago, and her work remains an inspiration in many ways. This book was more directly inspired by Anita Hill's courageous testimony during the hearings to confirm Clarence Thomas as an associate justice on the U.S. Supreme Court. Hill's writings since the hearings have played an important role in shaping my own thoughts about lynching and collective memory. I hope that my admiration for her comes through clearly in my chapter on the Hill–Thomas hearings and that my work does her justice.

Pat Ward Williams generously allowed me to include a reproduction of her work *Accused/Padlock/Blowtorch* in chapter 4. Mel Chin allowed me to include a reproduction of his work *Night Rap* in chapter 2 and provided me with his own interpretation of the work while encouraging alternative analyses. Jim Allen and the Special Collections Department of the Robert W. Woodruff Library at Emory University gave permission for reproductions of several lynching photographs in this book. The National Association for the Advancement of Colored People (NAACP) gave me permission to include several photographs from the collection of visual materials from the NAACP at the Library of Congress, and the staff at the Library of Congress Prints and Photographs division helped me to obtain reproductions of those images; I am very grateful for the permissions. Thanks, too, to James Huffman and the staff at the Photographs and Prints Division at the Schomburg Center for Research in Black Culture for their help in tracking down photographs.

I would like to thank my family for their unwavering support over the years. There were times when I did not know if I would ever complete this project. I can't believe they didn't harbor similar doubts, but if they did, they never let them show. The pleasure that my aunts, uncles, and cousins have taken in my accomplishments has always shone through and has been a source of great encouragement for me. My sister has always been interested in my work, and I have always known that I could count on her for anything. My parents have been enthusiastic readers and editors of my work, and their comments have always been helpful and encouraging, even when I chose not to heed them. Beyond that, I owe much of my love of learning and of language to them. The few puns in this book are, shameful as it ought to be to admit, points of particular pride and part of a family tradition. (I suspect at least one of my parents would prefer not to receive credit for passing on that tradition.) Both of my parents have provided important lessons about what matters in life, and many of the concerns that are addressed in this book reflect those lessons. This book is dedicated to them.

On Memory and Meaning

I n an effort to defeat the Dyer Anti-Lynching Bill in the 1921–22 congressional session, Representative Thomas Sisson from Mississippi declared that he "would rather the whole black race of this world were lynched than for one of the fair daughters of the South to be ravished and torn by one of these black brutes." House Minority Leader Finis Garrett agreed, arguing that the bill should be retitled "A bill to encourage rape."[1] Seventy years later, Clarence Thomas denounced the investigation by the Senate Judiciary Committee into allegations that he had sexually harassed Anita Hill by calling it a "high-tech lynching for uppity blacks who in any way deign to think for themselves, to do for themselves, to have different ideas," claiming that the hearings were "a message that, unless you kow-tow to an old order, this is what will happen to you, you will be lynched, destroyed, caricatured by a committee of the U.S. Senate, rather than hung from a tree."[2] When asked to elaborate, Thomas drew attention to a history of "the lynchings of black men" that shows that "there is invariably, or in many instances, a relationship with sex, and an accusation that that person cannot shake off." Thomas went on to say that he could not "shake off these accusations, because they play to the worst stereotypes we have about black men in this country."[3] This book attempts to explain the gulf that separates these speeches as it examines the struggles over meaning and memory that account for the evolution of a metaphor.

Lynching was always intended as a metaphor for, or a way to understand, race relations. While there were many different types of lynchings, lynch mobs typically worked to ensure that black audiences were aware of the strength of white supremacy and the costs of violating the boundaries of the racial order; at the same time, they wanted to reinforce images of white men as chivalrous protectors of white women. As I argue in chapter 1, the antilynching movement in the late nineteenth and early twentieth centuries forwarded an alternative set of meanings by arguing that lynchings were barbaric spectacles that provided evidence that white supremacy could only be maintained through the use of terrorist tactics that were justified by reference to viciously racist stereotypes of black men. Representatives Sisson and Garrett clearly relied upon the first set of meanings, while Thomas invoked the second. More accurately, each of the speakers relied upon various aspects of competing "common sense" understandings of lynching while ignoring other facets of the dynamics of lynching.

In their efforts to defeat antilynching legislation, it was important for Sisson and Garrett to claim that lynching was necessary to prevent rape, but they had no interest in suggesting that lynching provided evidence of the strength of white supremacy. Thomas's reference to lynching relied upon the antilynching movement's understandings of stereotypes and spectacle, but it divorced the notion of "an old order" from any concrete policies or programs that disproportionately affect African Americans. The most glaring difference between Thomas's reference to lynching and the antilynching movement's understanding of the same term is that by the time of Thomas's testimony, it had become possible to understand lynching as a phenomenon that could be confined to the realm of speech and politics and that did not necessarily involve the literal killing of a human being. I have only touched upon some of the differences between Thomas's use of the lynching metaphor and the understandings of lynching that were put forward by activists who were struggling to eradicate mob violence.[4] Even this cursory discussion should suffice, however, to establish that the meanings associated with lynchings have shifted in complicated ways over time.

I noted that apologists for lynching, and lynch mobs themselves, relied upon understandings of lynching that directly competed with the understandings put forward by the antilynching movement and invoked by Thomas. In fact, the contest is largely over, and the antilynching movement's understanding has won out. By 1991, Thomas could count on the fact that lynching had lost all of its publicly visible defenders and that his audiences would recognize that lynching was, as Charles R. Lawrence III says, the "most vivid symbol of racial oppression."[5] While Thomas needed to explain that lynching was justified via sexualized stereotypes of black men, it was clear that no one would contest his argument by claiming that lynching really did punish black rapists.[6] Lynching has become, as Wahneema Lubiano says of the relationship between women on welfare and black urban "pathology," a synecdoche, or the "shortest possible shorthand" for racism.[7] This book is concerned with the ways in which the lynching metaphor has acquired its meaning and has resurfaced, changed, and been deployed over time. I examine collective memories of lynching and attempt to explain how lynching became the "most vivid symbol" of racism, how exactly this symbol is understood, and what it means to subsume racism in its entirety under this one image. Most importantly, I argue that collective memories of lynching are intricately linked to understandings of a variety of racial categories and that the ways in which we remember lynching therefore help to shape the possibilities for contemporary racial politics.

The Metaphorization of Lynching

I examine lynching first as a material practice that was enacted primarily upon the bodies of black men and that was a central characteristic of race relations in the southern United States during the period that roughly spans the years 1880–1930. The definition of lynching in this sense of the term has been the subject of extended debate, but the most widely accepted definition was agreed upon by a meeting of antilynching leaders in 1940. According to this definition, the characteristics of a lynching are that "there must be legal evidence that a person has been killed and that he met his death illegally at the hands of a group acting under the pretext of service to justice, race or tradition."[8] I argue, though, that even during the years when lynching rates were at their peak, lynchings were never entirely confined to the physical realm and were instead always intended to be seen as a metaphor for race relations more broadly defined.

My argument that lynching has always been a metaphor is based on the definition of metaphor as "a device for seeing something *in terms of* something else."[9] While there were a variety of different types of lynching, lynchings in general, and public defenses of lynchings, were meant to provide a lens through which to view southern race relations.

They were really meant to be seen as a particular type of metaphor, a metonym, since seeing southern race relations in terms of lynching entailed "the reduction of the whole to the part."[10] But if lynchings could be seen as a microcosm of southern race relations, something was lost in the process of reduction. The vision that lynchings provided of southern society was inevitably partial, and the particular aspects of southern race relations that were meant to be invoked by lynching or by references to lynching were the subject of heated battle. I argue, in chapter 1, that both the antilynching movement and lynch mobs themselves were engaged in a struggle over how lynching would be understood and remembered and that our contemporary understandings of lynching owe much to these battles of the past.

In the past half century, as lynching has largely faded away as a material practice, lynching has become a metaphor in the more familiar sense: It is now possible to see lynching primarily as a figure of speech. While actual lynchings worked to provide lessons about the nature of southern society, the trope of lynching has been used to make implicit comparisons between the nature of particularly contentious events in the contemporary United States and what is now widely understood to be an exceptionally horrific part of our national past. Continuing struggles over the meaning of lynching as a metaphor highlight the political stakes in the process of metaphorization.[11] These stakes have come out quite clearly in several recent highly spectacularized political dramas. The metaphor of lynching has been invoked in a variety of arenas and for a wide range of purposes. Kenneth Burke's analysis of metaphors is useful here. Burke argues that

> [l]anguage develops by metaphorical extension, in borrowing words from the realm of the corporeal, visible, tangible and applying them by analogy to the realm of the incorporeal, invisible, intangible; then, in the course of time, the original corporeal reference is forgotten, and only the incorporeal, metaphorical extension survives . . . often because the very conditions of living that reminded one of the corporeal reference have so altered that the cross reference no longer exists with nearly the same degree of apparentness in the "objective situation" itself.[12]

This analysis is particularly appropriate for an understanding of contemporary invocations of lynching. The metaphor of lynching is extremely, though not infinitely, malleable and has been applied to situations that at first glance seem very distant from the historical phenomenon of racially based mob violence. Throughout the chapters on cinematic lynching, contemporary racialized violence, and the Hill–Thomas hearings, I examine the metaphor of lynching. I consider what it means to borrow language that was, in a previous era, inseparably connected to racist violence that was not only visible and tangible but also highly spectacularized, and to apply that language and associated imagery to a variety of contemporary dramas. We have not yet reached the point where, as Burke says, "the original corporeal reference is forgotten," but the very process of remembering lynching and of using those memories to help shape our understanding of the present are highly complex matters that are intimately linked to ongoing processes of national racial formation and "common sense" understandings of race.

Racial Formation and Common Sense

Michael Omi and Howard Winant understand race as "an unstable and 'decentered' complex of social meanings constantly being transformed by political struggle."[13] Their term "racial formation" addresses "the sociohistorical process by which racial categories are created, inhabited, transformed, and destroyed."[14] The notion of racial formation is indebted to Antonio Gramsci's discussion of "common sense." Gramsci argued that ruling groups consolidate and maintain their hegemony by putting forward a system of ideology that attempts to construct the most basic, taken-for-granted, or "common sense" assumptions about social life and to mobilize them in an effort to support the existing social order. "Racial formation" is a term that is meant to index the ways that racial categories become part of common sense. There are serious stakes involved in the struggle over common sense conceptions of the world, since any form of political opposition must be based upon the "refusal of the 'common sense' understandings which the hegemonic order imposes."[15] Common sense conceptions of race and racism provide the ideological foundations for the racial status quo, and antiracist movements therefore have a particularly pressing need to undermine their stability.

The idea that common sense is strictly imposed from above as a product of elite efforts to maintain hegemony is, however, somewhat of a departure from Gramsci's conception of the term. For Gramsci, hegemony is never complete, and common sense is therefore always open to contest. It is "fragmentary and contradictory," a "product of history," which contains traces of all of the struggles that have produced it.[16] Rather than refusing all common sense understandings of race, then, it becomes possible to see that at any given moment, there are competing common sense understandings of race in circulation and that some of them can be mobilized for antiracist purposes. This does not minimize the seriousness of the struggle over which conceptions of common sense will win out. Common sense is important because it "is the terrain of conceptions and categories on which the practical consciousness of the masses of the people is actually formed."[17] Anyone who wants to challenge existing social structures and practices must struggle against the systems of thought that legitimate and enable those structures and practices. Movements for social change are therefore contingent upon struggles over common sense.

As this discussion suggests, the fact that racial categories have no essential qualities and are instead socially constructed through political struggles does not make them any less real or meaningful. Rather, race is "a matter of both social structure and cultural representation,"[18] and racial categories have material repercussions for the ways that our daily lives are organized. In order to discuss the stakes of racial classifications, Omi and Winant use the term "racial project," by which they mean "simultaneously an interpretation, representation, or explanation of racial dynamics, and an effort to reorganize and redistribute resources along particular racial lines."[19] Racial projects, such as calls for welfare reform, attacks on affirmative action, and investigations into racially based employment discrimination, link the meanings of racial categories with the organization of social structures and everyday life. Lynching was itself a racial project that often linked punishment for violations of a racial order with conceptions of criminal and sexually monstrous black men, and collective memories of lynching have been enlisted in a variety of more recent racial projects.

Collective Memory and Lynching

While racial categories are in a state of constant flux, they are not constantly re-created from scratch. Instead, our understandings of race are based on cultural and political struggles of the past and the present. Anti-black mob violence and the struggle over the meaning of lynchings continue to play important roles in our understandings of race and racism. In the chapters that follow, I argue not only that lynching has become a metaphor for racism but also that the dynamics of lynching worked to construct basic ways of conceptualizing the world that are still relevant today: Lynchings have provided a "lens," or a way of seeing and understanding contemporary race relations and racial spectacles.

Thus, on the one hand, social actors like Thomas explicitly conjure up memories of mob violence by relying on lynching as a metaphor in order to suggest that particular contemporary political dramas should be assessed in light of our historical understandings of racial injustice. But because lynch mobs and the antilynching movement were actively engaged in racial projects that fundamentally altered the meaning of various racial categories, collective memories of lynching can be invoked even when lynching is not explicitly mentioned. A host of racial stereotypes that remain politically potent, including most importantly those of the black rapist and the sexually available black woman, were central components of turn-of-the-century discourse in defense of lynching. The lingering ability of this discourse to shape contemporary racial meanings can be identified by examining the sedimented traces of lynching narratives within recent racial spectacles. I argue in chapter 3, for example, that Susan Smith and Charles Stuart profited from racist stereotypes that gained power and resonance from earlier invocations of the mythical black rapist. Collective memories of lynching therefore played a central role in structuring the ways in which various audiences understood these stories, but they were only explicitly invoked once the true killers were revealed and the mass media and the African American press began to contextualize the killings by noting that the Stuart and Smith narratives were based on stereotypes of black male criminality that had been used to justify lynchings. Whether collective memories of lynching are used as metaphor or as lens, this book examines the ways in which contemporary social actors make sense of present racial dramas by relying on understandings of the past.

My use of the term "collective memory" follows Maurice Halbwachs's insistence that "the past is not preserved but it is reconstructed on the basis of the present."[20] For Halbwachs, collective memory differs from personal memory in that it refers to shared understandings of the past. Collective memory is therefore broader and more durable than personal memory. But while Halbwachs was one of the first theorists to argue that memory was the product of social interaction, he tended to write about ways in which entire societies remember and was thus largely inattentive to the contested nature of collective memory. Halbwachs saw memory primarily as a flawed and ephemeral version of history and was inattentive to the ways in which discourses of power influenced the selection of detail in historical narratives.[21] As an alternative to this conception of collective memory, Marita Sturken distinguishes between "history," by which she means "a narrative that has in some way been sanctioned and valorized,"[22] and what she calls "cultural memory," which is "a field that represents memory shared in some form, yet not officially sanctioned memory."[23]

Sturken's work is part of a growing trend of theorizing that seeks to address the stakes in the construction of collective memory.[24] These stakes are clearly addressed by Barbie Zelizer, who distinguishes between personal memory, "whose authority fades over time," and collective memories, which

> allow for the fabrication, rearrangement, elaboration, and omission of details about the past, often pushing aside accuracy and authenticity so as to accommodate broader issues of identity formation, power and authority, and political affiliation. Memories in this view become not only the simple act of recall but social, cultural, and political action at its broadest level.[25]

As this passage suggests, the construction and deployment of collective memories is a thoroughly political process validating some versions of the past while marginalizing others. Critical interrogation of collective memory is therefore crucial for an analysis of social relationships, since contemporary social structures and practices are based at least partly on often highly contested understandings of the past.[26]

Sturken's inquiries into the political struggles over collective memory are complemented by the work of theorists like Teshome Gabriel, who argues that "somewhere between [the] access to power and representation lies the battle between history and popular memory";[27] George Lipsitz, who addresses "the contested nature of historical memory in our time";[28] and Iwona Irwin-Zarecka, who addresses the roles played by a variety of "memory-workers" (including state actors) in the construction not only of collective memories but also of organized structures of forgetting.[29] All of these theorists demonstrate that decisions about what and how to remember and forget are far from automatic and are instead always open to contest and based on struggles over meaning and power.

The idea, though, that collective memory is socially constructed according to contemporary social needs requires some qualification. Michael Schudson and Barry Schwartz have expressed skepticism about the ability of contemporary social actors to reconstruct the past. They acknowledge that the past is continually reassessed in light of contemporary concerns, but they argue that this process cannot proceed arbitrarily.[30] However, while it is important to suggest that there are limits to the ways in which we can reconstruct the past, the collective memory literature has thus far said very little about how we can begin to assess those limits. At the same time, several British scholars writing under the name "the Popular Memory Group" have argued that "the cultural features of accounts [of the past] are not simply the product of individual authorship; they draw on general cultural repertoires, features of language and codes of expression which help to determine what may be said, how, and to what effect."[31] This statement marks another important gap in the collective memory literature: Very little has been said about how to determine the content of these "cultural repertoires." My examination of the collective memory of lynching speaks to each of these silences as it argues that some of the different limitations and possibilities for the construction of collective memory are imposed by political struggles of the past and present.

The Dynamics of Lynching and Race

Before discussing the construction of collective memories of lynching, some background is needed about lynching as a historical practice that was itself a racial project linking various ideas about race to efforts to maintain white supremacist social structures.[32] Lynching dates back at least as far as the American Revolution, but before the Civil War, the term "lynching" referred to a variety of forms of punishment, including beating, whipping, tar-and-feathering, and, only occasionally, killing. The term was used to describe the actions of mobs of American patriots who beat and, only occasionally, hanged Loyalists and British sympathizers. During the antebellum period, mob violence became increasingly widespread and was directed at abolitionists, Mormons, Catholics, and blacks.[33] In this period, though, the primary victims of mob violence were not blacks but whites who violated community standards. Whites who held unpopular moral or social beliefs or who engaged in behavior that was deemed inappropriate, such as spousal or child abuse, were likely targets of the mob.[34] Slaveholders had financial and political stakes in protecting their slaves from lynchings, and it was only during exceptional slave rebellions or periods of extreme white insecurity that blacks were lynched.[35] But during the Civil War, as communities throughout the South began to fear slave rebellions, slaves were occasionally executed in large numbers in order to terrorize the slave community into submission.[36] The meaning of the word "lynching" started to change around this time, and shortly after the Civil War was over, "lynching" had come to mean putting to death. Robyn Wiegman notes that it was at this time that "lynching" came to be understood "almost exclusively" as a method of punishment for newly enfranchised African Americans.[37]

During Reconstruction, whites were confronted with a new reality in which they could no longer count on a captive supply of black labor for the plantations that were so central to the southern economy. As blacks started to gain land and literacy, whites faced the real possibility of losing control of the black population, and violence was a potent weapon for shoring up white supremacy. Planters "whipped, shot, and killed thousands of blacks for arguing over crop settlements, wages, labor contracts, or simply for failing to display sufficient deference," while white violence was also used as a method of political terrorism to prevent any threat that newly enfranchised freedmen might pose to the Democratic party.[38]

Racial and political violence during Reconstruction was not, however, allowed to go unchallenged. Fitzhugh Brundage argues that Congress realized that mob violence threatened the success of Reconstruction and enacted measures that were aimed at curtailing the power of the mob and securing the stability of the federal government. Additionally, "vigorous campaigns against Klan violence in several states, particularly North and South Carolina, produced a dramatic decline in organized violence."[39] While these efforts met with only limited success, they were abandoned by the time that Reconstruction ended, and the last of the federal troops were withdrawn from the South in 1877.

In the years after Reconstruction, rates of lynching peaked. Stewart Tolnay and E. M. Beck have identified nearly three thousand victims of lynch mobs in the South between 1882 and 1930. And although some whites were lynched, lynching had clearly become a method of punishment for blacks, who accounted for nearly 85 percent of the victims.[40] After Reconstruction, "with each succeeding decade, the proportion of lynchings that occurred in the South rose, increasing from 82 percent of all lynchings in the nation during the 1880s to more than 95 percent during the 1920s," and the percentage of white victims dropped dramatically from 1880 to 1930.[41] Despite the fact that lynchings occurred throughout the nation and targeted whites, Native Americans, Mexicans, and Asians, by the late nineteenth century, lynching had become a distinctly southern phenomenon whose victims were primarily African American.[42]

Some scholars have argued that lynching was a response to white fears of the political power of newly enfranchised black men, but Tolnay and Beck point out that while this explanation might have some merit for the Reconstruction years, it makes less sense for the post-Reconstruction era, since whites were able to neutralize black political power legally during that time. Tolnay and Beck argue that if fear of black political power was a primary motivation for lynching, lynching rates would have declined drastically once blacks were just about completely disenfranchised by the early 1900s. This did not happen.[43] They are also able to dismiss the idea that lynchings were a result of the growing strength of opposition political parties, which may have threatened white supremacist hegemony under the Democratic Party, since their research shows that blacks who lived in regions with strong Populist or Republican Parties were actually somewhat less likely to be lynched than those who lived in uncontested Democratic strongholds.[44]

Ultimately, any explanation of lynching needs to account not only for explicitly political factors but also for economic and cultural motivations. The post–Civil War southern economy was dominated by cotton, and planters were willing to resort to violence in an attempt to recapture black labor in the wake of abolition; at the same time, white workers resented the need to compete with blacks for jobs. Tolnay and Beck provide the most convincing evidence to date that rates of lynching were most likely to increase during periods of economic stagnation and that mob violence occurred much less frequently when cotton profits were high.[45] They speculate that white workers used racial terrorism to decrease competition from blacks and that at the same time employers benefited from racial antagonism between workers, since racial violence limited the possibilities for potentially costly interracial worker alliances. They further demonstrate that lynchings were concentrated at the times when labor needs were the greatest, and they argue that landlords and merchants had a strong need for a "compliant labor force" during these periods. Lynching could help to secure this labor force by "demonstrating the consequences for those who would cause trouble and disrupt the production process. . . . [Lynching could also] heighten the general level of fear among black workers."[46]

While lynchings were often committed by relatively few people, the lynchings that were most effective as tools of political education and terrorism were staged as massive public spectacles, often drawing thousands of participants.[47] The lynching of Claude Neal on October 26, 1934, near the town of Greenwood, Florida, is a case in point. A report on Neal's lynching by the National Association for the Advancement of Colored People (NAACP) notes that after Neal was charged with the murder of a white woman named Lola Cannidy, "the word was passed all over Northeastern Florida and Southeastern Alabama that there was to be a 'lynching party to which all white people are invited,' . . . the information was broadcast from the radio station at Dothan, Alabama."[48] After subjecting Neal to incredible forms of torture, the mob of somewhere around one hundred men "decided just to kill him." But the drama did not end there. Neal's body was strapped to the back of a car and dragged over the highway to a site where a larger crowd, composed of somewhere between three thousand and seven thousand people, was waiting. The new mob transported the body to the nearby town of Marianna and "hung [it] to a tree on the northeast corner of the courthouse square [where] pictures were taken of the mutilated form." Postcards "were sold in large quantities at fifty cents each." But postcards were not the only way to remember the lynching, since "fingers and toes from Neal's body have been exhibited as souvenirs in Marianna." The following day a mob of white men started a campaign of terror as they systematically

> began driving Negroes from the streets and stores where some were engaged in buying and selling and working for white employers. An observer stated that "the mob attacked men, women and children and that several blind persons were ruthlessly beaten." Another observer said [that blacks] "came from the town in droves, some driving, some running, some crying, all scared to death." . . . After emptying the streets, stores, places of business, hotels, etc., of Negroes the mob started into the residential section to drive out the Negro maids. Some women sent their maids home, others hid them in closets. One man whose wife shielded her maid from the mob said, "Saturday was a day of terror and madness, never to be forgotten by anyone."

While it is true that not all lynchings were as much of a community spectacle as Neal's or were accompanied by the same kinds of subsequent violence, it is fair to say that lynchings were generally meant "never to be forgotten by anyone." Lynchings were intended to create collective memories of terror and white supremacy.

Twentieth-century lynchings by mass mobs, or "spectacle lynchings," such as the lynching of Claude Neal, should be understood not as barbaric relics of a bygone age but as a "peculiarly modern ritual" that relied upon virtually every form of communication and transportation technology.[49] Starting in 1893, railroad companies would make arrangements for special trains to bring spectators to lynching sites that had been already announced, and they would occasionally advertise these trains in local papers.[50] The photograph in Figure 1 is an indictment of the spectators in such "spectacle lynchings" as that of Claude Neal. The image, created between 1920 and 1930, seems intended as a visual pun, suggesting that the lynching literally shadows or hangs over the members of the mob. Even more important than the thousands of people who attended and participated in mass lynchings, though, were the much larger regional and national audiences who learned about these lynchings from newspapers, postcards, books, pamphlets, and even, as in the case of Claude Neal, radio announcements. These accounts were often presented by witnesses or participants in the lynchings, but "the experience for their listeners was mediated, a representation at least once removed from actual involvement," and even spectators who attended lynchings

Figure 1. This work by an unknown artist indicts the onlookers in "spectacle lynchings" such as that of Claude Neal. From the Visual Materials from the National Association for the Advancement of Colored People (NAACP) at the Library of Congress. Courtesy of the NAACP.

"were affected as well by the narratives constructed by reporters to describe and explain these events."[51]

The widespread circulation of representations of spectacle lynchings greatly increased their power to act as a method of terrorism or "to convey to black persons in this country that they had no power and nothing else whites were obligated to respect."[52] In important ways, the power of spectacle lynchings actually increased as their frequency declined, since modern communication technologies made it possible for images and narratives of lynching to be disseminated to ever-larger audiences.[53] Because representations of lynching worked to extend and magnify the surveillant functions and the terror of the mob, they should be understood not as entirely separate entities from lynchings themselves but as key components of the power of the practice.[54]

The specific form that spectacle lynchings took became routinized over time. The standard sequence of events included a hunt for the accused, the identification of the captured African American by the alleged white victim or members of the victim's family, the announcement of the upcoming lynching, selection of the site, and the lynching itself, which involved torture and mutilation, often including castration, followed by burning, hanging, shooting, or a combination of all three.[55] As familiar mass rituals, spectacle lynchings and representations of those lynchings worked not only to punish perceived transgressions of the racial order but also to impart lessons about the nature of that order. Wiegman has interpreted lynching as a symbolic revocation of the privileges of citizenship that might otherwise have been granted to newly enfranchised black men in the wake of the Civil War.[56] More generally, lynching worked to ensure that African Americans were aware that the color bar was still firmly in place and that "integrated spaces could prove deadly."[57] The culture of segregation presented a stark picture of a world divided into distinct races, but this image glossed over intraracial social divisions. By providing lessons about the power of segregation, lynching also worked to forge common bonds of "whiteness" between working-class and poor whites and white elites.[58]

Lynching rates began to shrink as the industrial war effort and the lack of immigrant laborers from southern and eastern Europe during World War I created incentives for blacks to migrate to northern states. Black migration meant that lynching began to pose a serious threat for southern employers, who had become desperate for laborers and who "reacted quite rationally to the threat of a shrinking labor supply" by taking "steps to reduce the level of violence directed against local blacks."[59]

Some of the starkest changes in the southern economy were a result of New Deal agricultural programs in the 1930s. Initiatives like the cotton and tobacco crop-reduction and subsidy programs, which were administered by the Agricultural Adjustment Administration, led to increased reliance upon mechanization and wage labor in agricultural production.[60] Together with tenant evictions and increasing reliance on hired labor, mechanization led to capital-intensive agriculture in the South. Black migration to urban centers and the North increased as growing numbers of black farmers were unable to find work as hired laborers. Southern planters did not abandon violence as a means of ensuring an adequate labor supply but increasingly counted on law enforcement agencies and the courts to limit any resistance to their power.[61] Ultimately, "rural modernization had the salutary effect of sharply diminishing the socioeconomic roots of mob violence."[62] Lynching rates steadily declined during the 1930s and 1940s, and in the 1950s, "lynchings became so extraordinary that each incident provoked national outrage. The lynchings of Emmett Till in 1955, of Mack Charles Parker in 1959, and the murder of three civil rights workers in 1964 became national causes célèbres."[63] It is in this new context that it becomes possible to see lynching primarily as memory and metaphor.

Organization of the Book

There is no one privileged site that reveals the contours of collective memory. Instead, collective memory is a tricky thing to pin down. It is re-generated and re-created constantly, and although recording technologies and relations of power imbue it with a degree of stability, its meaning is never fixed.[64] The problem is only exacerbated when discussing collective memories of a part of our not-too-distant history that is as volatile as lynching. As I have argued, lynching has become one of the most powerful metaphors for racism in contemporary society. There is virtually no aspect of American culture that has not engaged with memories of lynching in one form or another. Lynching has been the subject of countless works of visual art and literature.[65] We know about lynchings because of the ways they were publicized by local and national newspapers at the turn of the century and because of the ways they have been invoked by recent antiracist movements. One particularly well-known lynching has even become the subject of a Broadway musical.[66] An analysis of collective memories of lynching could look to any, and all, of these sites and still not hope to provide a complete picture of how we remember and understand lynching.

Since it is therefore impossible to provide a comprehensive overview of the ways in which collective memories of lynching have been constructed and deployed, I have instead chosen to address a variety of sites where collective memories of lynching have played important roles in a process of national racial formation. Chapter 1, "Antilynching and the Struggle for Meaning," examines the struggles that the antilynching movement (which consisted of a wide variety of activists and organizations, including Ida B. Wells, the NAACP, the Commission for Interracial Cooperation [CIC], and the Association of Southern Women for the Prevention of Lynching [ASWPL]) waged over how lynching would be understood and remembered. I argue that it is largely because of this movement that it became possible to see lynching as a metaphor for racism. While it is difficult to determine the precise effect that the antilynching movement had either on the reduction of the actual numbers of lynchings or on a national process of racial formation, this was a mass movement spanning more than half a century and devoted to challenging common sense understandings of race and conceptions of lynching. Contemporary collective memories of lynching and racial terror are thoroughly indebted to the efforts of this movement.

Chapter 2, "Cinematic Lynchings," examines representations of lynching in mainstream Hollywood films and in independently produced films by black directors. While there are many sources for our understandings of lynching, cinematic depictions of lynching have been particularly widely circulated and are therefore of central importance for determining how a national collective memory of lynching has been shaped. The history of cinema is littered with figures from traditional lynching narratives, including the mythical black rapist, the heroic white avenger, the pure white female victim, and the oversexed black woman. Cinematic images are particularly potent sources for the creation and rearticulation of collective memory, and mainstream Hollywood films have always been key sites in the production and elaboration of various racial categories. But Hollywood's ability to construct and deploy racial images has never been uncontested. The struggles of the antilynching movement were complemented by the work of some early black directors, and I analyze the importance of their films for contests over how lynching would be remembered.

Increasingly, the mass media construct representations of "blackness" within the context of discussions of racialized violence. Chapter 3, "Lynching as Lens: Contemporary Racialized Violence," examines a series of cases of either alleged or actual racialized violence that rely upon and reconfigure collective memories of lynching. Lynch mobs and representations of lynching that were put forward by both the public defenders of lynching and the antilynching movement worked to instruct national audiences about the nature of the racial order. I argue that these lessons continue to be influential and that they help determine how contemporary audiences interpret racial dynamics in the United States. This chapter analyzes the enduring power of racial stereotypes; the relationships among race, fear, and memory; and the ways history works to structure credibility and common sense understandings of race.

Chapter 4, "The Hill–Thomas Hearings and the Meaning of a 'High-Tech Lynching,'" examines collective memories of lynching in the Senate hearings to confirm Clarence Thomas's nomination to become an associate justice of the U.S. Supreme Court. The portion of those hearings devoted to Anita Hill's allegations that Thomas had sexually harassed her became one of the most watched political dramas in television history. The political stakes of the lynching metaphor came out in bold relief in Thomas's charge that he was the victim of a "high-tech lynching," which was arguably the most powerful rhetorical moment of the hearings. I argue, though, that collective memories of lynching were in play even before Hill's allegations were made public. The Hill–Thomas hearings therefore provide the occasion for an extended consideration of the meaning and the power of the lynching metaphor and of the relationships between political struggles in the past and the present.

My Conclusion, "Not Just Memory," brings together some final thoughts about the possibilities for constructing and deploying collective memories and metaphors over time as part of a process of national racial formation. This discussion draws on the earlier chapters while considering discussions of lynching surrounding a recent exhibition of photographs of lynchings organized by James Allen. As a material practice, lynching has been embedded within a complex web of social relationships. I argue that contemporary invocations of lynching conjure up some of those relationships while neglecting others and that the metaphor of lynching is therefore never fixed. Yet this does not mean that lynching is an infinitely malleable metaphor, available for any use at all. Instead, I argue that the range of possible meanings attached to lynching is determined in relation both to the constraining influences of history and to current configurations of power and knowledge. The Conclusion addresses the ways in which struggles that were waged in the past have provided discursive resources that can be accessed for contemporary purposes. I also assess the questions of who is able to access these resources, and under what circumstances. Finally, I provide a caution against understanding contemporary lynchings as located solely within the realms of memory and metaphor.

Chapter 1

Antilynching and the Struggle for Meaning

Lynchings as Lesson and Memory

When a white woman in Selma, Alabama, gave birth in 1893, she was forced to disclose the fact that she had been involved in a relationship with a black man named Daniel Edwards. Despite the fact that the consensual relationship had been going on for over a year, Edwards was arrested for rape. He was then "taken by a mob of one hundred neighbors and hung to a tree and his body [was] riddled with bullets." A note was pinned to his body saying, "Warning to all Negroes that are too intimate with white girls. This the work of one hundred best citizens of the South Side." While the note clearly suggests that the killers were punishing Edwards for an interracial affair, press accounts claimed that he was lynched for rape. The antilynching crusader Ida B. Wells publicized this lynching in her pamphlet *A Red Record* in order to draw attention to some of the most important dynamics of lynching.[1] Her account sets the stage for a consideration of the challenges faced by antilynching activists.[2]

The lynching of Edwards was intended to send a message to black audiences about the power of white supremacy and the costs of transgressing the boundaries of the racial order while simultaneously reinforcing images of white men as chivalrous protectors of white female sexual virtue. The newspapers refined the message and made the lynching fit into a more recognizable narrative by reporting only the official criminal charge and invoking the figure of the black rapist. In the context of Wells's pamphlet, however, all of these meanings shift. Instead of merely signaling the strength of white power, the note that was pinned to Edwards's dead body now provides evidence that white supremacy is maintained through the use of terrorist tactics. Wells's retelling represents the white woman as far from a passive victim; she is instead presented as an active sexual agent who chose to maintain an illicit affair with a black man. The "black rapist" is revealed as an innocent victim, and the "one hundred best citizens" are figured as the true source of brutality and barbarism. Perhaps most important, the newspapers are seen not as objective sources of information but as manipulative organs of propaganda, complicit in disseminating racist images of black men and furthering the terrorist functions of the mob.

A Red Record foreshadows much of the work done by antilynching activists in the first several decades of the twentieth century. The most important organizations in the antilynching movement, including the NAACP, the CIC, and the ASWPL, did not always agree about tactics. They argued about a variety of issues, including even the potential value of federal antilynching legislation. But they agreed that the struggle against mob violence had to be waged largely in the realm of public opinion and that they could not allow traditional lynching narratives to stand uncontested.

Many lynchings were staged as massive public spectacles, so drawing attention to the *fact* of lynching was never a problem for the antilynchers. In fact, as the note pinned to Edwards's body suggests, lynch mobs often wanted as broad an audience as possible. In the wake of Reconstruction,

> lynchings were carefully designed to convey to black persons in this country that they had no power and nothing else whites were obligated to respect. Black people were made to feel that their lives were their own only as long as whites were not in a whimsical mood to take them. Black males were especially made to feel that they had no right to take care of their families to any degree beyond that of bare subsistence, and no right to assume any other claims to manhood as traditionally expressed in this country. Lynchings became, then, the final part of an emasculation that was carried out every day in word and deed. Black men were things, not men, and if they dared to claim any privileges of manhood, whether sexual, economic, or political, they risked execution.[3]

The idea that lynching was meant to serve as "a tool of psychological intimidation aimed at blacks as a group"[4] finds support in a speech by a man who identified himself as the mayor of a small town during the New Orleans race riot of 1900.[5] The mayor explained that "[t]he only way that you can teach these Niggers a lesson and put them in their place is to go out and lynch a few of them, and the others will trouble you no more. That is the only thing to do—kill them, string them up, lynch them!"[6]

As a method of political education and terrorism, "never to be forgotten by anyone,"[7] lynchings worked to create collective memories of terror and white supremacy. The antilynching movement shared an awareness with members of the mob that lynchings were meant to broadcast particular understandings of the nature of the racial order. Both groups were thus concerned with the metaphorical functions of vigilante violence, that is, with the ways in which lynching could provide a lens into broader social relations. The antilynching struggle challenged the meanings and metaphorical associations of the memories attached to lynching. I have noted that historical metaphors by necessity rely upon incomplete comparisons with the past. The struggle between the public apologists for lynching, on the one hand, and the antilynching activists and organizations, on the other, helped to determine which historical aspects of the dynamics of lynching would be linked to lynching as a metaphor.

This chapter examines the antilynching movement as a struggle that was fundamentally concerned with discourse and with resisting prevalent conceptions of race and gender. I take issue, therefore, with theorists who have argued that a concern with representational politics is a recent addition to the repertoire of social movements.[8] At perhaps no moment in American history were the stakes of symbolic struggles starker, higher, or more direct than during the peak years of lynching. Lynchings were only possible as a result of powerful discourses of race and gender, and the effort to eradicate lynching required multifaceted struggles against racist representations.

The specific form that these struggles took is also important. In the pages that follow, I demonstrate that antilynching activists were concerned with racist representations of, and racist violence directed against, black men *and* black women. But I argue that because lynching was justified by referencing myths of black *male* sexuality and criminality, antilynching activists were forced to devote the bulk of their resources toward combating these myths and were therefore less able to confront racist representations of black women. This discussion of rhetorical strategies is important not only because it highlights an interesting historical issue that has received fairly scant attention but also because the movement's representational struggles played a role in setting the terms of debate for a variety of later political contests. The movement helped to shape not only how contemporary audiences remember and understand lynching itself but also how we think of a variety of racial categories and stereotypes. In recent years, significant research has addressed the structure, tactics, and successes of the antilynching movement, but fairly little has been said about the legacies left by the movement and the ways antilynching discourse works to help shape the contours of contemporary activism.[9] By starting to address that topic, I hope to shed light upon the continuing impact of social movements often thought of as neatly confined to the dustbins of history.

Antilynching Activists and Organizations: The Makeup of the Movement

Wells was one of the earliest antilynching activists, and she waged a tireless campaign against lynching from the 1890s through the early years of the twentieth century. She urged African Americans "to boycott, vote, and agitate against white oppressors,"[10] but she directed the bulk of her resources toward the realm of public opinion as she sought to challenge the attitudes that made lynching socially acceptable. Her 1894 speaking tour through England focused tremendous amounts of publicity upon lynching and produced international condemnation of what was seen as a distinctly American form of barbarism.[11] National religious conventions in England issued critiques of lynching, and British reformers organized antilynching societies in response to Wells's lectures.[12] Eventually, American elites were forced to respond to British criticism of lynching, and many politicians and newspapers wound up taking antilynching stances as a result of Wells's efforts. Wells's work was particularly powerful when it came to challenging attitudes in the northern United States toward lynching, and by 1895 most northern newspapers and periodicals rejected the idea that lynching was a response to rape and had started treating lynching as a "barbarous" practice that "hurt America in the eyes of the 'civilized world.'"[13] Wells's tireless campaign provided a blueprint and precedent for later antilynching activism, most notably that of the NAACP.[14]

The NAACP was founded as a direct reaction to the 1908 race riot in Springfield, Illinois, and from its inception, the organization has been devoted to the struggle against racist violence. The antilynching struggle became a central part of the NAACP's organizing efforts and a way to shed light upon the broader struggle for racial justice. The importance of antilynching work to the NAACP is reflected in its financial data, which show that by 1919 the organization was prepared to devote nearly one-fifth of its total operating budget to the antilynching campaign.[15] Jacquelyn Dowd Hall provides an indication of the extent of the NAACP's antilynching efforts when she writes that

> after 1910, the NAACP had expanded Ida B. Wells-Barnett's one-woman anti-lynching crusade into a multifaceted offensive against mob violence. Access to funds and legal talent had enabled the organization to respond swiftly to lynching incidents—publicizing the facts, urging the incorporation of anti-lynching planks in national party platforms, and lobbying for the passage of state and federal anti-lynching legislation.[16]

The NAACP's antilynching drive lasted nearly half a century and led to the passage by the U.S. House of Representatives of antilynching legislation on three separate occasions, in 1922, 1937, and 1940. Each of these measures was ultimately defeated in the Senate, but the struggle for antilynching legislation generated an unprecedented amount of publicity about the problem of mob violence.[17] By the 1940s, the NAACP was largely responsible for the fact that southern communities could no longer "rest assured of the security of relative anonymity or of only a brief spasm of condemnation following a lynching; instead there was the certain prospect of a flood of hostile national publicity."[18]

Starting in 1919, the NAACP's antilynching work was complemented by that of the southern-based Commission on Interracial Cooperation (CIC). The CIC started as the result of a series of meetings between black ministers and an organization of white ministers in Atlanta called the Committee on Church Cooperation. These meetings were designed to "discuss and find solutions for the range of urban ills that bore down on blacks" and eventually to lead to "more formal meetings of the Christian Councils, comprised of representatives from both races and officials of the YMCA, YWCA, and the Salvation Army, which endeavored to stimulate communication between white and black congregations."[19] The group struggled to find enough money to expand across the South, and by 1920 it had obtained funding from the Laura Spelman Rockefeller Memorial and was formally organized as the Commission on Interracial Cooperation.[20] The CIC had become the major southern interracial reform organization by the mid-1920s,[21] and it struggled for the eradication not only of lynching itself but also of "the mythologies that condoned it."[22] The CIC conducted some of the most important research about lynching under the auspices of the Southern Commission on the Study of

Lynching, which it sponsored. The organization publicized its findings in a series of press releases and pamphlets and was responsible for the publication of two of the most important early books on lynching, Arthur F. Raper's *The Tragedy of Lynching* (1933) and James H. Chadbourn's *Lynching and the Law* (1933). Perhaps the most important contribution that the CIC made to the antilynching struggle, though, was its responsibility for the founding the Association of Southern Women for the Prevention of Lynching (ASWPL).

The ASWPL started as part of a CIC women's committee and became an independent organization under the leadership of Jessie Daniel Ames in 1930.[23] The organization received funding from the CIC, but Ames also relied upon "an existing network of women's church and civic groups with their own program budgets."[24] As a group of southern white women who were opposed to lynching, the ASWPL realized that it was well positioned to launch an attack on the notion that lynchings worked to provide protection for white women from black rapists. Its denunciations of the myth of the black rapist carried a special weight that was difficult to ignore. The ASWPL came along fairly late in the antilynching struggle, after numerous gains had been made, but lynching was still a defining feature of southern race relations, and significant portions of the population still believed that mob violence worked as an appropriate form of punishment for black men who had raped white women. In this context, the power of a group of white women devoted to challenging the myth of the black rapist cannot be overstated.[25] The ASWPL was successful in deterring a number of lynchings and in helping to change the political climate that tolerated lynching. By 1942, the ASWPL had gathered the signatures of over 43,000 white women on an antilynching pledge, and numerous commentators had credited them with reducing the numbers of lynching throughout the South.[26]

Movement Strategies and the Contested Meanings of Lynching

Wells closed *A Red Record* by noting that after her lectures, she was often approached by people wanting to know what they could do to help end lynching. She wrote that "[t]he answer always is 'Tell the world the facts.' When the Christian world knows the alarming growth and extent of outlawry in our land, some means will be found to stop it."[27] Wells wanted African Americans to use a variety of tactics, including boycotts and voting, to challenge racism. But she believed that it was essential to confront the white press in order to eliminate lynching, since this was the most direct method of reaching white people and changing the public sentiment that made lynching possible.[28]

Wells-Barnett's work marked the beginning of a continuing tactic of antilynching activists, which was to gather evidence from sources that white audiences considered credible in order to attack the popular justifications for lynching.[29] Antilynching activists felt that lynching was possible only so long as it was supported by white popular opinion. The CIC expressed its hopes most directly in a report that stated, "We expect lynchings ultimately to be eradicated by the growth of a healthy public opinion that will no longer tolerate them. It is a matter of major importance to stimulate this growth."[30] In order to foster a climate in which lynchings would no longer be acceptable, antilynchers set out to systematically refute popular justifications for lynching.

Like Wells-Barnett, the NAACP launched a campaign to "expose injustices. . . . [The campaign] rested on their belief that a democratic society would respond constructively if only it had the facts at its disposal. This commitment to disclosure marked the organization's campaigns against lynching for the next forty years."[31] Publicity was a central concern of the NAACP, and it used its campaign against lynching as a way to mobilize support for a broader struggle against racism. The NAACP, along with the rest of the antilynching movement, attempted to gather publicity in every way possible: Its members wrote pamphlets, editorials, and articles; organized antilynching art exhibitions; and even engaged in mass demonstrations.[32] In an early example of symbolic protest and civil disobedience, members of the NAACP stood with nooses around their necks in Washington, D.C., in order to focus attention on the failure to include lynching on the agenda of a national crime conference (see Figure 2). In another instance, members of the NAACP Youth Council demonstrated in front of the Strand Theatre in Times Square for antilynching legislation (see Figure 3). While these protests were hardly typical, the effort to gather support for antilynching campaigns by publicizing the brutality of lynching was a hallmark of the struggle and was also a way to address broader issues of race. The "antilynching effort became a number-one priority of the Association's public programs and the issue best conceived to redirect white America's perceptions of interracial realities."[33] For the NAACP, as for the lynchers themselves, lynchings were always meant to symbolize something larger. Antilynchers and lynchers were united in their efforts to establish lynching as the most easily recognizable symbol of race relations. Of course, the understandings that they wanted their audiences to have of the racial order were diametrically opposed. A central part of the antilynching struggle was based on challenging the various racial stereotypes that had become standard parts of traditional lynching narratives.[34]

Figure 2. Howard University students protest the December 1934 National Crime Conference in Washington, D.C., for its refusal to address lynching. From the Visual Materials from the National Association for the Advancement of Colored People (NAACP) at the Library of Congress. Courtesy of the NAACP.

"The Usual Crime": The Myth of the Black Rapist

Despite the fact that rape was only cited as the reason for a minority of lynchings, the need to punish black rapists was the justification most widely cited by the public apologists for lynching. A South Carolina senatorial candidate named Cole Blease issued a typical defense of lynching in a 1929 campaign speech when he exclaimed, "[W]hen the Constitution of the United States comes between me and the chastity of white women, to hell with the Constitution!"[35] A more elaborate version of this defense was expressed in a letter to the *Reader's Digest:*

> As long as your negroe men violate white women, no hope of real
> emancipation may be shown you by the white race. This animal char-
> acteristic of negroes as is shown almost daily in the newspapers, will
> forever stamp a stigma on your race. . . . you know as well as I that as
> long as white men lynch blacks for sex crimes, the negroe has no hope
> of gaining Caucasian respect. Now instead of trying to get laws to
> prevent lynchings (which are just punishments for the vicious crimes
> of the black rapers), why not reform your own race?[36]

Figure 3. Demonstration by the NAACP New York City Youth Council for anti-lynching legislation, September 1937. From the Visual Materials from the National Association for the Advancement of Colored People at the Library of Congress. Courtesy of the NAACP.

The letter was unusual only in that it explicitly linked a defense of lynching to an argument against emancipation. The expression of absolute certainty that lynching acted solely as a punishment for rape was commonplace. As Brundage argues, "the 'unspeakable crime'—rape—gripped the imaginations of whites to a far greater extent than any other offense. Ignoring statistics that showed that sexual offenses did not spark most lynchings, white southerners maintained that rape was the key to lynching."[37]

The defenders of lynching were often so committed to the notion that lynchings were always and only a way to punish black men who raped white women that they ignored all evidence to the contrary. For example, when George W. Chamlee wanted to argue that, in his editor's words, "lynching is the most effective deterrent to brutal assaults upon white women," he had no difficulty confronting the NAACP's statistics demonstrating that rape had been charged in less than a third of all lynchings, since "the North does not realize that the Southern white men in the rural communities have a special haunting uneasiness about leaving their homes unprotected even though all the statistics in the world may show such fears ungrounded."[38] Facts were equally unimpressive to a white woman who was asked by the ASWPL to investigate a lynching that "was reported by the press to have been the result of an 'improper proposal to a white woman.'" In her response to the ASWPL, the woman said,

> I cannot help you in this matter. The only lynchings I have heard of in the State of Mississippi have been Negroes for the most horrible crime that can be committed—"rape on a white woman"—far worse than murder. I thank God for the courage of the men who protect us.

The ASWPL investigated the matter on its own and found that the local consensus was that the victim had been lynched "'for greed' . . . and that the purported cause was merely framed up because the white man knew no officer would move to investigate the death for such alleged reasons."[39] Charges of improper sexual conduct were often tacked on as a secondary justification for lynching when the primary reason for the lynching was economic or political.[40] The unwillingness of the ASWPL's correspondent to even consider the possibility of another cause in this case suggests, however, that rape was such an integral part of white southerners' common sense understanding of lynching narratives that tacking on a rape charge might have been unnecessary: Rape was so readily assumed as a motivation for the mob that it hardly needed to be stated explicity.

The rape of a white woman by a black man was regarded as such a serious crime that to say it enabled public apologies for lynching is too mild. Instead, the myth of the black rapist made it possible to gain political mileage not by excusing but by publicly *advocating* lynching as a form of extralegal terror. South Carolina's Governor Ben Tillman has been widely cited for his argument that the law is incapable of dealing with so monstrous a crime as a black man's rape of a white woman:

> Shall men coldbloodedly stand up and demand for him [the black rapist] the right to have a fair trial and be punished in the regular course of justice? So far as I am concerned he has put himself outside the pale of the law, human and divine. . . . Civilization peels off us, any and all of us who are men, and we revert to the original savage type whose impulses under any and all circumstances has always been to "kill! kill! kill!"[41]

While this speech represents the most famous defense of lynching, its sentiment was widely shared. For example, Representative Sisson exclaimed that he "would rather the whole black race of this world were lynched than for one of the fair daughters of the South to be ravished and torn by one of these black brutes,"[42] and during a debate on an antilynching bill, Representative William C. Lankford argued that the bill's supporters should "quit howling about lynchings and begin preaching against rape."[43]

Shaking the Foundations: The Struggle against Stereotypes

The fact that the mythical black rapist was so readily invoked as a justification for lynching meant that the antilynchers were compelled to devote a good deal of their energies toward, as one NAACP campaigner put it, "exploding the rape myth."[44] In antilynching pamphlets and in congressional testimony in favor of antilynching legislation, leaders of the struggle against lynching commonly noted that fewer than one-third of all lynching victims were even charged with rape by the mobs themselves.[45] As Walter White, the executive secretary of the NAACP, noted in his testimony in favor of the Costigan-Wagner Anti-Lynching Bill,

> There are . . . certain misconceptions which need again to be corrected, untruths and half-truths being as persistently long-lived as they are. The first of these misconceptions which is still believed by otherwise well-informed and fair-minded persons is that there is some connection between lynching and sex offenses by Negroes on white women. In a statistical study of the crime . . . [it was shown that] less than one-fifth of the colored men done to death by lynching mobs were even accused of the usual crime. It should be remembered that a mob's accusation is by no means equivalent to conviction or even to an indictment by a regularly constituted jury.[46]

The CIC consistently repeated its findings that "less than one-fourth of those lynched since 1890 were accused of assaults upon women, the 'usual crime' commonly supposed to be the chief occasion of lynchings."[47] At times, the antilynchers expressed frustration that the public defenders of lynching continued to reference rape despite overwhelming evidence that it was not cited as the reason for most lynchings. White noted in his 1946 testimony before the House Judiciary Committee that

> I wish to refer very briefly to the charge which is sometimes but fortunately not as frequently true as the lynch mobs would have you to believe: That those victims have been guilty of sex offenses against white women.
>
> That charge has been repeatedly exploded. Out of more than 5,000

lynchings which have disgraced America since 1889, less than 1 in 6 of the victims have even been charged by the mobs themselves with sex offenses of any character whatsoever.

Yet, as has already been referred to by a previous witness, last night in my native State of Georgia the Ku Klux Klan held a meeting claiming they were coming back into being in order to "protect white womanhood." I believe that white womanhood in the North and the South is in no great danger and wants no violation of the laws of God or man for their protection.[48]

White's argument that rape is cited as a defense for lynching despite the fact that the rape charge "has been repeatedly exploded" resonates with Wells's much earlier claim that "[n]obody in this section believes the old thread bare lie that Negro men rape white women."[49] White and Wells both suggested that lynching's apologists were disingenuous in their references to rape, since they had every opportunity to know that rape was not the reason for lynching.

The antilynchers' frustration at the persistence of the assumed link between rape and lynching was largely due to the power of the rape charge within popular culture.[50] "Thread bare lie" or not, allegations of rape were remarkably effective at silencing dissent. Frederick Douglass argued that

> [t]he crime which these usurpers of courts, laws, and juries, profess to punish is the most revolting and shocking of any this side of murder. This they know is their best excuse, and it appeals at once and promptly to a prejudice which prevails at the North as well as the South. Hence we have for any act of lawless violence the same excuse, an outrage by a negro upon some white woman. . . . it is not with them the immorality or the enormity of the crime itself that arouses popular wrath, but the emphasis is put upon the race and color of the parties to it. . . . The appeal is not to the moral sense, but to the well-known hatred of one class towards another. It is an appeal that not only stops the ears and darkens the minds of Southern men; but it palliates the crime of lawless violence in the eyes of Northern men. The device is used with skill and effect, and the question of guilt or innocence becomes unimportant in the fierce tumult of popular passion.[51]

Wells noted that "this cry has had its effect. It has closed the heart, stifled the conscience, warped the judgement and hushed the voice of press and pulpit on the subject of lynch law throughout this 'land of liberty.'"[52] She later elaborated by arguing that

[h]umanity abhors the assailant of womanhood, and this charge upon the Negro at once placed him beyond the pale of human sympathy. With such unanimity, earnestness and apparent candor was this charge made and reiterated that the world has accepted the story that the Negro is a monster which the Southern white man has painted him. And today, the Christian world feels, that while lynching is a crime, and lawlessness and anarchy the certain precursors of a nation's fall, it can not by word or deed, extend sympathy or help to a race of outlaws, who might mistake their plea for justice and deem it an excuse for their continued wrongs.[53]

This passage provides some sense of the urgency that antilynchers felt about the necessity of refuting the myth of the black rapist. As Wells argued, the effort to gain support for antilynching struggles was made considerably more difficult as long as lynching was represented as the only way to curb the sexual monstrosity of black men. If it had not challenged the rape charge, the antilynching movement would have had much greater difficulty overcoming political isolation.

One of the most important methods of "exploding" the association between rape and lynching was to attempt to expose the rape charge as a veil that was valuable to lynchers because it covered up less honorable motivations for mob violence. Ames, from the ASWPL, argued that

[t]he surest method to follow in developing hate and fear to the point of violence, whether in precipitating a lynching or a war, is the use of stories of sex crimes committed by the people who are to be killed on the women of the people who are to do the killing. Men and women alike see in outraged womanhood their own mothers or wives or sisters, and they are moved by an invincible force to mete out punishment to the vandals. Something of Arthurian chivalry stirs men's minds; they wear the colors of their own womanhood into a battle for all womanhood.

As it is in war, when true stories of sex violation are lacking, fictitious accounts of imaginary assaults against innocent women by brutish enemies are published, so it is in lynchings. As wars have their roots in economic conditions, greed and avarice, so also have lynchings. "My country right or wrong" furnishes the motive in wars; preservation of white supremacy, in lynchings. In both, a whole people lose for the benefit of the few.[54]

James Weldon Johnson of the NAACP agreed that defenses of lynching that were based on rape diverted attention from the fact that lynching was really a method of securing white supremacy:

[B]odies of leading Southern white women in various states have publicly, on several occasions, repudiated the implication that their salvation depended upon the burning alive of Negroes and thrown out of court the plea that "lynching" was a necessary or defensible safeguard for the honor of "white womanhood." . . . Of course, lynching is not and has not been a "protection to the honor of white womanhood." It dishonors those who practice it and those in whose behalf it is practiced. Rather it has been part of the post-slavery and post-Reconstruction system of terrorization by which the Negro has been disfranchised, kept in peonage, robbed, maltreated, denied justice in the courts and decent accommodation in schools and public places for which he is required to pay. The "white supremacy" in whose defense lynching is invoked is denied by the horrors of lynching itself, which could come only from inferiors in any known scale of civilization.[55]

This passage is typical of the antilynching strategy of attempting to strip away the rape charge in order to reveal lynching as a terrorist method of limiting black economic and political power.

Coercion versus Consent: Voluntary Interracial Relationships

Aside from arguing that the rape charge was a method of cloaking the true purposes of lynching, some antilynchers attempted to undermine the charge by formulating and publicizing alternative interpretations of the relationships between black men and white women. One way of doing this was to emphasize that the stereotype of the black rapist was a new invention and that there had been no similar concerns about the safety of white women as recently as the Civil War. Wells argued that

[t]he thinking public will not easily believe freedom and education more brutalizing than slavery, and the world knows that the crime of rape was unknown during four years of civil war, when the white women of the South were at the mercy of the race which is all at once charged with being a bestial one.[56]

She suggested that it was absurd to think that black men could suddenly turn into dangerous sexual monsters just at the moment when their humanity was legally recognized, and she elaborated by hammering home the point that the rape charge was utterly without precedent:

During all the years of slavery, no such charge was ever made. . . . Likewise during the period of alleged "insurrection" and alarming "race riots," it never occurred to the white man, that his wife and children were in danger of assault. Nor in the Reconstruction era, when the hue and cry was against "Negro Domination," was there ever a thought that the domination would ever contaminate a fireside or strike to death the virtue of womanhood.[57]

While Wells argued that rape was a new charge, she did not suggest that black men and white women kept to entirely separate sexual worlds. Instead, she argued that instances of what lynch mobs referred to as rape were often, in fact, voluntary sexual relationships. She argued that "[w]ith the Southern white man, any mesalliance existing between a white woman and a colored man is a sufficient foundation for the charge of rape,"[58] and she devoted most of one chapter of her first antilynching pamphlet, *Southern Horrors: Lynch Law in All Its Phases*, to examples culled from the mainstream white press that "substantiate the assertion that some white women love the company of the Afro-American [man]."[59] She discusses the lynching of Daniel Edwards, which I addressed at the beginning of this chapter, as only one of "hundreds of such cases [that] might be cited" of black men who were lynched as a response to consensual sexual relationships with white women.[60]

The Role of White Women in the Antilynching Movement

When mobs used violence to patrol the sexual boundaries separating black men and white women, the obvious victims were the black men, who were often lynched for their transgressions of the southern racial order, but the code of chivalry also limited white women's behavior. Because lynching "was not just a punishment for forcible assault; it was also a severe sanction against voluntary sexual relations," it was an effective method of constraining white women's sexual freedom.[61] The code of chivalry carried an additional cost for white women, since "the right of the southern lady to protection presupposed her obligation to obey."[62] The role of lynching as a terrorist tactic intended to keep blacks in a subordinate status was paralleled by the role of the discourse surrounding rape in generating fear meant to control white women. The code of chivalry imposed a "legacy of terror" upon white women that reinforced their dependency upon white men.[63] As Jane Addams said, "[The] woman who is protected by violence allows herself to be protected as the woman of the savage is protected, and she must still be regarded as a possession of man."[64] White women thus occupied a precarious position within the traditional lynching narrative. While lynchings were said to be carried out in their names and for their honor and security, mob violence helped to reinforce a system of white male domination that severely curtailed white women's mobility. White women who were opposed to mob violence were therefore uniquely motivated and positioned to intervene in the debate over lynching.

African American antilynchers recognized the contribution that concerned white women could make to their struggle early on. In 1915, the *New York Amsterdam News* pleaded

> Great God . . . is there in Georgia no woman bold enough to take up the cudgels for her sex? Will not Georgia's womanhood fight the new pastime of the mob? Will not Georgia women organize and draw the line somewhere in this disgraceful business? Women have captured the ear of the public before and can do so now. Can Southern white women sit still and see women, of whatever race, manhandled and insulted, lynched and riddled with bullets?[65]

And in 1920, Charlotte Hawkins Brown addressed a Southern Women's Conference sponsored by the CIC. She argued that

> [t]he Negro women of the South lay everything that happens to the members of her race at the door of the Southern white woman. . . . We all feel that you can control your men . . . that so far as lynching is concerned . . . if the white women would take hold of the situation that lynching would be stopped.[66]

These calls were eventually answered by the Association of Southern Women for the Prevention of Lynching.

The ASWPL agreed with other parts of the antilynching movement that the most important method of combating lynching was to destroy the myth of the black rapist. They realized that as a group of southern white women, "they were strategically placed to make maximum use of the cultural symbol of the southern lady"[67] and that their denunciations of this myth would therefore have a kind of authority that was denied to groups like the NAACP. The ASWPL membership pledged,

> We, the undersigned, believe that the crime of lynching undermines all ideals of government and religion which we hold sacred and which we try by our lives and our conduct to implant into the minds of our youth. We recognize that all lynching will be defended so long as the public generally accepts the assumption that it is for the protection of white women. We hold that we owe it not only to our own times, but to posterity to repudiate the acts of mobs and lynchers and to declare that if the Constitution, our law, our courts cannot protect women, then our civilization is a travesty and our religion is a mockery. We pledge ourselves to arouse public opinion to the menace of the crime

of lynching by educating the youth of our own communities to an understanding of the consequences of such lawless acts, by calling upon press, pulpit, schools, and every patriotic citizen to join us in a campaign against such violations of law and civilization and the teachings of religion.[68]

In an ASWPL pamphlet that explained the origins of the organization, Ames explains the logic of this pledge and of all of the ASWPL's work by saying that since

[l]ess than 29% of [the people lynched between 1922 and 1929] were charged with crimes against white women . . . the first and most necessary move on the part of white women was to repudiate lynching in unmistakable language as a protection to Southern women. Unless this idea of chivalry could be destroyed, lynchers would continue to use the name of woman as an excuse for their crimes and a protection for themselves . . . [so] emphasis at all times was to be placed on the repudiation of the claim that lynching is necessary to the protection of white women.[69]

The members of the ASWPL understood that white women's silent complicity was a crucial factor in the power of lynching narratives, and thus they devoted the bulk of their efforts over their twelve-year history to debunking the idea that lynching provided a necessary or desired defense against rape by black men.[70]

While the ASWPL's argument against rape as a justification for lynching was nothing new, the organization was right to think that their claims would be received differently than had those of the NAACP. An article in the *Birmingham Age-Herald* noted that

[s]ince the main defense of mob law is the protection of womanhood, there is a special force in this disavowal from women who know that the lyncher is in very truth the most vicious debaucher of spiritual values. Even a stagnant public opinion must respond to such a challenge.[71]

Other antilynching campaigners realized that the ASWPL's antilynching work could lend their own arguments an extra layer of credibility. Thus, it became standard practice to reference the ASWPL's work in a variety of publicity drives, fund-raising appeals, and political forums. For example, during hearings for antilynching legislation in 1934, Albert E. Barnett testified that

[t]he idea that lynching is regularly, or to any great degree, the result of indignities by Negro men against white women is . . . untenable. Not

more than one sixth of the more than 3,700 victims of mob violence between 1889 and 1932 were charged with rape, and it is more than likely that many of those so charged would never have been judged guilty even in a southern local court. Southern women have repeatedly opposed the use of this pretext as a justification for the barbarous practice of lynching.[72]

While white women's repudiation of the rape charge helped to expose the hollowness of the arguments made by lynching's public defenders, antilynchers also attempted to highlight the sexual vulnerability of black women in order to present the claim of chivalry as hypocritical.

Black Women's Role in the Antilynching Movement

In the years following Reconstruction, black women who were raped by white men could not name their assailants without endangering the lives of black male relatives who might seek vengeance and who might thus end up the victims of mob violence.[73] Thus, in addition to limiting black male economic and political mobility, the terror of lynching also worked to enforce silence about the sexual victimization of black women. Because it was difficult to discuss the sexual victimization of black women at the hands of white men, lynching "helped reinforce a myth of the sexually available black woman."[74] Antilynching activists from Wells-Barnett on recognized that, as Hazel Carby writes, "black women were relegated to a place outside the ideological construction of 'womanhood.' That term included only white women; therefore the rape of black women was of no consequence outside the black community."[75] Antilynching activists sought to challenge this construction as they simultaneously focused on the role of white rapists and worked to further erode the idea that mobs were composed of chivalrous men who wanted only to defend women's sexual virtue.

Wells referenced the rapes of black women to argue that chivalry was merely a transparent excuse used by white men in order to avoid criticism for their own crimes:

> [I]t is [white women's] misfortune that the chivalrous white men of [the South], in order to escape the deserved execration of the civilized world, should shield themselves by their cowardly and infamously false excuse, and call into question that very honor about which their distinguished priestly apologist claims they are most sensitive. To justify their own barbarism they assume a chivalry which they do not possess. True chivalry respects all womanhood, and no one who reads

the record . . . will for a minute conceive that the southern white man had a very chivalrous regard for the honor due the women of his own race or respect for the womanhood which circumstances placed in his power. That chivalry . . . can hope for but little respect from the civilized world, when it confines itself entirely to the women who happen to be white. Virtue knows no color line, and the chivalry which depends upon complexion of skin and texture of hair can command no honest respect.[76]

As proof for the claim that white men who claimed to be acting under the code of chivalry were hypocritical, Wells noted that rape

committed by white men against Negro women and girls, is never punished by mob or the law. A leading journal in South Carolina openly said some months ago that "it is not the same thing for a white man to assault a colored woman as for a colored man to assault a white woman, because the colored woman had no finer feelings nor virtue to be outraged!" Yet colored women have always had far more reason to complain of white men in this respect than ever white women have had of Negroes.[77]

Rather than making this claim abstractly, Wells provided a variety of examples contrasting the different treatment accorded the rapes of white and black women. She discussed several cases of rape that would probably have resulted in lynchings if the victim had been white, and she suggests that because the victim was black, there was not even any legal sanction. Wells provided numerous examples of black women and girls who were brutally assauted and raped without any intervention on the part of the legal system or the broader community. In one case, a black girl was raped by a group of white men, and when "her father went to have a warrant for their arrest issued . . . the judge refused to issue it."[78] Perhaps the starkest case Wells discussed is of a little black girl in Baltimore who was raped by a white man. Wells noted that

it was rumored that five hundred colored men had organized to lynch him. Two hundred and fifty white citizens armed themselves with Winchesters and guarded him. A cannon was placed in front of his home, and the Buchanan Rifles (State Militia) ordered to the scene for his protection. The colored mob did not show up.[79]

This case is about as different from the traditional response to a white woman's rape at the hands of a black man as can be. As in the traditional scenario, a white mob was mobilized, but in this case, the mob was formed not to lynch the accused rapist but to provide him with an armed defense.

As powerful as these examples are, it is important to note that Wells's descriptions of the rapes of black women are much more subdued than are her descriptions of the lynchings of black men. This is not accidental and is indeed typical of other writers of the times. Black women writers in particular were constrained by "restrictions on womanly decorum," and black writers in general "would not hesitate to represent graphically the violence of lynching as used against black men especially, as proof of the danger of white supremacy. . . . the representation of the rape of black women could not be discussed in similar terms."[80] Sandra Gunning provides a sense of the ways that Wells attempted to work within these narrative constraints when she says that

> Wells curtails considerably her account of black female victims so as not to offer up for public display the details of black female victims' bodily suffering. As a negotiation of indecorous accounts that threaten her claims to virtue and thus credibility, Wells seeks to publish the facts of *Southern Horrors* in order to effect a rewriting of the public record on race, women, and rape, without doing damage to the image of black women in general; by the same token, in her narrative strategies, Wells also seeks to protect herself from indictment as an unwomanly speaker.[81]

I would add to this that despite Wells's clear concern with the plight of black women, it was not necessary for her to depict their suffering in graphic detail because her primary goal was always to undermine popular justifications for lynching. The rapes of black women were discussed for this purpose, and even relatively mild descriptions could undermine the notion of white male chivalry.

Rape was not the only form of victimization facing black women, and the antilynchers noted that occasionally black women were lynched. The fact that the photograph of the lynching of Laura Nelson (Figure 4) was widely circulated as a postcard provides evidence that the lynchings of black women could be used as part of an effort to boast of white supremacy in much the same manner as were the lynchings of black men.[82] In a petition to President Franklin D. Roosevelt in support of the Costigan-Wagner Anti-Lynching Bill, the NAACP argued that

> there have been 5,070 lynchings since 1882. Less than one-sixth of the victims have even been accused of rape. Since 1889, 83 women have been lynched. Lynchers are rarely arrested; almost never convicted. The States will not stop lynching. A Federal law is necessary.[83]

COPYRIGHT - 1911- G.H.FARNUM
OKEMAH.OKLA - 2096-

Figure 4. Postcard of the lynching of Laura Nelson at Okemah, Oklahoma, on May 25, 1911. Allen-Littlefield Collection, Special Collections Division, Robert W. Woodruff Library, Emory University.

In comparison to black men, black women were lynched in relatively low numbers. But their lynchings provided compelling evidence that rape was, at the very least, not the sole reason for mob violence.[84] References to the lynchings of black women therefore became one more tool to disprove the myth of the black rapist. An excerpt from an antilynching memo by James Weldon Johnson is illustrative of the ways in which the lynchings of black women were mentioned:

> The charge that rape is the principal cause of lynching can best be shown to be untrue by the following figures of the fourteen southern states in which more lynchings have taken place than in other states. The figures are self explanatory. . . . From 1889 through December 19, 1921 there have been 3,434 known lynchings in the United States. Of that number, 570, only 16.6 percent have been lynched for rape. It is especially emphasized in this connection that there have been many lynchings where the victim was not even accused of rape but in which cases the lynchers gave rape as a cause. . . . They did this because they felt that the . . . American public would not censure them for lynching . . . [if] the crime of rape against the victim of the mob could be placed. *From 1889 through 1921 64 women (11 white, 53 colored) have been lynched. Certainly, no charge of rape could have been the cause of these lynchings.* [My emphasis][85]

Johnson presents a familiar litany of refutations of the rape charge: Only a small percentage of lynchings were based on allegations of rape; the rape charge is a method to avoid public criticism; and finally, the fact that some women have been lynched is conclusive proof that rape is not always a factor in lynching. Johnson's memo is representative of the antilynching movement's concern with black women's experiences at the hands of white mobs. (Figure 5, an ad placed in the *New York Times* by the NAACP to support the Dyer Anti-Lynching Bill, addresses many of the same themes.) Lynchings of black women were rarely discussed in their own right but were instead used as one more method of "exploding" the black-rapist myth.

Lynching as Spectacle: Civilization versus Barbarism

One of the reasons that the antilynchers devoted so much energy to challenging the assumed link between lynching and rape was that as long as lynching was seen as a defense of white womanhood, it was difficult to gather any sympathy for the victims of the mob. The hope was that all of the different methods of debunking the myth of the black rapist would make it possible for people to see lynchings not as heroic acts of protection but as barbaric attacks upon defenseless victims that were meant to secure a system of economic and political domination by terrorizing black communities. In order to help people accept this vision, the antilynchers

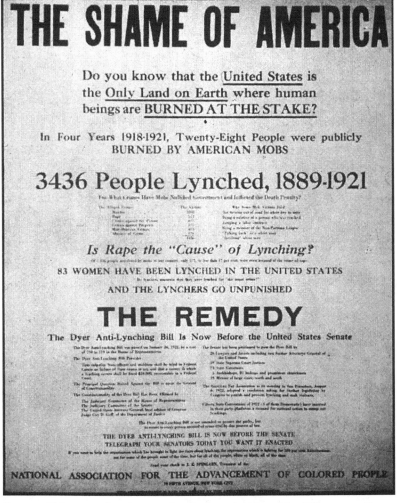

Figure 5. This 1922 advertisement for the Dyer Anti-Lynching Bill answers the question "Is Rape the 'Cause' of Lynching?" by noting that "Of the 3436 people murdered by mobs in our country, only 571, or less than 17 per cent were even accused of the crime of rape" and "83 women have been lynched in the United States." It then poses the rhetorical question of whether it is possible that these women were lynched for "the usual crime." The lynchings of women provided the antilynching movement with compelling evidence to refute the idea that lynching is always a punishment for rape.

drew as much attention as they could to the victims of the mob and to the support that supposedly respectable communities provided for horrible acts of cruelty.

Journalists in the 1890s drew upon Victorian ideologies about male sexuality in order to portray lynching as a struggle between white "manly civilization" and black "unmanly savagery."[86] A central component of the antilynching activists' agenda was to reverse these characterizations and shed full light upon the barbarity of lynching. In *A Red Record,* Wells urged blacks to defend themselves by disclosing

> to the world that degree of dehumanizing brutality which fixes upon America the blot of a national crime. . . . It becomes a painful duty of the Negro to reproduce a record which shows that a large portion of the American people avow anarchy, condone murder and defy the contempt of civilization.[87]

In order to construct this record, antilynching activists detailed not only the incredible brutality of lynchings but also the community support for and involvement in mob violence.

Antilynching activists were at pains to argue that the responsibility for lynchings did not rest merely with the people who actually hunted down and killed the victim but was shared among entire communities that aided the mobs, either through active participation (which could include publicizing lynchings, coming to the town square to watch someone hang, getting wood for the fire that would burn a victim alive, hiring sheriffs who had no qualms about turning prisoners over to mobs, failing to convict members of mobs, and so on) or through silent complicity. For example, in its analysis of lynching from 1882 to 1927, the CIC noted that

> [m]any of the victims were tortured, mutilated, burned at the stake, with a ferocity unbelievable among civilized people. . . . [one woman], for example, was hung to a limb by her feet, her body was riddled with bullets and then ripped open with knives. Not infrequently, multitudes of men and women have gathered to see human victims tortured with hot irons, slashed with knives, and slowly roasted to death. Even children have sometimes been the witnesses of these horrors. In some cases newspapers have announced in advance the exact time and place at which lynchings would occur: yet no steps were taken to prevent them. . . . Sometimes officers sworn to uphold the law have themselves taken part in lynchings. Hundreds of prisoners have been turned over to mobs without an effort for their protection.[88]

While it is unusual for antilynching literature to discuss a black *woman's* suffering in this kind of graphic detail, in other respects this passage is quite common. The effort to indict as wide a variety of culpable parties as possible was an especially important part of the antilynching strategy of questioning the very nature of southern "civilization."

While the antilynchers never failed to address the failure of the police or the courts to secure rights for victims and potential victims of mob violence, their overarching concern was always with popular opinion, and thus much of their work was devoted to criticizing practices of spectatorship, by the media as well as the mob.

Thus, in her discussion of the lynching of Lee Walker in Memphis, Tennessee, Wells quoted a local paper's description at length, noting that "the crowd looked on with complaisance, if not with real pleasure," and that after Walker was killed, his body was burned, and

> the comments of the crowd were varied. Some remarked on the efficacy of this style of cure for rapists, others rejoiced that men's wives and daughters were now safe from this wretch. Some laughed as the flesh cracked and blistered, and while a large number pronounced the burning of a dead body as a useless episode, not in all that throng was a word of sympathy heard for the wretch himself.[89]

Wells's critique was not limited, though, to the mob itself. Instead, she noted that the *Memphis Public Ledger* had sent her a telegram the day before the lynching asking her to come to Memphis "to write it up." She noted that "this telegram shows that the intentions of the mob were well known long before they were executed" and suggested that part of the crime was the fact that no one tried to intervene.[90]

Figures 6 and 7, from the NAACP antilynching publicity campaign, present the two sides of the antilynching critique of spectatorship. Figure 6 is a photo used in an NAACP antilynching fund-raising flyer. The text that accompanies the photo reads in part:

> Do not look at the Negro. His earthly problems are ended. Instead, look at the seven WHITE children who gaze at this gruesome spectacle. Is it horror or gloating on the face of the neatly dressed seven-year-old girl on the right? Is the tiny four-year-old on the left old enough, one wonders, to comprehend the barbarism her elders have perpetrated? Rubin Stacy, the Negro, who was lynched at Fort Lauderdale, Florida, on July 19, 1935, for "threatening and frightening a white woman," suffered PHYSICAL torture for a few short hours. But what psychological havoc is being wrought in the minds of the white children? Into

Figure 6. "Do Not Look at the Negro": Photograph of the lynching of Rubin Stacy, July 19, 1935, Fort Lauderdale, Florida. Allen-Littlefield Collection, Special Collections Division, Robert W. Woodruff Library, Emory University.

what kinds of citizens will they grow up? What kind of America will they help to make after being familiarized with such an inhuman, law-destroying practice as lynching.

The manacles, too, tell their own story. The Negro was powerless in the hands of the law, but the law was just as powerless to protect him from being lynched. Since 1922 over one-half the lynched victims have been taken from legal custody. Less than one percent of the lynchers have been punished, and they very lightly. More than 5,000 such instances of lynching have occurred without any punishment whatever, establishing beyond doubt that federal legislation is necessary, as in the case of kidnaping to supplement state action.[91]

Figure 7 is taken from the NAACP's pamphlet about the lynching of Claude Neal that I discussed in the Introduction. While much of the pamphlet is devoted to descriptions of the dynamics of the lynching, Figure 7 is a collage of newspaper articles from around the country (including Florida, Arkansas, Georgia, Ohio, and Wisconsin, among other places) announcing the impending lynching. The collage could, perhaps, speak for itself, but the NAACP has added one line of text at the top, a line that is no less damning for its simplicity: "All of America Knew of Lynching in Advance."

At first glance, the photograph in Figure 6 and its accompanying text might seem more powerful than the newspaper collage. After all, the dead body, the description of brutality, the glee on the faces of the spectators, and the plea for change leave little to the imagination. But however gruesome the photograph is, the spectacle and the crime appear somewhat isolated. It is easy to imagine that parts of the NAACP's national audience might have been revolted at the lynching but comforted by the stark difference between themselves and the mob. The collage, on the other hand, offers no such reassurances, for while it indicts the thousands of people who attended the lynching of Claude Neal, it suggests that the problem is far greater and that the media worked to create a national audience as an extension of the mob. "All of America" knew and is held accountable in the NAACP's indictment of American "civilization."

Concluding Remarks: The Impact of the Movement

As I noted in the Introduction, there were many reasons for the decline and near-elimination of lynching by the 1950s, including the mechanization of agriculture, industrial expansion, and black migration. It is impossible, therefore, to measure the effect of the antilynching movement with any degree of precision. Still, as Brundage writes in his study of lynching in Georgia and Virginia,

> the cumulative effect of the various efforts to suppress lynchings is apparent. . . . The accelerating shift from outright glorification of mob violence to defensive embarrassment can be traced across the early

Figure 7. Newspaper collage from "The Lynching of Claude Neal," pamphlet. From the NAACP Antilynching Publicity and Investigative Papers. Courtesy of the NAACP.

twentieth century. . . . with each passing year, the defenders of mob violence moved toward the periphery of southern society, no longer able to claim the unquestioned allegiance of the mob.[92]

For more than half a century, a devoted movement published hundreds of pamphlets, wrote countless articles and editorials, pressured local law enforcement agencies, and struggled in legislative battles and mass demonstrations, all in an effort not only to eliminate lynching but to challenge common sense understandings of race. When Robert Zangrando writes of the NAACP that they "sought to change public attitudes, stir politicians to corrective action, and generally redefine the settled contours of American race relations," his words apply equally to the entire antilynching movement.[93]

While it is not possible to determine just how successful the movement was, it is worth noting that journalists writing from the 1920s through the 1940s often credited the antilynchers with creating a political climate in which lynching was widely seen as unacceptable. For example, one article in 1939 noted that

> [m]ob violence, masquerading as the champion of southern womanhood, is petering out below the Mason Dixon line. And the weaker sex is largely responsible. Nine years ago a small group of thinking [women] who had long realized that there was more bloodthirst than knight-errantry in howling mobs, organized the Association of Southern Women for the Prevention of Lynching. . . . [The group was dedicated to] Demolishing the Myth of Mob Chivalry. . . . [To the question] "Isn't the primary purpose of lynching to protect white women?" . . . "thousands of southern women have answered for nearly ten years with an emphatic, "NO."[94]

Another article considers economic reasons for lynching's decline and black migration but concludes that

> [u]nderneath all there has been the constant agitation conducted by the Christian forces of the country, culminating during the past few years in the constructive efforts of the Committee on Interracial Cooperation. Service of this kind is not spectacular, but it evolves slowly that change of mind out of which alone there can come a permanent improvement of the relations between the races.[95]

In the time between the peak years of lynching in the late 1880s and early 1890s, and its virtual disappearance by the 1950s it had become widely understood as a very different kind of phenomenon. Few would deny the importance of the antilynching movement in fostering this "change of mind."

It is, however, difficult to assess the precise nature of this change. I noted at the beginning of this chapter that lynch mobs and antilynching activists were united in their efforts to ensure that lynching would be seen as the ultimate symbol of southern race relations, even though they had wildly divergent hopes about the ways in which their various audiences would understand the relationships between mob violence, race, and white supremacy. Lynching has now become a commonly used metaphor for racist injustice. Certainly this is an indication that at least to some extent, the antilynchers won their struggle over meaning. There are, after all, now virtually no publicly recognized speakers who would defend lynching or who would dispute the idea that lynch mobs represent a particularly appalling part of our national history. And while it is true that the antilynchers were not alone in fostering this shift in understanding, their efforts were clearly an important component of the change. Still, while the antilynchers' primary goal was always to challenge the logic behind mob violence, in order to meet this goal, they needed to refute a variety of racial stereotypes associated with lynching. It is important to note that they did not devote equal amounts of attention to all of their targets, nor did they resist them with the same amount of vehemence.

In the course of their struggles, the antilynchers sought to undermine the ideas that white men who joined lynch mobs were heroically defending white female virtue; that white women were sexually passive victims in need of male protection; that black women were sexually insatiable, virtually unrapeable, and in no need of defense; and, of course, that the black men who were killed by vigilante violence were sexually monstrous rapists. Ultimately, though, the antilynchers were generally forced to devote the bulk of their energies to debunking the myth of the black rapist, and their contribution to changing configurations of race has to be understood in this light.[96]

This point is particularly important when considering the relevance of the antilynching movement for contemporary antiracist struggles and racist stereotypes. I have argued that the antilynchers often challenged stereotypes of black female sexuality and emphasized the victimization of black women not only at the hands of white rapists but also, occasionally, by lynch mobs themselves. But I have also shown that they issued these challenges as part of a larger effort to challenge the myth of the black rapist. They referenced the rapes of black women to show the hypocrisy of the mob and to argue that white men's concern with rape was a sham, and they used the lynchings of black women to provide concrete proof that at least some lynchings were not motivated by the rape of white women. I am not suggesting that the effect of the antilynching campaign upon representations of black women was negligible, but it is important to note that antilynching activists seldom discussed black women in their own right. In the end, it is safe to say that the figure of the black rapist is the only stereotype in our nation's history that was systematically targeted by an antiracist movement spanning more than half a century. There is simply no similar history for challenges to stereotypes of black women. The antilynchers helped ensure that lynching would be remembered as a brutal crime against black men that relied upon the racist stereotype of the black rapist. The movement's impact on collective memories of black women is less clear and is certainly considerably less powerful. In later chapters on contemporary racialized violence and on the Hill–Thomas hearings, I examine the ways that the tactical choices and rhetorical strategies of the antilynching movement reverberate within national political processes at the dawn of a new century.

The antilynching movement and lynch mobs themselves were engaged in a struggle over how lynching would be understood and remembered, and our contemporary understandings of lynching owe much to these battles in the past. Contemporary invocations of lynching are also heavily indebted to these historical struggles that have helped to establish the meanings that have been attached to the lynching metaphor. In the past half century, however, as lynching has largely faded away as a material practice, the most important discursive battles over memories of lynching have generally been waged not over actual victims of vigilantism but in the realm of metaphor and popular culture. In chapter 2, I examine the cinematic construction of collective memories of lynching and racial terror.

CHAPTER 2

Cinematic Lynchings

"There's only one more question I need to ask you. . . . The man with
you appeared to be not entirely in his pants at the time of impact. Can
you tell me what happened just before you went off the road?"
    "Well, he became [whispers] Motherfucker this, motherfucker that."
    "Like in the movies?"
    "Exactly. And um . . . the next thing I knew . . . I only remember
bits and pieces of it, but he, uh, the gist of it was he was going to
uh . . . impale me with his . . . big . . ."
    "Ohh."

—The Last Seduction, *John Dahl, 1993*

"I ain't never been with a black man in my life. . . . [Pause, some
thought] Oh bloody hell. Oh Jesus Christ. Oh my. [Breaks down into
tears] I'm sorry, sweetie. I'm so ashamed . . . I can't look at you. I
didn't know, sweetheart. Honest, I didn't know you was black."
    "Who was he?"
    "You don't want to know, darling. . . . Listen, I want to be honest
with you, but I can't tell you that, sweetheart. I'm sorry. I'm sorry."

—Secrets and Lies, *Mike Leigh, 1996*

These two scenes from recent, highly successful independent films
give some indication of the variety of ways in which figures from
traditional lynch narratives have been invoked in recent cinema.
The first exchange occurs after Linda Fiorentino's supremely manipulative Wendy Crow has foiled a black private eye's kidnapping attempt by
tricking him into lowering his pants while she drives her car into a tree.
While Crow is recovering in the hospital, a policeman questions her
about what happened. Her answers take full advantage of the racism that
is prevalent in her area of rural New York State (the town's population
is almost completely white, and Crow had noticed earlier that any black
people were immediately seen as suspect), as she is completely confident
that her charge of attempted rape will be believed. The officer's reference to the movies suggests that the community's belief in the myth of
the black rapist is based, at least in part, on cinematic representations of
black men.

The second exchange is between Marianne Jean-Baptiste's Hortense
and Brenda Blethyn's Cynthia. Hortense is a black woman who was put
up for adoption at birth and who has gone on a quest in which she has

33

discovered that Cynthia, a white woman, is her birth mother. As the dialogue suggests, Cynthia is initially incapable of accepting Hortense's claims because she's unaware of ever having slept with a black man. When she finally *does* understand how Hortense could be her child, she is devastated by the realization. As the film progresses, the relationship between Hortense and Cynthia becomes more and more intimate, and a great number of secrets and lies are shared and revealed. Still, even at their closest, Cynthia is unable to reveal the identity of Hortense's father. Finally, Hortense gives up on finding out anything specific about her father, but suspecting the truth, she bitterly asks, "Was my father a nice man?" Cynthia is still unwilling to discuss him and responds by saying, "Oh, don't break my heart darling." Though he is never explicitly named as such, the figure of the black rapist is a constant presence throughout the film, never seen but always lurking at the edges of consciousness, haunting and threatening to disrupt the relationship between these two women.

Ever since Flora Cameron attempted to "preserve her honor" by throwing herself off a cliff while being chased by the ex-slave Gus in D. W. Griffith's 1915 film *The Birth of a Nation*, Hollywood has had a particularly strong fascination with imagery associated with interracial rape and lynching.[1] Whether exposing racist stereotypes as dangerous myths, as in *The Last Seduction*, or relying upon them for dramatic tension, as in *Secrets and Lies*[2] and *The Birth of a Nation*, cinematic representations of the rape/lynching narrative have been of central importance for the production of collective memory and a national process of racial formation.

Collective memory is constructed within the realm of representational politics and can be powerfully shaped and widely disseminated through cultural narratives involving photography, television, and cinema. But the production of collective memory is inextricably bound with processes of cultural amnesia, for representations of the past also work as "screens, actively blocking out other memories that are more difficult to represent."[3] While a variety of forms of cultural representations are involved in national processes both of constructing collective memory and of forgetting, Hollywood films have a particularly interesting role. As cultural artifacts, Hollywood films offer unique insight into the cultural anxieties and "value crises" of the periods in which they were made.[4] More important, the emotional investment that viewers bring to films and the massive circulation of Hollywood films in particular enable commercial films to powerfully influence social agendas as they "reposition us for the future by reshaping our memories of the past."[5]

The stakes over cinematic representations of the past are nowhere more evident than where race is concerned. Hollywood films have helped to shape audiences' understandings of race, and by representing African Americans in "every possible manner" of demeaning and marginalized position, they have worked to "glorify and relentlessly hold in place the white-dominated symbolic order and racial hierarchy of American society."[6] But because racial categories are fluid and subject to ongoing challenge and negotiation, "Hollywood's unceasing efforts to frame *blackness* are constantly challenged by the cultural and political self-definitions of African Americans, who as a people have been determined since the inception of commercial cinema to militate against this limiting system of representation."[7] Hollywood films are key sites in the struggles over the meaning not only of the category of "blackness" but also of a variety of other categories of race.

The process of representing race is closely linked to the construction of racial metaphors. Ella Shohat and Robert Stam argue that debates surrounding political and cultural representation of oppressed groups are based on "the semiotic principle that something is 'standing for' something else, or that some person or group is speaking on behalf of some other persons or groups."[8] This analysis of the stakes in struggles over representation resonates strongly with Burke's definition of metaphor as "a device for seeing something *in terms of* something else."[9] Indeed, *some* representations are automatically caught up in what we can see as processes of metaphorization. A tendency to reduce racial minorities to a series of essentialist characteristics works to ensure that "any negative behavior by any member of the oppressed community is instantly generalized as typical, as pointing to a perpetual backsliding toward some presumed negative essence. . . . each negative image of an underrepresented group becomes, within the hermeneutics of domination, sorely overcharged with allegorical meaning."[10] Representations of members of oppressed groups are unavoidably caught up in a process whereby they stand for something broader than themselves. The relative dearth of varied representations of oppressed groups, particularly in mainstream Hollywood cinema, helps to ensure that these representations automatically become metaphors for, or devices for seeing, the oppressed group itself.[11] Struggles over how various racial categories are represented in mainstream film are thus inseparable from broader social understandings of various racial groups and policies.[12] Cinematic representations of lynching and rape present these struggles in their starkest terms.

While many of the most enduring of the films that have dealt with lynching have already received widespread scholarly attention, the last decade has seen a host of new films that self-consciously invoke, manipulate, and attempt to reconfigure a collective memory of lynching and racial terror.[13] The selection of films in this chapter is not meant to be exhaustive. Because I am interested in the films that are most likely to have a substantial impact upon a national collective memory, this chapter is primarily concerned with mainstream films.[14] Practical considerations have forced me to further limit the bulk of this discussion to Hollywood films that have been released recently. As I have noted, representations of lynching have been central to the history of cinema since the inception of the studio system. The virtually endless supply of films to consider forced me to make difficult choices when determing which films to address.[15] Still, Hollywood's ability to construct and deploy racial images has never been uncontested, and to focus solely upon mainstream cinematic depictions of lynching would be to deny a critical part of the history of resistance against racism. The antilynching struggle waged by Ida B. Wells and groups like the NAACP and the ASWPL was complemented by the work of some early black filmmakers. I turn now to a brief discussion of their work.

From *The Birth of a Nation* to *The Birth of a Race* and Beyond: "Race Films" and Countermemory

Even before *The Birth of a Nation* opened in 1915, it was the subject of widespread outrage and protest throughout many black communities. The film's release during the peak years of lynching and Jim Crow posed an immediate and material threat to African Americans.[16] The film's glorification of the Ku Klux Klan "most certainly contributed to the public's tolerance of Klan criminality and its expansion to its greatest membership ever, about 5 million, by 1924."[17] The action that took place on the screen was often reflected on the streets. For example, when the film opened in Atlanta on Thanskgiving night in 1915, 25,000 Klansmen staged a march to celebrate.[18] Ed Guerrero observes that "African Americans had every reason to fear that what was depicted on the screen could easily be acted out against them in reality."[19] The recently formed NAACP responded to the threat posed by *Birth* by attempting to have it censored or banned. While these efforts were ultimately unsuccessful, protests against the film did result in having several of the most inflammatory scenes (including footage of black soldiers attacking white women) cut from the work print and in pressuring President Wilson to withdraw his support for the film.[20]

The NAACP's struggle to prevent the screening of *The Birth of a*

Nation should be seen as a component of antilynching movement activism. Certainly, the NAACP's critiques of *Birth* were not limited to the fact that the film might inspire or justify mob violence against blacks. But the concern with the material effects of racist representational practices is perfectly in line with the antilynching movement's recognition, as outlined in chapter 1, that representational politics constituted a crucial arena of struggle against lynching and that in order to eradicate lynching, it was necessary to challenge racist cultural projects, particularly those involving images of the black rapist.

Antiracist cultural activism was not limited to efforts to censor films like *The Birth of a Nation*. An important part of the struggle against racism in general and lynching in particular was waged by people who are not always thought of as engaged in social activism, namely, the growing numbers of black cultural producers who worked to create their own representations of black life. Independent black filmmakers attempted to challenge the racial representations of *Birth* on their own terms.

Toward the end of 1915, the NAACP was forced to recognize that its protests against *Birth* had not been nearly as effective as its members had hoped. One member of the group, May Childs Nerney, claimed that the "political signficance" of *Birth* was so important that blacks needed to "create a powerful public opinion against this [outmoded] idea of the Negro," and she argued that "we cannot create it except in some such spectacular way [as movies]."[21]

At the same time as Nerney and the NAACP were considering a cinematic response to *Birth*, Booker T. Washington proposed using his autobiography, *Up from Slavery*, as the basis of a "counter-irritant" to *Birth*. Similarly, W. E. B. Du Bois proposed a project that would be "a pageant of Negro history and some plays of my own and in moving pictures based on them."[22] Debates between Washington's camp and the NAACP's made it difficult to present a unified front to the Hollywood studios, and ultimately, the NAACP gave up on the project because of problems in finding sufficient funding. Eventually, Emmett J. Scott, who had been one of Booker T. Washington's secretaries, decided to produce *The Birth of a Race*, which was meant to counter the racist stereotypes in *The Birth of a Nation* by highlighting black aspirations and accomplishments.[23] In order to get the film produced, Scott needed financial support from white backers, who forced him to make thematic changes that drastically limited any ideological challenge the film might have posed to *The Birth of a Nation*.[24] While the resulting film was disappointing and a box-office bomb, this initial effort drew attention to the possibilities that cinema presented as a vehicle for social change and critique and provided a spark for other black independent filmmakers. Most notable among this group was Oscar Micheaux.

In 1918, Micheaux started a career in film that would span three decades, during which time he would write, direct, and produce thirty-four films.[25] Unfortunately, only three of Micheaux's silent films survive today.[26] His surviving films, along with publicity materials and reviews of the remainder of his work, provide clear evidence of Micheaux's long-standing concern with representations of racism, lynching, and interracial rape.

Micheaux was a witness to the lynching of Leo Frank in Marietta, Georgia, in 1915,[27] and he portrayed a fictionalized version of the case in *The Gunsaulus Mystery* (1921), in which an innocent man is accused of murdering a white woman.[28] He is said to have had the same case in mind when he filmed *Harlem after Midnight* (1934).[29] He addressed the antilynching movement explicitly in *The Brute* (1920) by focusing on a black boxer who "struggled against lynching"[30] and in *The Dungeon* (1922), which was publicized as addressing the Dyer Anti-Lynching Bill.[31] *The Symbol of the Unconquered* (1920) highlighted the KKK's use of terrorism as a strategy to overcome economic competition from blacks.[32] But it is perhaps Micheaux's best-known film, *Within Our Gates* (1919), that provides the most direct refutation of the rape and lynching narrative in *The Birth of a Nation*.

Lynching is not an issue in *Within Our Gates* until the final moments, when we gain some insight into the ways in which the family background of Sylvia Landry (the film's black protoganist) has structured her feelings about race and romance. Starting with an intertitle that refers to "Sylvia's Story," we learn that Landry's parents were lynched following a fight with a planter over money. Landry's father had earned enough money to pay off his debt to the planter. The planter responded violently to Landry's attempt to remove himself from financial bondage. During the ensuing scuffle, a white enemy of the planter shoots him, and Landry is blamed for the crime. Landry's entire family flees, while a lynch mob gathers and moves "off to the swamps" in pursuit.

Before Landry is caught, Efrem, the black man who reported Landry, is killed by the frustrated mob, on the grounds that one black victim is nearly as good as the next. (One of the members of the mob proposes, "While we's waitin', what ya say we grab this boy?") The local newspaper refers to Efrem as the "recent victim of accidental death at unknown hands," despite the fact that the film's audience has witnessed the clearly intentional beating and lynching of Efrem at the highly recognizable hands of some of the town's best-known leaders. When Landry is finally caught, we see what appears to be a headline reading

> *Proclamation: Hanging of the Negro Murderers of Philip Gridlestone* [the planter]. The murderer Jasper Landry, having been captured and having confessed to the crime of which he is accused, will be brought under guard by the citizens of Lawrence to the place of execution.
> —The Committee.

While Landry's wife and son are also caught by the mob, his son manages to escape. Landry and his wife are less fortunate and are both lynched. We see nooses over their heads and watch as two teams of people, including women, pull as hard as they can to raise the bodies. Jane Gaines writes of this scene, "That the man and wife are to be hanged together is signalled by one of the most unsettling images in the history of African-American cinema: a low-angle close-up of a wooden bar frames two dangling ropes against a cloudy sky."[33]

As the Landrys are being lynched, another group of white men is shown working on a pyre, dousing it with kerosene and putting twigs at the base. We learn that after being hanged, the Landrys were "incinerated in the bonfire." While the lynching is going on, the film crosscuts back and forth between the lynching and a scene in which Gridlestone's brother is attempting to rape Sylvia. Sylvia is thus shown as "being molested *at the same moment* in which her parents are being executed for crimes they did not commit."[34] Gridlestone eventually abandons his efforts because of the strength of Sylvia's struggle and because he sees a scar on her chest that reveals that Sylvia was actually his daughter—"his legitimate daughter from a marriage to a woman of her race—who was later adopted by the Landrys."

This narrative summary is sufficient to show many of the elements of Micheaux's critique of lynching and rape. Not only is lynching represented as a barbaric practice, marked by the highly spetacularized violence of the bonfire that follows the hanging, but it is also presented as a community event involving women and children as well as leading figures from the town, supported by the legal system, and publicized by the press.[35] Perhaps most important, the "thread bare lie" that Wells so famously exposed, that lynching is a response to the rape of white women by black men, is refuted. Not only is it clear that lynching has nothing to do with rape, but the only time that rape comes up as an issue is as a white man's attempted rape of a black woman. This scene was a direct response to the scene in *The Birth of a Nation* in which the mulatto leader Silas Lynch corners Elsie Stoneman. Toni Cade Bambara, speaking of Micheaux's scene, remarks that "[t]here are several things about that scene that are really kind of interesting. One is its obvious echo of the rape scene in *The Birth of a Nation*. Same gestures. Same lighting. But clearly what he is trying to do is correct, challenge, protest, set the record straight on who rapes who."[36] In this short little ending to *Within Our Gates*, a segment that almost seems to have been tacked on, Micheaux has systematically refuted virtually every element of the traditional lynch narrative and has done so along very much the same lines as did the more formally organized branches of the antilynching movement.[37]

The power of Micheaux's critique of traditional representations of rape and lynching was blunted, however, by the fact that his film was seen by relatively few people. All of Micheaux's early films were independently produced, and therefore they did not have nearly the distribution of a film like *The Birth of a Nation*.[38] Moreover, *Within Our Gates*, released the year after the "Red Summer" of 1919, met with strong resistance in a number of cities. Micheaux was often required by city officials to edit out parts of the film because of fears that the film would incite race riots.[39] Gaines contrasts the different treatments accorded *Within Our Gates* and *The Birth of a Nation*, arguing that

> the case of *Within Our Gates* brings home one of the lessons of the
> NAACP campaign against *The Birth of a Nation*. Whereas *protest* against
> a film in this period did not mean that it would be banned (and it might
> even insure that it drew crowds), the threat of a race *riot* meant that ex-
> hibitors and city officials would cooperate to keep a film off the screen.[40]

Gaines sees the concern with race riots as a "smoke screen" that was used as a way to silence the film's protest against lynching and as a way to "suppress active protest against worsening housing and employment conditions in the North."[41] Even without such explicit forms of censorship, Micheaux's work and other "race films" would not have had nearly the power to influence popular culture or to intervene in the creation of national collective memories of interracial rape and lynching as did the more widely viewed Hollywood films.

In the wake of the controversies surrounding *Within Our Gates* and *The Birth of a Nation*, cinematic depictions of race relations tended to avoid explicit scenes of racialized violence. The political pressure of black protest worked to prevent most directors from engaging in outright glorification of lynching and Klan terrorism, and while antilynching narratives influenced a variety of films, from the Academy Award–winning *To Kill a*

Mockingbird to the blaxploitation-era *Mandingo* (Richard Fleischer, 1975), it was not until a new wave of black filmmakers emerged in the 1980s and 1990s that many of the themes that were so central to Micheaux's work would find a mass audience.[42] Micheaux's films may not have had the kind of distribution that was necessary to truly blunt the impact of a film like *The Birth of a Nation*, but they did help to create and maintain a powerful set of countermemories that would resonate decades later with the work of contemporary directors such as John Singleton and Spike Lee.

Lynching in Bed-Stuy: Spike Lee's *Do the Right Thing*

Spike Lee's 1989 film *Do the Right Thing* has been widely seen as one of the most important films of the past twenty years. Its popularity "opened the door for the new rush of black films to come in the 1990s,"[43] and the film received more attention in the national media than any other film in recent memory, with the possible exception of Oliver Stone's *J.F.K.* (1991).[44] *Do the Right Thing*, dedicated to the families of famous victims of police brutality, uses lynching imagery as a way to critique modern-day racism.

A Day in Brooklyn: A Narrative Summary

The film's opening scenes set the stage. After a sequence in which Rosie Perez dances to Public Enemy's "Fight the Power," we hear a very loud alarm clock going off and Samuel L. Jackson's DJ, Mister Señor Love Daddy, telling his radio audience to "Waaaake Up! Wake UP! Wake UP! Wake UP! Up ya wake! Up ya wake! Up ya wake!" Thus, the film literally broadcasts its intentions to serve as a wake-up call, and the prominence given to Public Enemy's lyrics suggests that racism and the necessity for antiracist struggles will be an underlying subtext for the remainder of the film.

Do the Right Thing takes place on "the hottest day of the summer"[45] and is set entirely on one block in the Bedford-Stuyvesant section of Brooklyn. As the film follows many of the block's residents throughout the day, we see that eventually just about everyone winds up at Sal's Famous Pizzeria. Sal's Famous is run by Sal (played by Danny Aiello) and his two sons Vito and Pino (Richard Edson and John Turturro, respectively). Sal's Famous and the Korean-owned grocery store across the street are the only businesses on a block where many of the black residents appear to be either un- or underemployed. (A trio of unemployed black men who sit on the corner—ML, Coconut Sid and Sweet Dick Willie—make up, in Spike Lee's words, a "Greek chorus" offering commentary throughout the film.) The grocery seems to be a family-only business, so Sal's is the only place on the block that employs any local residents. Spike Lee plays a pizza deliverer named Mookie. Sal's economic power and the question of the debt that he owes to the community are primary concerns throughout the film. Two characters in particular—Buggin' Out and Radio Raheem—clash with Sal and his sons over the pizza parlor's policies (see Figure 8).

The first sign of conflict comes when Buggin' Out notices that the pizza parlor's "Wall of Fame" is covered with eight-by-ten photos of famous Italian Americans and decides that the predominately black clientele entitles the black community to have photos of African Americans too: "[R]arely do I see any *Italian* Americans eating in here. All I've ever seen is Black folks. So since we spend *much* money here, we do have some say. . . . Put some brothers up on this Wall of Fame. We want Malcom X, Michael Jordan tomorrow."[46] When this appeal doesn't work (Sal's answer is to take out a baseball bat), Buggin' Out decides to organize a boycott. Initially, the proposal to boycott Sal's is rejected by the rest of the community. Most of the people with whom Buggin' Out discusses the boycott reject it out of hand. The block's elder statesman (Ossie Davis's unemployed and drunk "Da Mayor") dismisses it as "foolishness," while the block's group of teenagers tell him that they were raised on Sal's food and that Sal has done nothing wrong. Mookie's sister Jade (played by Lee's sister Joie Lee) agrees with Buggin' Out that something

Figure 8. The "Wall of Fame" in *Do the Right Thing* (1989). Left to right: John Turturro as Pino, Danny Aiello as Sal, Giancarlo Esposito as Buggin' Out, and Spike Lee as Mookie.

needs to change, but she does not see the sense in Buggin' Out's target or strategies. She tells Buggin' Out to "direct your energies in a more useful way" and claims that she is "down for something positive in the community" instead of for what she clearly sees as a meaningless boycott.[47] Still, Buggin' Out is really the *only* character who has a plan to challenge racism, and eventually he is able to recruit Radio Raheem to his cause.

We always hear Radio Raheem before we see him. He carries around a huge radio that only plays one song—Public Enemy's "Fight the Power." (He explains, "I don't like nothin' else.") We gain our clearest sense of his identity in a scene in which a group of young Puerto Rican men are sitting on a stoop, listening to salsa music from a radio placed on top of a car. The camera focuses on their radio, but we soon hear the salsa giving way to Public Enemy's rap, and the camera pans to a close-up of Radio Raheem's radio, which is clearly bigger and shinier than the Puerto Ricans' radio. As Radio Raheem comes closer to the men, the camera pans up his body until his upper torso and face fill most of the frame. Bill Nunn, who plays Radio Raheem, is a very large man, and he is wearing a T-shirt that exposes his muscles, so this shot clearly shows an imposing figure. To further emphasize this point, the camera moves away from Radio Raheem and toward the group of men, who are all visibly upset as they seem to fit nicely into the same size frame as was occupied by Radio Raheem alone. The framing suggests some sort of battle and equivalence between this one, lone, radio man and a group of five men. In a classic Hollywood showdown, one of the members of the group walks up to his radio, faces Radio Raheem, says, "You think you got it like that bro'?" and turns up the volume, drowning out Raheem's radio. Far from defeated, however, Radio Raheem simply smiles, holds his own radio at waist level, reaches down, and twists up the volume. The pretender realizes his plight, turns off his radio, frowns, and says, "You got it, bro'" as Radio Raheem walks off into the horizon, fist raised in triumph. Thus, Radio Raheem is presented as a mythic figure. He is hypermasculinized, and his radio is a central part of his masculinity. This information is important for an understanding of Radio Raheem's relationship with Sal.[48]

The first time we see Radio Raheem enter Sal's, his radio is blasting as he orders: "Two slices." Sal needs to yell to be heard as he tells Radio that there will be "no service until you turn that thing off." Radio ignores him at first and just demands two slices again, but Sal yells that "I can't even hear myself think. You are disturbing me. You are disturbing my customers."[49] Radio pauses for a moment, contemplating his next move, but he ultimately decides to turn off his radio and order the pizza again.

Sal takes full advantage of this victory, and he proceeds to lecture Radio Raheem: "You come into Sal's, there's no music. No rap, no music, no music, no music. Capiche? Understand?" A close-up shot of Radio's face suggests that he understands perfectly well and that this is not a slight that will soon be forgotten.

It is, therefore, no surprise that when Radio Raheem runs into Buggin' Out later that night, he is open to the idea that something needs to be done about Sal. Buggin' Out mentions the boycott, and Radio replies, "I almost had to bust him in the head today man. Gonna tell me, tell *me*, Radio Raheem, to turn down my box and shit, man, and didn't even say please. Who the fuck he think he is? Don Coreleone and shit?" The two of them agree on an alliance. They walk into Sal's right after closing time, radio blasting (Sal had reopened the place for some late customers and had not gotten around to locking it again). Sal yells, "What'd I tell you about that noise?" and Buggin' Out answers, "What'd I tell you about the pictures?" They get into a screaming match, during which Sal says, "Turn that jungle music off!" Until this moment, Sal had resisted overt racism. He had even lectured his son Pino about the problems with stereotypes and told him how proud he was that the kids in this neighborhood had grown up on his food. When push comes to shove, however, his racism comes out, and Buggin' Out calls him on it: "Why it gotta be about jungle music? Why it gotta be about Africa? It's about the fucking pictures!" Sal ignores the charge of racism and focuses on the issue of turf, saying, "It's about turn that shit off! And get the fuck out of my place." But Radio Raheem refuses to comply: "This is music. MY music!" The confrontation escalates as Sal says, "Fuck your music!" and Radio Raheem answers by putting his radio on the counter and defying Sal to "turn it off then!" After a little more yelling, Sal pulls out a bat and says, "You black cocksucker. I'll fucking tear your nigger ass." Sal's open embrace of racism at this point is too much for the rest of his customers. While they had earlier defended Sal and refused to take part in the boycott, now they start yelling at Sal: "Oh, we're niggers now?" There is a little more yelling before Sal finally hauls off, raises his bat, and, in what Mark Reid describes as a "virtual castration," repeatedly bashes Radio Raheem's radio, totally destroying it.[50] When he is done, there is complete silence, which is broken by Sal's declaration, "I just killed your fuckin' radio." There is silence again, until Radio Raheem examines his radio, throws it to the ground, yells, pulls Sal over the counter, throws him to the ground, and starts to beat and choke him. Everyone in the pizza parlor gets involved in the fight (Sal's sons try to pull Radio off Sal, and some of the customers try to stop them), and it soon spills out onto the street, where a much larger crowd gathers. Radio Raheem is so strong that none of the crowd can pull him off Sal, and it looks for a moment as if he might actually kill Sal.[51] Thus, when the police come, they actually appear to be justified in using force to pull Radio Raheem away from Sal. This initial appearance gives way almost immediately, however, to a clear sense that they are being unnecessarily brutal, for one cop uses his nightstick in a choke hold on Radio Raheem.[52] At this point, close-ups of Raheem's face reveal that he is clenching his teeth, and it looks as if he is choking. His distress is obvious, and the three older men from the corner yell at the cops, "You're killing him! You're killing him." Other spectators yell for the cops to stop, and finally even one of the cops says, "Gary, that's enough; Gary, that's enough, man." Gary does not stop, however, and we see a classic lynching shot: As the choke hold is used to lift Radio Raheem off the ground by the neck, the camera focuses on his feet, which are dangling over the street and shaking in the air as he goes through his final convulsions before death. Finally, the shaking stops, and Buggin' Out starts yelling "Radio! Radio Raheem!" Recognizing that they have gone too far, the cops drop Radio's body, and one starts yelling at him to "[g]et the fuck up." One cop even kicks the corpse, yelling at him to "quick faking it."

Of course he is not faking it, and as it becomes clear to everyone what has happened, the cops load Radio Raheem's body into a squad car, shove Buggin' Out into another car, and start to beat a hasty retreat from what is rapidly turning into an angry mob. As the cops leave, initial expressions of rage and distress (Buggin' Out was screaming, "You can't kill us all. You can't fuckin' kill us all" while another character was in the streets howling in pain) give way to a highly stylized sequence in which one member of the crowd after another addresses the camera directly against a background of total silence. The first member of the crowd to speak notes, "They killed him. They killed Radio Raheem." But it is clear that Radio's death is not meant to be seen in isolation, for the other members of the crowd place Radio Raheem in a larger context of racist police brutality: "Murder. They did it again. Just like Michael Stewart." "Murder. Eleanor Bumpurs."[53] "Murder." Finally, one of the old men says, "It's as plain as day. They didn't have to kill him." There is one final moment of silence and tension when it is clear that *something* is about to happen, but it is not clear what. Finally, Mookie picks up a garbage can and hurls it through the pizzeria's window. Most of the crowd follows his lead, and they proceed to trash Sal's. Finally, the place is set on fire, and everybody runs out.

Once Sal's is nearly gutted, the fire department shows up, along with what seems like an army of police officers in full riot gear. The police ask the crowd to disperse, but after one warning, in a scene that was intended to evoke the police brutality during the civil rights movement,[54] the police instruct the firefighters to turn their hoses on the crowd. Pandemonium breaks out as people run from, or are knocked over by, the water or are arrested or beaten by the police.

Black Lynching/White Rage: Lynching as Warning?

By setting much of the film's action in and around a white-owned pizza parlor, Lee was alluding to the 1986 incident in Howard Beach, Queens, in which a group of white teenagers beat and chased three black men after hunting them down in a pizza parlor.[55] One of the men, Michael Griffith, was forced to run onto the Belt Parkway, where he was killed by traffic. This incident received national media attention and was referred to by then-mayor Ed Koch as "a modern lynching" and "the worst crime in the recent history of the city."[56] Governor Mario Cuomo also got involved. He appointed a special prosecutor for the case, and he proposed new civil rights legislation because of the incident.[57] Thus, there was already a powerfully institutionalized collective memory of Howard Beach as a signifier of modern-day racism.

While Lee is clearly invoking some of the most powerful memories of racist police brutality and extralegal racist mob violence, he has changed the context of these events in important ways. Most notable are the shifts in geography and time. By locating the white-owned pizza parlor in a predominantly black section of Brooklyn in the 1980s (instead of the largely white Howard Beach or the southern United States in the 1950s), Lee allows for a new range of possibilities, at the same time as he divorces racist violence from much of its underlying logic.

The fact that Radio Raheem's "lynching" occurs in a black neighborhood means, first of all, that there is a dramatic change in terms of spectators. Bell hooks argues that this change has important implications for the ways the film conceptualizes the possibilities for antiracist resistance:

> A distressingly nihilistic ritual of disempowerment is enacted when a large crowd of black people watch as a "few" policemen brutally murder a young black man. Such a scene delivers a powerful message in a white supremacist society. The message is not about police brutality and how outraged citizens should be that the law does not protect black people deemed dangerous; it is instead that the white supremacist system of policing and control is intact and black people are powerless to assert any meaningful resistance. The crowd symbolically re-enacts the lynching mob, only with black victims as spectators.[58]

I think that hooks is right to suggest that this scenario presents a horrify-ing portrait of helplessness, but the idea that race is the "only" difference between these spectators and those in a traditional lynch mob misses the complexity of this substitution. The difference between audience as vic-tims and audience as willing, even enthusiastic, participants is striking. Traditional lynchings, with white mobs, served as mechanisms of con-tainment. They were meant to paralyze blacks and to "convey to them that there was always someone watching over their shoulders ready to punish them for the slightest offense or the least deviation from accept-able lines of action."[59] The white mob (and widely circulated newspaper photographs of the mob) strengthened the disciplinary power of the spectacle, since it suggested that any laws that might otherwise provide a measure of safety for blacks would be flagrantly flaunted and that kill-ing black people was a community affair. By making the mob black, Lee inverts this scenario and suggests that lynchings can be a source of community outrage and horror.[60] While the publicity surrounding tra-ditional lynchings served to extend "the function of lynching as a mode of surveillance by reiterating its performative qualities,"[61] the spectacle of Radio Raheem's death is clearly a key component of Lee's wake-up call, which is meant to put a very different audience on notice. The hor-rified black mob *rejects* the performative qualities of Raheem's death and attempts to send the message that racist killings will not be tolerated.

I would argue, in fact, that it is precisely this rejection that was re-sponsible for so much of the outrage that the film provoked. As I have noted, Joe Klein's review of *Do the Right Thing* in *New York* magazine warned that the riot scene would add to New York's climate of racial hostility and could produce race riots. Lee anticipated this reaction. In the first days of his film journal, he writes, "I know I'll come up against some static from the white press. They'll say I'm trying to incite a race riot."[62] The controversy over the film's potential for inciting violence among blacks prefigured the 1992 controversy over Ice-T's song "Cop Killer." The song was eventually removed from Ice-T's album because of fears that it would actually lead to assassinations of police officers. In both of these cases, I think it is reasonable to suggest that a good deal of the outrage is likely based upon a reaction to the suggestion that perpe-trators of racist violence might have something to fear.[63]

Hooks is right to suggest, though, that *Do the Right Thing* presents this warning in only the most tentative terms. The crowd could not prevent Raheem's death, *avoided* violence in favor of property destruction (Sal and his sons were safely escorted to a stairwell, from which they watched the proceedings), offered only token resistance against the forces that were allied against it, was safely contained (the crowd channeled all of its rage into the destruction of Sal's), and was easily dispersed.[64] When the crowd leaves and Sal's is left to burn, we see a close-up of Radio Raheem's broken radio, as we hear his favorite song, "Fight the Power," growing louder and louder. While the sound track suggests that Radio Raheem is thus resurrected in fighting spirit, the film never follows up with any kind of organized antiracist movement in the wake of the riots. Lee's use of civil rights–era imagery therefore falls flat, for the fire hoses that are used to douse the flames in the pizza parlor and to drive back the rioters in the streets appear to be much *more* successful at extinguishing the sparks of resistance than were the fire hoses that were used during the height of a well-organized mass movement for civil rights.

Racism without Rationale: Mindless Violence

Part of the reason that antiracist resistance seems so impotent here might well be the fact that Lee's depicition of racism itself lacks clear definition. Certainly, the film suggests that there are powerful institutional forces that will support racist brutality. Radio Raheem may have been killed accidentally, but the police and fire department acted quite purposefully to quell dissent, and it is clear that the city government placed a higher priority on white property rights than on black life.[65] But the fact that Radio Raheem's death *was* apparently accidental is indicative of the fact that the film presents no clear rationale as to why anyone might have *wanted* to kill him.[66] Again, Lee's use of lynching imagery is instructive here.

I have already noted that Radio Raheem's violence was prompted by what we can see as a direct assault on his masculinity: the destruction of his radio. Wiegman argues that lynching and castration as spectacle served the symbolic function of revoking black men's claims to patriarchal entitlement in the years following emancipation:

> In severing the black male's penis from his body . . . the mob aggressively denies the patriarchal sign and symbol of the masculine, interrupting the privilege of the phallus and thereby reclaiming, through the perversity of dismemberment, the black male's (masculine) potentiality for citizenship.[67]

This violent denial involved "a perverse level of physical intimacy between the white male aggressor and his captive ex-slave," which is clearest in the historical accounts of lynchings in which the mob kept pieces of the victim's genitals as souvenirs.[68] Wiegman writes, "In the image of white men embracing . . . — . . . with hate, fear, and a chilling form of empowered delight—the same penis they were so over-determinedly

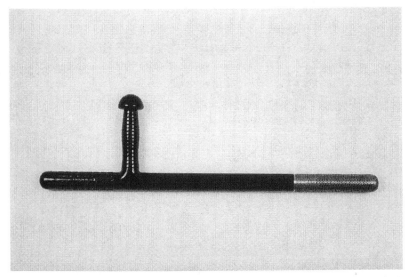

Figure 9. Mel Chin, *Night Rap,* 1993. Modified black polycarbide nightstick with nickel-plated mike head of perforated steel. Collection of the artist. Used with permission of the artist.

driven to destroy, one encounters a sadistic enactment of the homoerotic at the very moment of its most extreme disavowal."[69] Mel Chin's sculpture *Night Rap* (1993; see Figure 9)—a phallic police nightstick that has been converted into a microphone—suggests that modern-day police brutality incorporates the mob's desire to appropriate black male sexuality and, at the same time, reproduces aspects of a lynch mob's surveillant functions. Using Chin's sculpture as a lens to understand the film, I would argue that the intense death embrace between Radio Raheem and his white killer, mediated by a black nightstick, suggests that some of the sexual dynamics of lynching are very much in play in *Do the Right Thing.* But it is not clear what kind of threat is posed by Radio Raheem's masculinity or why the police would want to either revoke or reappropriate it. Racism might be institutionalized, but the film presents little indication of whose interests it serves. Even though the film presents Radio Raheem's death in the context of fairly widespread racist police brutality, it fails to present that brutality within the larger context of institutionalized inequality and white supremacy.[70]

The fact that Raheem's death is not clearly linked to broader racist social structures also means that Lee's critique of the mythology of dangerous black men is blunted.[71] As I have noted, the initial police intervention is presented here as really quite *reasonable*: Radio Raheem may have been killed unnecessarily, but he was on the verge of killing Sal and was therefore no innocent victim. The role that Raheem played in necessitating police action ultimately prevents Lee from demonstrating that black men were lynched for *trumped-up* charges and from debunking the myth of the black man as beast.[72] While this may not have been Lee's agenda, to the extent that Raheem is responsible for his own death, *Do the Right Thing* serves to perpetuate rather than challenge stereotypes of black men as unthinkingly brutal.

Hanging Signifiers: The Shifting Contours of Lynching in *Just Cause* and *A Time to Kill*

Just Cause (1995) and *A Time to Kill* (1996) follow *Do the Right Thing* insofar as they rely upon lynching imagery to dramatize stories about race and justice in contemporary America. But the similarity ends there. While Lee's film can be faulted for failing to provide a rationale for racist violence and for consequently reinforcing racist stereotypes, it presents itself as a fairly straightforward critique of modern-day racism. *Just Cause* and *A Time to Kill*, in contrast, destabilize the traditional lynching narrative and re-present its central figures in ways that are simultaneously immediately recognizable and completely new. In the process, the lines between lyncher and lynched, rapist and rape victim, and mob violence and legal justice are blurred while the meaning of racism is presented as ever shifting and indeterminate.

Just Cause opens in rural Florida with the arrest of a black man (Bobby Earl Ferguson, played by Blair Underwood) who has been charged with the rape and murder of an eleven-year-old white girl. We immediately begin to suspect that there is something wrong with the case against him as we see the beginning of Earl's interrogation (he is consistently referred to as Earl or Bobby Earl; his last name is mentioned only once during the film and is not mentioned in the credits) and beating in police custody. The next scene is meant to confirm our suspicions; in it, we see Paul Armstrong (a former trial lawyer turned Harvard law professor, played by Sean Connery) debating the death penalty in a posh lecture hall, presumably at Harvard University. Armstrong, who is arguing against the death penalty, notes that "this justice system has killed at least twenty-three innocent men, and sentences blacks who kill whites seven times more than whites who kill blacks." Ultimately, his scathingly sarcastic conclusion is that "from 1890 to the 1990s [there have been] over a hundred years of progress." By referencing the peak years of antiblack mob violence, Armstrong is suggesting that racism is as prevalent as ever and that what used to be extralegal violence has now been embraced by the legal system in the form of legal lynchings. As the debate concludes (a clearly victorious Armstrong is greeted with thunderous applause and is informed by his opponent that "you changed my mind, I'll tell you that"), Armstrong is approached by Earl's mother (played by *A Raisin in the Sun*'s Ruby Dee, whose almost iconic status lends the film a veneer of civil rights credibility), who informs him, "[T]hey're going to kill my boy." She enlists Armstrong in the fight for her son's life, and the stage appears to be set for an antiracist courtroom battle in the long-standing tradition of films like *To Kill a Mockingbird.*

Armstrong's first meeting with Earl supplies more evidence that the more things change, the more they stay the same. Earl claims that his confession was coerced by a black cop (Tanny Brown, played by Laurence Fishburne), who had threatened to kill him if he did not confess. Again, racism has changed forms, but only slightly. Earl argues, "This is the New South and now they've got black cops to come and torment your black ass. It's called affirmative action." The flashback to Earl's interrogation confirms this, as we see Brown put a gun in Earl's mouth and pull the trigger. The gun does not fire, but the clear implication is that the next shot will be for real if Earl doesn't start talking. When Earl *does* finally confess, Brown says, "[Y]ou strange fruit, Bobby Earl. Strange fruit indeed." "Strange fruit" is a reference to the Abel Meeropol song about lynching ("Southern trees bear a strange fruit / blood on the leaves and blood at the root / Black Body swinging in the Southern breeze / Strange fruit hanging from the poplar trees"), and Brown's words confirm that Earl was the intended victim of a lynching.[73]

In case there is any doubt that Earl's death sentence was *not* due to "just cause," we soon learn that the legal case was as flimsy as it could be. The coroner did shoddy work, the arresting deputy was brutal and corrupt, and Earl's defense attorney was only minimally competent. None of this really mattered during the trial because, as Earl's original defense attorney says, the notion that "truth will prevail" is "naive." He elaborates by noting that "the people in this town were sick with grief over that poor little girl, and they wanted their revenge. The end." Ultimately, he suggests that even the minimal defense that he offered may have been too much, noting, "I paid for it dearly. I've lost half of my business in this county because I tried to defend that son of a bitch. And he got the chair. Can you imagine what it'd be like for me here if I'd a gotten him acquitted?" Community outrage over the murder and rape of a white girl provided a lynch mob atmosphere that ensured that the jury's verdict was predetermined.[74]

Figure 10. Laurence Fishburne as Tanny Brown and Sean Connery as Paul Armstrong in *Just Cause* (1995).

Lest we get too complacent, however, what looks in the movie like a new antilynching narrative soon begins to crumble. Brown informs Armstrong that Earl had been arrested a year before the murder for an earlier case in which a white girl was kidnapped (Figure 10). The charges against Earl were dropped for lack of evidence, but Armstrong is clearly concerned about the possibility that there is a pattern here. He is somewhat reassured when he confronts Earl with the earlier kidnapping case, but Earl's anger and sarcasm in this scene add new dimensions to his character and suggest that we still do not know the whole story. Earl explains that the first arrest changed his life, since it provided an excuse for Cornell University to revoke a scholarship that it had offered to him.[75] He claims that Cornell had only wanted him as a token black man, to foster an image of diversity, but the kidnapping charges made him more of a liability than an asset. While this charge is a serious one, Earl's hesitation in this scene suggests that there is more behind his anger than the loss of the scholarship.

Armstrong does not linger on the earlier kidnapping case or on Earl's anger because he is given a new lead. Earl claims that another inmate, Blair Sullivan (played by Ed Harris), who is a confessed serial killer in the same prison, is the person who really murdered the girl that Earl was accused of killing. Sure enough, Sullivan tells Armstrong how to find the murder weapon and admits to the murder. With the murder weapon and confession in hand, Armstrong easily wins the appeal that he has filed on Earl's behalf. The photographers, joyful music, and Armstrong's loving embrace with his wife all testify that justice has at last been done and that a racist miscarriage of justice has been adverted. Finally, Armstrong's father-in-law is able to toast "the triumph of truth over appearance," but we see Tanny Brown frowning in the distance, and we are led to suspect that, for now, it is only the appearance of truth that has triumphed.

Almost immediately after the trial, our suspicions are confirmed as we learn that Sullivan's confession was fabricated. He had agreed to take the rap for Earl if Earl would kill his parents for him after being acquitted. Earl agreed to Sullivan's terms not simply for freedom but for revenge. It turns out that Earl had not selected Armstrong as a champion because of his brilliant legal mind or liberal politics but because his wife had been the prosecutor in the first case in which Earl was accused of kidnapping. Earl did, apparently, tell Paul Armstrong the truth when he claimed that he was innocent in that case, but he hid the extent of his suffering. In her zeal to win her case, Armstrong's wife had managed to have Earl held over in jail for one night, despite the fact that she knew her star witness was a liar. While in jail for charges of kidnapping and attempted rape of a white girl, Earl not only was "beat up" (as Armstrong's wife put it) by the white prisoners, but he was castrated. In this earlier scenario, Earl really is figured as the classic lynching victim: He is an innocent black man subjected to a highly sexualized form of mob (as opposed to legally sanctioned) violence on the basis of an unreliable charge of rape. His innocence is largely immaterial, however, since there is no longer any doubt about his guilt in the case for which he has been convicted and since his actions subsequent to his appeal and acquittal render him more monstrous than even his original jury had suspected.

Armstrong finds out about the true nature of Sullivan's confession and about Earl's motivations too late to prevent Earl from kidnapping Armstrong's wife and daughter, but with Tanny Brown's help, he is able to track Earl to his lair. During the course of their final confrontation, Earl reveals his plans to rape and murder Armstrong's wife and daughter, thus enraging the otherwise passive Armstrong and forcing him to finally adopt strong-arm tactics as he fights and eventually stabs Earl, leaving him to be eaten by a crocodile in the Florida swampland.

This film is interesting not merely because it is centrally concerned with the iconography of various figures surrounding lynching discourse but also because of the ways it reconfigures and deploys those figures, and in the process thoroughly blurs the boundaries between what we might otherwise have seen as clearly hegemonic or counterhegemonic subject positions. Armstrong as liberal lawyer is revealed as a dupe who is redeemed only when he assumes the mantle of the truly heroic White Avenger. The myth of the black beast/rapist is simultaneously exposed as a dangerous and racist myth that is at the heart of mob violence (Earl was castrated for a rape he did not commit) and endorsed (Earl becomes the very monster the mob feared).[76] White women are positioned as willing participants in the lynching of black men (Armstrong's wife had Earl kept in prison for careerist reasons) and as potential rape/murder victims of oversexed (even when castrated) black men.

The film is clearly weighted toward the second set of readings here. Armstrong the liberal lawyer *becomes* Armstrong the White Avenger in the triumphant final scene; any offenses his wife had committed are shown offstage, whereas her terror at her impending fate is registered in full view for maximum dramatic effect; and any suffering that Earl might have gone through pales in comparison to the full exposition of his machinations and monstrosity that takes up the bulk of the film's ending. Still, the presence of the first set of readings undermines the stability of the second set and suggests that contemporary racial discourse occurs on highly contested terrain in which the definitions of racial justice are very much up for grabs.

Like *Just Cause*, Joel Schumacher's 1996 film, *A Time to Kill* (based upon John Grisham's novel), relies upon lynching imagery for a southern trial about race and sexuality, and like *Just Cause*, *A Time to Kill* recognizes and inverts many of the traditional roles in the lynching scenario.

A Time to Kill opens with two white thugs driving around town, abusing blacks in a variety of ways. They throw a beer bottle at two black boys playing basketball and ask them if they "wanna get shot? You wanna get shot?" They throw another beer bottle at someone else's house in the black neighborhood, knock over groceries in a black-owned grocery store, and order a young black man in the store to "clean up that mess, boy." All of this serves to establish their racism and to confirm that what follows is a racial as well as a gendered crime. As they see a ten-year-old black girl, Tonya, with a bag of groceries, one of them says, "[Y]ou know what I always say—if they're old enough to crawl, they're in the right position." They attack and sexually assault the little girl. By the end of the film, we will have learned about this attack in graphic detail, but for now, we see only a montage of quick cuts that show her being tied up, her clothes being ripped, her feet being lifted off the ground as she is being hung, a tree branch splintering and breaking under her weight, and her bloodied leg as she is dragged out of their truck. While most of the violence is kept offscreen, there is enough here to suggest that the girl is the victim not only of a rape but also of a lynching (or at least an attempted lynching). The traditional lynch narrative is thus abandoned, as *white* men are presented as rapists, and lynching is clearly presented as a racist crime with black girls as the primary victims. This lynching is, however, only the *first* in the film, and it serves to set the stage for later lynchings whose narratives are not nearly so straightforward.

When the girl's father, Karl Lee Hailey (played by Samuel L. Jackson), finds out what has happened, he rushes home in tears and desperation, and he attempts to comfort his daughter, saying, "Oh no . . . I'm here baby, Daddy's here." His desperation quickly turns to steely resolve and determination, and as he carries his daughter to the ambulance, he is surrounded by members of the black community who are clearly united in their horror and in their support for Hailey and his family (Figure 11). This support will be called upon later in the film as Hailey embarks upon a crusade for justice.

After making sure that his daughter will receive proper medical attention, Hailey visits the office of a young white lawyer (Matthew McConaughey's Jake Briggance). He notes, "They worked her over something good, Jake," and he then goes on to ask, "You remember them four white boys raped that little black girl over in the Delta last year? They got off, didn't they?" When Briggance answers affirmatively, Hailey changes the subject: "Jake, um, if I's in a jam, you'd get me out, wouldn't you?" Jake answers that he would, but asks, "What kind of jam you talking about?" Hailey's answer is, "You got a daughter, Jake; what would you do?" Hailey's subsequent preparations for retaliation are, therefore, presented as the only way for a black father to achieve justice

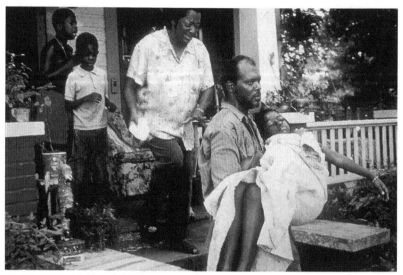

Figure 11. Samuel L. Jackson as Karl Lee Hailey and Rae'ven Kelly as Tonya Hailey in *A Time to Kill* (1996).

for his victimized daughter given a racist legal system that fails to punish white men who rape black girls.

The next day, as the rapists are being led into the courtroom, Hailey commits the film's second "lynching," shooting them to death as they walk across the floor, which has a giant painting of the Mississippi state seal. In a clear indication of the film's sympathies, the men land in a crumpled heap in the middle of the state motto: *Virtute et armis* ("By valor and arms"). Lynching as vigilante justice is thus separated from and *opposed* to lynching as racist and sexist crime, as the film suggests that the only way that a black man can protect his family is to take the law into his own hands.

When Hailey is arrested for the murders, the final phase of the film begins. Briggance takes his case, and Hailey's trial becomes a litmus test for the state of contemporary race relations in the South. Briggance announces in his televised press conference that his goal is to "show that the good men and women of the South can look past color and see the truth—that here in the South, the new South, justice is and will be color-blind."

Clearly, though, there is nothing color-blind about this case. Thus, Briggance's first move is to propose a change of venue because, as the prosecutor (played by Kevin Spacey) explains, "It's quite simple. This county's 26, 30 percent black, give or take. Almost every other county's 40, 45, in some cases 70 percent black. Blacks are more sympathetic to other blacks. If he gets it moved, he gets a greater chance of 'coloring' the jury box, and we know what that means. If the trial stays here, it's an all white jury for sure."[77] Briggance's motion is rejected, however, by the aptly named Judge Omar Noose, who agrees that the probable jury pool will be unlikely to sympathize with a black man but who reasons that this is, after all, Mississippi and that any other venue would be just as racist.

Judge Noose is not the only one who is convinced that a black man is unlikely to receive justice in a Mississippi courtroom. The NAACP argues that the proceedings amount to a legal lynching, since "Karl Lee Hailey is on trial because he's black, no other reason." Of course, the fact that Hailey shot and killed two men and shot a police officer in full view of many witnesses provides a very compelling reason for his trial completely independent of race. The NAACP's charge of racism is therefore presented as empty and nonsensical. But that reason is ultimately beside the point because, as the NAACP's representative explains, "Mr. Hailey's case has far-reaching ramifications. Karl Lee's acquittal for the killings of two white men will do more for the black people of Mississippi than any event since we integrated the schools. His conviction, on the other hand, will be a slap at us—a symbol of deep-seated racism. Perhaps enough to ignite a nation. See how important this case is?" The NAACP hires a law firm notorious for the publicity it generates and the martyrs it creates, and also attempts to manipulate the local black reverend into helping convince Hailey to change lawyers. When manipulation fails, the NAACP resorts to bribery: "Obviously we would expect you to take a modest administrative fee for your troubles." These behind-the-scenes machinations reveal that the NAACP is concerned with Hailey *solely* for his symbolic value and that it is completely insensitive to the needs of Hailey or his family (its fund-raising appeals on Hailey's behalf in the black community promised that the money would go to Hailey's family to prevent them from starving while Hailey was in jail and out of work, but it was actually planning on channeling all of the money to the new legal team). The charge of racism is merely a tool that the NAACP is cynically attempting to use to further its own ends.[78]

The NAACP is not the only group that objects to the particulars of the trial. The local racists agree that the courtroom is an inappropriate forum in which to achieve justice, and they express a nostalgic yearning for the days when "that nigger'd be hanging by the end of a noose with his balls in his mouth."[79] They feel so strongly that Hailey should not receive a trial that they enlist the aid of a nearby cell of the KKK to intimidate Hailey's defense team. To this end, the Klan kidnaps Briggance's assistant Ellen Roark (played by Sandra Bullock). As a white liberal—she has written briefs for the American Civil Liberties Union (ACLU) and plans "to spend a glorious career stomping out the death penalty"—defending a black man, Roark is singled out for special blame by the Klan, and as her clothing is ripped off and she is strung up on a tree and left to die, she is accused of being a race traitor: "You can't blame a nigger for being a nigger, no more than you can blame a dog for being a dog, but a whore like you—comingling with mongrels, betraying your own, that makes you worse than being a nigger. So I'll tell you what I'm gonna do. I'm gonna leave you tied up here naked—first it'll just be bugs eating at you. A day, maybe two . . ." She survives, but only because she is rescued by a renegade Klan member turned government informant.

Roark's abduction and a growing Klan presence in town (Klan members stage rallies against Hailey and firebomb Briggance's house) eventually force Briggance to abandon his earlier stance on color-blind justice in favor of a more realistic approach. His closing argument openly acknowledges racial differences in the hopes of transcending them:

> I set out to prove that a black man could receive a fair trial in the South—that we are all equal in the eyes of the law. That's not the truth. Because the eyes of the law are human eyes, yours and mine, and until we can see each other as equals, justice will never be evenhanded. It will remain nothing more than a reflection of our own prejudice. So until that day, we have a duty under God to seek the truth—not with our eyes and not with our minds, where fear and hate turn commonality into prejudice—but with our hearts, where we don't know better. . . . Now I want to tell you a story, and I'm gonna ask y'all to close your eyes while I tell you this story. . . . This is a story about a little girl walking home from a grocery store one sunny afternoon. . . . I want you to picture this little girl. Suddenly a truck races up. Two men jump out and grab her, and drag her into a nearby field and they tie her up and they rip her clothes from her body. Now they climb on, first one, then the other, raping her, shattering everything innocent and pure with a vicious thrust and a fog of drunken breath and sweat, and when they're done, after they've killed her tiny womb, murdered any chance for her to have children—to have life beyond her own—they decide to use her for target practice. They start throwing full beer cans at her. They throw them so hard, it tears her flesh all the way to her bones. And they urinate on her. Now comes the hanging. They have a rope, tie a noose, imagine the noose going tight around her neck, a sudden blinding jerk she's pulled into the air, and her feet and legs go kicking, and they don't find the ground. The hanging branch isn't strong

enough, it snaps and she falls back to the earth, and they pick her up, throw her in the back of the truck, drive out to Foggy Creek bridge, pitch her over the edge. And she drops some thirty feet down to the creek bottom below. Can you see her? Her raped, beaten, and broken body, soaked in their urine, soaked in their semen, soaked in her blood and left to die. Can you see her? I want you to picture that little girl. Now imagine she's white.

Throughout the speech various people in the courtroom start to cry or express some form of emotional distress. The last line, however, shocks people (heads that are bowed in contemplation or sorrow jerk upward, eyes widen, etc.). It is not clear whether this reaction is due to the recognition that Briggance has chastised the jury for seeing a white girl's victimization as substantially more horrific than that of a black girl or whether it is due to the fact that the jury *is* more horrified when they are forced to imagine a white girl's victimization. Either way, Briggance obviously felt that the full extent of the black girl's suffering could only be expressed indirectly through the body of a white girl.[80] The speech seems to have worked, because what had been a largely unsympathetic jury (earlier in the trial, the foreman had announced, "That nigger's dead, you all," with very little protest from the other jurors) returned a "not guilty" verdict for Hailey. In the film's triumphant conclusion, which suggests that the verdict is the first step in a larger process of national racial healing, Briggance brings his family to Hailey's house in an attempt to bridge what had been an unbreachable racial divide because "I thought our kids could play together."

The superficiality of this gesture is emblematic of the film's politics in general. Everything is surface here; there is virtually no depth to any of the imagery. Thus, Tonya's rape and lynching suggest that sexism and racism are thoroughly intertwined and that our legal system is incapable of addressing the victimization of a black girl, but this suggestion is really not much more than a plot device to kick off a much larger narrative about the possibilities of justice for a black man in a southern courtroom. The lynching of Ellen Roark, in turn, reveals that the Klan's image as shining knights protecting the virtue of white womanhood is a fiction. At the same time, it both obscures white women's role in perpetuating this fiction[81] and enables Briggance to assume the role abandoned by the Klan, as he rushes off to avenge Roark's victimization while simultaneously intervening in the legal lynching of Karl Lee Hailey. Briggance wins his case through an elaborate series of substitutions and displacements in which a white girl's body stands in for a black girl's victimization, which in turn serves as evidence that a guilty verdict would be tantamount to the racist lynching of a black man. This aborted lynching is also, however, only a lynching in the most superficial of ways. It is clear that without Briggance's white knight, Hailey would have been found guilty by a racist jury/lynch mob (recall the foreman's words here), but he *was*, after all, guilty, so whatever their motivations, the jury would have secured a legally appropriate form of justice. The traditional lynch narrative's rape charge is displaced here away from the black man and onto the bodies of two white men, but while this displacement might debunk the mythic figure of the black beast rapist, it also obscures the dynamics of real lynchings and serves to deny the basis for black men's claims of racism, legal or otherwise. (Ultimately, the Klan's desire for mob justice appears to be based on a *realistic* assessment that the legal system allows black men to kill white men with impunity.) The NAACP's claim that the trial *was* in fact a legal lynching is presented as superficial and opportunistic precisely because there is no recognition that this displacement makes the trial substantially *different* from real lynchings, in which black men were the *victims* rather than the *instigators* of vigilante justice. The next two films present historical investigations that are intended to make sure that this kind of recognition becomes an accepted part of our understanding of the past.

Memories of Terror, Struggles for Justice: *Ghosts of Mississippi* and *Rosewood*

Two recent high-profile historically based films have suggested that the only way to achieve racial justice in the present is by addressing the history of lynching and vigilante justice in the past. Rob Reiner's 1996 *Ghosts of Mississippi* and John Singleton's 1997 *Rosewood* are both highly self-conscious attempts to intervene in the production of a national collective memory about the racial struggles of our fairly recent past.

Like *Mississippi Burning*[82] before it, *Ghosts of Mississippi* is predominately the story of a white protagonist's quest to bring the perpetrator of racial violence to justice after the fact. As the title indicates, the film suggests that we are haunted by the horrors of our past. The most important "ghost" in the movie is the memory of the civil rights leader Medgar Evers, who was murdered by Byron De La Beckwith in 1963. The film's opening credit sequence suggests, however, that Evers's death needs to be seen within a much larger context of American race relations. The credits are superimposed over an ever-changing series of images of our national racial past. (We see a diagram of the "cargo hold" of a slave ship, with black bodies crammed into every available inch, footage of the

KKK on horseback in full regalia, guard dogs and fire-hoses being used to attack civil rights protesters, black people voting for the first time, Jim Crow–era separate-facilities signs, photos of Martin Luther King Jr. and Malcolm X, the text of the Fourteenth Amendment, a lynching, a civil rights march on Washington, and a burning cross, to name only some of the more interesting images.) Clearly, then, the events in the film are meant to be seen in historic proportions, as they take their place alongside some of the most vivid images and important events of the American racial imaginary.

The bulk of the film is set between 1989 and 1994, as Evers's wife, Myrlie Evers (played by Whoopi Goldberg), convinces the local district attorney to reopen the case against De La Beckwith thirty years after two previous attempts to convict him had ended in mistrials. The original trials were so thoroughly racist as to be farcical. In the movie's depiction of the first trial, the former governor comes into the courtroom and shakes hands with De La Beckwith (played by James Woods in an Academy Award–nominated performance) in front of the jury as Myrlie Evers is testifying against him. An exchange between court reporters sums up the situation: "'There's not a court in America would stand for that.' 'What's America got to do with anything? This is Mississippi.'" As the new prosecuting attorney, Bobby DeLaughter (Alec Baldwin) watches old video footage from the 1960s, Medgar Evers himself offers the clearest explanation for De La Beckwith's mistrials. In the video, Evers is making a speech about "the horrific deaths of Emmet Till . . . and a variety of other atrocities [for which] no one has been convicted," and he notes that "those guilty of having committed those ungodly acts had the feeling of assurance that nothing ever *would* be done. For you see, ladies and gentlemen, white juries have yet to convict a white man in Mississippi guilty of a crime against a Negro." DeLaughter hopes to change this, and his case is premised on the hope that the Mississippi of the 1990s is more in tune with the rest of the country than was the Mississippi of the 1960s. (The idea that De La Beckwith could *only* have been let off the hook in the South is never questioned.)

The case is a political hot potato, though, as various actors fear the results of reopening the wounds of the past. DeLaughter's father-in-law is infuriated by "these damn liberals [who have] been trying to rewrite history," and he asks, "When are these people going to get it through their heads that the '60s are over? The 1860s *and* the 1960s." DeLaughter's wife is even more upset, and she eventually leaves DeLaughter because she is angry at him for taking the case. Meanwhile, the district attorney feels the need to satisfy Myrlie Evers (for fear of alienating the black community in an election year), but he is reluctant to actually retry De La Beckwith. He asks DeLaughter, "What if you lose? The whole state which is supposed to have changed so much over the past twenty-five years gonna be looking at the worst damn public relations disaster since that little black kid Emmet Till bobbed out of the Tallahatchie. . . . I'm telling you, you're dealing with the past. In the state of Mississippi that's not a place you want to be." While Evers had earlier referenced Emmet Till's lynching as a symbol of horrific racial violence that provided the rationale for continuing struggles for civil rights, the district attorney is using the same image as part of an argument in favor of the status quo. He presents chasing up the ghosts of the past as a dangerous business that can only make the present more difficult. De La Beckwith's defense attorney agrees that the past is best left in the past, as he argues in his closing statement that the entire case is problematic, since "to my knowledge, this jury is being asked to look further into the past than any jury in the history of American jurisprudence [and] that places [the jury] at a considerable disadvantage."

DeLaughter stands against these forces of "organized forgetting"[83] as he attempts "to make the past start living again" and argues that "this whole case is one big resurrection." Memory is presented as unequivocally aligned with the forces of justice here. An ex-Klansman turned government informant ultimately decides to testify against De La Beckwith because of the memories of his own racist past and of the killings of "them three kids . . . them freedom riders" (James Chaney, Andrew Goodman, and Michael Schwerner).[84] Meanwhile, Medgar Evers's brother notes that "nobody hardly even remembers Medgar Evers—whites or blacks— and that's a crying shame, 'cuz whatever rights a black man has around here now he's got because of something called the civil rights movement, and for a long time . . . my brother Medgar *was* the civil rights movement." Ultimately, DeLaughter asks the jury if it is "ever too late to do the right thing?" and says, "For the sake of justice and for the hope of us as a civilized society, I sincerely pray it is not." His argument that a modern-day (antiracist) civilization is reliant upon an honest reckoning with the past is rewarded by a guilty verdict for De La Beckwith and by Myrlie Evers's confession to DeLaughter that "you remind me of Edgar" (Figure 12).

While *Ghosts of Mississippi* suggests that a white prosecutor can achieve racial justice in the present by wrestling with the racist ghosts of the past, and while it suggests that racism is a widespread phenomenon (at least in Mississippi, though not as widespread as in days past), its focus on Bobby DeLaughter rather than on Medgar Evers presents blacks as

Figure 12. Alec Baldwin as Bobby DeLaughter and Whoopi Goldberg as Myrlie Evers in *Ghosts of Mississippi* (1996).

somewhat peripheral to (at least modern-day) antiracist struggles and does very little to explain the underlying *reasons* for racist violence. John Singleton's 1997 *Rosewood* is an attempt to address exactly these problems in Hollywood's collective memory of racist terror.

Rosewood is a fictionalized account of a racist massacre that occurred in Rosewood, Florida, in 1923. The real-life massacre had been largely ignored by Florida's state government, as well as by the national and local press, until journalist Gary Moore, while in Florida on assignment for the *St. Petersburg Times* in 1982, started to hear rumors about what had happened. His investigation turned up several survivors of the massacre who, because of fear and a sense of futility, had remained largely silent about the incident until that time. In the wake of Moore's investigative efforts, the Rosewood survivors started a campaign to get Florida's state legislature to pass a law to award reparations to the survivors. In 1993, the state accepted their demands and passed the "Rosewood Law." The struggle for reparations and official acknowledgment brought some national attention to the story, but John Singleton clearly thought that it deserved far more attention than it had received. The film is, therefore, an attempt to establish the Rosewood massacre as an important part of U.S. national collective memory.

The film had disappointing results at the box office, but it received an extraordinary amount of attention in the national press. Some of the most important events surrounding this film were a PBS documentary on Rosewood called *The Rosewood Massacre: The Untold Story*, an episode of *The Oprah Winfrey Show* devoted to the film (Winfrey spent more than a week urging her audience to see the film and referred to Singleton as "the director who brought this once-forgotten piece of history to life"), and Michael D'Orso's book *Like Judgement Day*, with an introduction by Singleton on the making of the film. Everybody involved with publicizing the film agreed that it was important that the Rosewood story finally be told. One of the survivors of the massacre who was interviewed for the PBS documentary said, "What I wanted from the whole thing was recognition of it. I wanted them to at least say when it did happen, and to recognize when they go with the history books that my Uncle Sammy was the first person killed there for no reason at all. Now I wanted that known." The documentary's final voice-over recognizes this desire and says, "Although Rosewood could never come back to life, at least its memory had been restored, and its skeletons had escaped the national closet. And maybe . . . all the victims of Rosewood could now rest in peace." The film's importance was not meant, however, to be limited to calming the spirits of the past. As Singleton says, "So much in *Rosewood* is relevant. You can deconstruct the Susan Smith case, where a woman who killed her two children in 1994 blamed it on a black male carjacker, and say that Susan Smith is a direct descendant of Fannie Taylor [the white woman in *Rosewood* whose claim that she was beaten by a black man ignited the massacre]." Singleton mentions several other events that he argues can be better understood in light of *Rosewood*. Clearly, then, while the film is unlike *Ghosts of Mississippi* in that it is firmly a story about the past (there is no effort here to tell the story of the later struggles for reparations and justice), one of its central purposes is to create and mobilize a collective memory of racism in order to explain and intervene in contemporary understandings of racial struggles.

Early in the film, we get a hint of what is to come, as Sylvester Carrier (played by Don Cheadle) confronts a white man who has whistled at his cousin. With a rifle in his hands, he says, "I come to have a word with you about my cousin. Now I expect you to show her some respect. . . . I don't like Scrappy feeling scared around nobody. . . . I don't mess with your peoples, I don't want you messing with mines." This gesture is stunning in its defiance of a white man's presumed entitlement to indiscriminate sexual access to black women. When Sylvester tells his mother (Aunt Sarah, played by Esther Rolle) what happened, she fears for him and argues that such defiance is life threatening: "Sylvester, you can't talk to white folks like that and not expect a rope around your neck." The film thus supports the argument that lynching helped to secure the myth of sexually available black women by placing any of their possible male defenders in jeopardy of their lives.[85] Sylvester is reluctant to accept the claim that lynching is a viable threat, and he responds to his mother by arguing that "times is changing, Momma. Now I ain't no sharecropper. I'm a music teacher," but his mother rejects this argument: "Times ain't never changing for no Crackers, boy. Don't you forget—they *burned* a colored man over in Raleigh last summer for *winking* at a white woman."[86] This admonition proves prophetic as the rest of the film unfolds and a white woman's claims of black brutality bring destruction and terror upon the town.

We first see Fannie Taylor (played by Catherine Kellner) having sex with a white man who is not her husband. As the man starts to leave Taylor's house, they get into an argument, and he brutally beats her. Later in the day, Taylor realizes that she needs a way to explain her bruises to her husband, so she goes out into the street and cries for help. As a crowd starts to gather, she continues to yell: "Somebody please help me. . . . it was a nigger! He broke in my house and he beat me up. He was a nigger!!!!" As she continues to ask for help, word of her beating moves through town, and the rumor spreads that "she was raped by a nigger." When the sheriff (played by Michael Rooker) finally arrives on the scene, he asks, "Who raped you?" Taylor corrects him, by answering that "Oh, jeez . . . I sure wasn't raped. I just got beat." But her response is irrelevant, as some of the members of the crowd ask, "Did she say she got raped?" and others answer affirmatively. The sheriff asks Aunt Sarah (who works in Taylor's house and who witnessed the beating) what happened, but Sarah knows that her answer will be ignored, so after a moment of consideration she decides to say that she did not see anything.

Despite having been told directly by Fannie Taylor that there had been no rape, the sheriff organizes a group of men to hunt down her rapist. (He asks his first "suspect," "Did you rape Fannie Taylor?") They find several black men who they know are innocent, but they terrorize and nearly kill these men in an effort to get them to turn in the "real" rapist. Ultimately, they are led to Sam Carter (played by Kevin Jackson), who is accused of having given the rapist a ride out of town. When Carter is unable to provide the mob with the rapist's identity, he is shot and then hung from a tree. The sheriff makes some attempt to dissuade the mob, but he is taken away from the tree by a man who tells him that "a white woman was beat and raped by a colored boy. Now you want to tell her husband . . . that this boy don't have to pay for that?" While this statement seems to suggest that the mob is motivated by a desire to get vengeance for Fannie's rape, the mob's actions suggest that there are very different motivations at play. No one in the mob actually believes that Carter was responsible for, or even knew about, the rape, but this does not stop the mob from cheering as he is lynched. Similarly, the first suspect was clearly innocent, but the mob still thoroughly enjoyed the preparations for his death and laughed out loud at the comment, "He don't need to talk. . . . He need to hang from one of those trees out there."

The motivations for the violence become clearer the following day as members of the lynch mob are sitting around discussing their plans and the possibility that Sylvester Carrier is somehow involved. One of the men says, "That nigger, he hates us white folks," and another notes with outrage, "You know he's got a piano? A nigger with a goddamn piano. . . . I been working all my life, I ain't got a piano. . . . Now how that look?" Aunt Sarah had stated earlier that "most of us [black people in Rosewood] doing better than those [white] folks over in Sumner," and as the film progresses it becomes clearer that the charge of rape is really just an excuse for the mob's members to vent the frustration and resentment that they feel because of the economic disparity between the two towns. Eventually the mob hangs the film's heroic Mr. Mann (played by Ving Rhames; Figure 13).[87] Mann has apparently survived an earlier lynching attempt, and he survives this one too; while he is hanging from the tree, the crowd loses interest, and Mann uses his last bit of energy to grab a knife from his pants and cut through the noose that is choking him. During the hanging, the sheriff says that Mann "prob-

Figure 13. Ving Rhames as the mythically heroic Mr. Mann in *Rosewood* (1997).

ably didn't have nothin' to do with it. Truth be told, none of them did." Fannie Taylor's husband asks, "What the hell does that mean?" The sheriff responds, "It means, James, that you know as well as I do what Fannie's been doing lunch times. Some of you all know better than others. I should have never listened to her." The crowd laughs at this point, indicating that they doubted the rape charge all along. The sheriff says, "This thing's gone far enough. . . . Deep down, I don't think I believed it from the start." Of course, the sheriff is at least a little disingenuous here, since he knew all along that Fannie had not been raped. Still, his explanations for his actions (he says that he organized the mob despite his reservations because as sheriff, he had no choice) ring true. As a representative of the legal system, he had an institutional imperative to act as if a white woman's charge of victimization at the hands of a black man was beyond question, no matter its plausibility.

The sheriff's newfound willingness to openly express his doubts is insufficient to put an immediate end to the violence, and during the rest of the night, many other people are killed as most of the black population attempts to flee Rosewood. As the violence begins to wane and the new day dawns, the film's final moments include a written postscript that notes that "[t]he official death toll of the Rosewood massacre, according to the state of Florida, is eight . . . two WHITES and six BLACKS. The survivors, a handful of whom are still alive today, place the number anywhere between 40 and 150, nearly all of them AFRICAN AMERICAN." The film (which has presented far more than eight deaths) thus makes a final argument for its importance as an intervention into the historical record. The statement suggests not only that officially sanctioned history is racially suspect[88] but also that it can be challenged through the use of survivors' testimony and organized resistance.

Conclusion: Reel Memories

There is no one clear and stable set of meanings attached to cinematic representations of lynching. Instead, lynching is represented in a seemingly endless variety of ways for a variety of different reasons. There are, however, some patterns that are worth reiterating. In *Within Our Gates, Do the Right Thing, Ghosts of Mississippi,* and *Rosewood,* lynching is used as a metaphor for racism more broadly defined. By drawing upon, and working to reconfigure, a collective memory of racial terror, each of these films attempts to shed light on contemporary configurations of racial injustice.

For the most part, these films are concerned with the racist victimization of black men, which makes sense given black women's conspicuous absence from traditional narratives about lynching, whether put forward by apologists for the mob or by the antilynching movement. While "black women were routinely lynched, burned, and summarily mutilated," generally, "the corporeal violence attending black female bodies has been expulsed from public view."[89] Certainly, none of the films that I have considered here has a black female protagonist. Still, black women's victimization is not entirely absent here. *Within Our Gates* presents rape and lynching as parallel forms of racist barbarity. *Rosewood*'s primary motivation is to dispel the myth of the black rapist, but in the process, it suggests that lynching worked as a disciplinary mechanism that prevented black women from complaining about their sexual victimization at the hands of white men. Aunt Sarah's death provides clear evidence that lynch mobs were equally capable of killing black men and black women. *A Time to Kill* plays around with the traditional lynching narrative so much as to render it virtually unrecognizable, but it places a black girl's rape and beating at the center of a narrative of race and (in)justice.

Perhaps the most interesting films that I have considered here are *A Time to Kill* and *Just Cause*. By separating lynching from its roots in white supremacy and by changing the gender and race of its victims and perpetrators, these films help to sever lynching from its historical ties. In the process, the metaphor loses some of its specificity and weight, as its weightlessness enables it to truly become a floating signifier whose meaning is indeterminate. If *Rosewood* was intended to secure a collective memory of lynching and racism, *A Time to Kill* and *Just Cause* serve precisely the opposite purpose, as they work to empty the lynching metaphor and the category of "racism" itself of any clear logic.

In the Introduction, I noted that historical metaphors necessarily rely upon incomplete comparisons with the past. Assessing the particular aspects of history that are referenced when a metaphor is invoked is, however, no simple matter. I hope that this discussion has provided some sense of the ways in which recent Hollywood films have helped to determine the historical baggage that is associated with the lynching metaphor. In chapters 3 and 4, I examine the consequences of these processes of historical selection, as I argue that decisions to either acknowledge or ignore various aspects of lynching's history have had serious repercussions for our understandings of contemporary racial violence and for the Hill–Thomas hearings.

CHAPTER 3

Lynching as Lens:
Contemporary Racialized Violence

Increasingly, the mass media construct representations of "blackness" within the context of discussions of racialized violence. The Rodney King beating and aftermath and the O. J. Simpson trials are only two of the best-known examples. Whether African Americans are the victims or the perpetrators, spectacularized racial violence provides opportunities for rearticulations and reconfigurations of common sense understandings of race. In the previous chapters, I have argued that lynch mobs and representations of lynching put forward by both the public defenders of lynching and the antilynching movement worked to instruct national audiences about the nature of the racial order. Here, I argue that these lessons continue to be influential. The dynamics of lynching worked to construct basic ways of conceptualizing the world that are still relevant today: Lynchings have provided a "lens," or a way of seeing and understanding contemporary race relations and spectacles of racialized violence.

In the Conclusion of this book, I discuss several recent murders of African Americans that have been widely understood as modern-day lynchings.[1] The links between each of those cases and collective memories of lynching are fairly straightforward. The incidents often involved mobs of white men, the use of explicit racial epithets, and even notes that (mis-leadingly) attributed the violence to the Ku Klux Klan. In this chapter, I examine a series of cases of either alleged or actual racialized violence that rely on and reconfigure collective memories of lynching in somewhat less straightforward and more nuanced ways. My consideration of the cases of Bernhard Goetz, Susan Smith, Charles Stuart, and Tawana Brawley examines the enduring power of racial stereotypes; the relationships among race, fear, and memory; and the ways history works to structure credibility and "common sense" understandings of race. Mobilizations around racialized violence demonstrate that there is no singular mean-ing attached to lynching as a metaphor but, rather, that lynching can be invoked as a method of historical comparison with varying degrees of depth, depending in part upon the purposes for which, and audiences to whom, the metaphor is addressed.

Bernhard Goetz and the Politics of Fear

On December 22, 1984, Bernhard Goetz, a thirty-seven-year-old white man, was asked for five dollars by four eighteen- and nineteen-year-old black men on the number 2 IRT express train in the New York City sub-way system. In response, Goetz shot each one of the young men. Barry Allen, Troy Canty, and James Ramseur would eventually walk out of the hospitals they were taken to. But the bullet that hit Darrell Cabey severed his spinal cord and left him paralyzed for life. As the train came to a halt in the tunnel before the next stop, Goetz told a conductor, "[T]hey tried to rip me off," and then he jumped onto the tracks and escaped.[2] Within a day, the New York City Police Department established a Vigilante Task Force to identify and bring in the gunman, and by Christmas Day the story occupied central stage in the New York media. On December 31, Goetz surrendered to the state police in Concord, New Hampshire, and by then, every major paper in the country had started discussing developments in the Goetz case on their editorial pages and presenting them as first-page news. Over the next three years, as the case made its way through the legal system, Goetz was the subject of unceasing public scrutiny and fascination. In 1996, the case became front-page news once again when Cabey was awarded $43 million in a civil suit against Goetz.[3] Throughout all of this time, the debate in the mass media over Goetz tended to focus on whether he was a hero who had done what most of "us" fear to do, by finally standing up to street criminals, or a danger-ous vigilante who acted irresponsibly, possibly endangering "innocent" passengers, by taking the law into his own hands. There was even some concern that his actions would spawn copycats who had no regard for the law and whose actions would therefore threaten the very basis of our civilization. The mainstream media occasionally gave voice to people who insisted that not only was Goetz a vigilante, but his actions were the equivalent of a lynching and the support for his actions was evidence of a racist mob mentality.

The extreme violence that Goetz used, coupled with the fact that he was white and his victims were black, quite possibly made this last explanation inevitable. And in light of the tremendous amount of popular support that Goetz received, the idea that Goetz's actions were the modern-day equivalent of a lynching raised troubling questions about the prevalence of racism in the United States. When Goetz's identity was revealed, the New York Guardian Angels organized a fund-raising drive for his defense, and they had collected over $700 in cash donations by the end of their first day. By this time, they had also received two hundred phone calls asking where donations could be sent.[4] One man even offered to pay Goetz's bail with a $50,000 cashier's check, which represented his life savings.[5] Even before Goetz turned himself in, the hotline that the police set up in order to determine his identity was immediately flooded by callers "expressing sympathy and offering to help pay his legal fees."[6]

This section examines the ways the Goetz case, which so forcefully drew the attention of a national audience to matters of "vigilante" violence and fear, has been represented and understood within a variety of settings. I argue that the case sheds important light upon the often unacknowledged, and at times unintentional, ways in which the national media and legal system work to reinforce and legitimate racialized understandings of crime, and I suggest that the politics of fear constitute a crucial arena for struggles over race and justice.

Goetz as Popular Hero

The mainstream media's extensive attention to the kind of information mentioned above made it seem as though Goetz's support was simply overwhelming, and indeed, a *New York Times* editorial about Goetz's indictment claimed that "by charging him only with lesser offenses, [the grand jury] expressed what 110 percent of the American public has already expressed: support for the subway vigilante."[7] This statement was made despite the fact that less than a week earlier, the first national poll results about Goetz's actions had been released and had shown that only "roughly half the people 'generally approved' of what Goetz did."[8] The poll results were consistently downplayed throughout the national media in order to further the relatively unquestioned representation of Goetz as a popular hero.[9] The *Washington Post* presented the support for Goetz as almost gleeful when, for example, it chided its readers by claiming that "[t]he first reaction even among the most militantly non-violent [people who heard what he did] was, alas, 'Hooray' followed by sheepish second thoughts."[10] This quote is particularly telling because it suggests that whatever problems there are with popular support for Goetz have to do with an unproblematic acceptance of violence. Goetz's supporters are noticeably *not* chided for their thoughts about race.

Instead, Goetz's support is seen as the product of commonly shared, nonracialized fear of crime, while Goetz's actions were, in turn, portrayed as eminently reasonable. Part of this portrayal is intrinsic to the idea that Goetz was a "vigilante." When the New York City police set up the Vigilante Task Force to determine Goetz's identity, they were surely suggesting that Goetz had acted outside the bounds of the traditional legal system. But at the same time, they were reinforcing the view that Goetz's victims were the real criminals. *Webster's Dictionary* defines a vigilante as "a member of a volunteer committee organized to suppress and punish crime summarily (as when the processes of law appear inadequate)" or more broadly as "a self-appointed doer of justice," and the idea that Goetz's actions were the only way to deal with street criminals who would otherwise elude the criminal justice system was absolutely taken for granted within the mainstream media.[11] So despite the fact that Goetz was the only person on that IRT subway train who was actually accused of committing a crime (or series of crimes) that day, he is consistently presented as having taken a stance *against* crime. This is why his actions inspired a series of articles and editorials not about racial violence but about subway muggings. When the *Times* said that "much can be done about subway crime," it was not suggesting that more needed to be done to reign in people like Goetz but was instead arguing for a better-organized transit police force that would keep "muggers and chain snatchers," as well as "graffiti, vandalism, [and people who are] harassing passengers for handouts," under control.[12] The *Times* consistently implied that Goetz's victims were the real criminals, when, for example, it asked "why hasn't government undertaken any serious new anti-crime program" and used this rhetorical question to explain Goetz's popularity: "No wonder the public supports the Goetz Anti-crime and Self-Defense Act of 1984. No wonder people applaud someone taking the law into his own hands."[13] The image of Goetz as victim instead of criminal was furthered by then-president Ronald Reagan's statement that it "seemed that we got overzealous about protecting the criminal's rights and forgot about the victim"[14] and by Senator Alfonse D'Amato's statement that "Mr. Goetz was justified in his actions . . . [since] the issue is not Bernhard Goetz. The issue is the four men who tried to harass him. They, not Mr. Goetz, should be on trial."[15]

Victims as Villains: Allen, Canty, Ramseur, and Cabey in the Press

In fact, there was no need to try Goetz's victims, since as far as the press was concerned, the possibility that they might be innocent was never seriously entertained, despite the absence of formal criminal charges against them.[16] Even before Goetz's identity was determined, the press reported details about the criminal records of each of the four victims, noting that Cabey had been arrested on charges of armed robbery, that Ramseur and Canty had each served sentences for petty thievery, and that Allen had pled guilty to two charges of disorderly conduct.[17] The media also continued to report the erroneous information from police that all four of the victims were carrying sharpened screwdrivers, "dangerous weapons capable of killing," when they were shot.[18] Even when Jimmy Breslin managed to get the police to admit that only two screwdrivers had been recovered and that they were *not* sharpened, most of the press continued to refer to the sharpened screwdrivers as part of the basis for Goetz's fear. A full week after the police corrected their statement, Phil Donahue told a national television audience that Goetz's actions were a reaction to reasonable fear generated by the sharpened screwdrivers, despite the fact that Goetz never even claimed to have seen the two screwdrivers that *were* in his victims' possession. As the case progressed, one of the victims, Ramseur, was arrested and convicted for rape, and this fact was mentioned prominently in most of the subsequent coverage of the case.[19] If there had been any doubts about the fact that Goetz had chosen worthy victims, Ramseur's rape conviction seemed to erase them.[20]

The criminal records of Goetz's victims were thus used as a crucial part of the explanation for the public approval of Goetz's actions. And despite the fact that constant references to Ramseur's rape conviction surely helped to justify the shootings by invoking ages-old stereotypes of black male sexuality and bestiality, for the most part, the media argued that race was at most a peripheral issue in the case. Again, the mainstream press *did* allow space to quote people like New York City Police Commissioner Benjamin Ward, who argued that Goetz's actions were comparable to Klan activity:

I have a little different definition of a vigilante. I would equate—maybe it's my background—I think those fellows wearing those pointy hats and white sheets call themselves vigilantes, too. When we asked them where the black people hang out around here, they would very frequently point to the highest tree and say "Right there."[21]

The *Times* even included Ward's later critique of Goetz's supporters:

I'm not surprised that you can round up a lynch mob. . . . We were always able to do that in this country. I think that the same kind of person that comes out and applauds the lynching is the first that comes out and applauds someone that shoots four kids.[22]

For the most part, however, this perspective was accorded little space within the mainstream media. When the idea that Goetz's support might be due to racism was brought up, it tended to be found in letters to the editor or toward the end of longer articles on the inside pages of the papers.

Instead, the more common explanation for Goetz's support had to do with a largely nonracialized, universal fear of crime.

Equality of Fear?

The *New York Times* consistently suggested that Goetz's support came from diverse segments of the population who were fed up with, and afraid of, crime. It noted, for example, that "[m]any people—from Chicago to Hawaii to Canada—have responded passionately and vehemently to an event that seems to have embodied their fears and frustrations about crime in their own cities," and it claimed that "citizens have responded with overwhelming appreciation for the anger that apparently motivated Mr. Goetz to shoot the youths."[23] Note that "citizens," Goetz, and "the youths" are all addressed without reference to race. In its explanation of the differences between the verdicts in Goetz's criminal and civil cases, the *Times* claimed that the criminal trial was conducted in a different climate: "In 1987 New York was in the middle of a drug-fueled crime wave that made *everyone* feel like a potential victim" (my emphasis).[24] Another article explained the first verdict by stating that "Mr. Goetz epitomized the frustrations of many New Yorkers about crime."[25] An editorial analyzing Goetz's actions in the context of a criminal justice system in which "your chance of arrest is 1 in 10, [and] of imprisonment 1 in 50" for committing a felony posed the rhetorical questions "What to do if I think someone is going to mug me? Why do I have to surrender meekly?" and claimed that "Mr. Goetz's angry answer evoked a primal response from millions."[26]

The *Times* did not merely ignore the relevance of race; it specifically downplayed it by arguing that Goetz's support was based on a fear of crime that cut across racial lines. An article by Columbia law professor George P. Fletcher considers both of Goetz's trials and concludes that "our effort to give both sides their due weighs more heavily in these results than does racial politics." Part of his evidence for this is that "[b]lack jurors played an important role in Mr. Goetz's 1987 acquittal," and he speculates that if the "civil trial had taken place in Manhattan, instead of the Bronx [or if there had been a predominately white jury for the civil trial], my sense is that the judgment would have gone against Mr. Goetz" because "violent felonies in the subways" in 1996 were "down 50 percent compared with 1984," and so New York no longer had the same climate of fear.[27] The fact that the two black jurors helped to acquit Goetz of most counts in the criminal trial is consistently taken as evidence that Goetz's fear and support for Goetz were universal. This idea is echoed in articles that discuss the support Goetz received from black New Yorkers. The claim that "the day of the subway shootings, it seemed there was hardly a person in New York, black or white, who couldn't relate [to] the story of a mugging inflicted on himself or a friend or family member" is typical.[28]

This image of Goetz's cross-racial support is only partially borne out by poll results. A Gallup poll conducted for *Newsday* in March 1985 showed that 57 percent of the respondents approved of Goetz's actions, but when the results are broken down by race, only 39 percent of non-whites supported Goetz.[29] In early January, blacks and whites supported Goetz by roughly the same percentage (49 percent of blacks and 52 percent of whites surveyed approved of the shootings), but an ABC poll conducted in March showed that "by March 1, a sharp shift was in progress, with the black approval rate dropping by 12 percent and the white rising by 5 percent: 37 percent of blacks approve compared with 57 percent of whites."[30] If Goetz's support had at one time cut equally across racial lines, this was clearly no longer the case. As the director of the ABC polling unit said,

> The issue is definitely no longer color-blind. Blacks now disapprove of what he did; whites now approve. Blacks think he went too far and should have been indicted for attempted murder; whites don't. There were no significant differences in attitudes along racial lines in the first poll. Now there are.[31]

The mainstream media found little space in which to report this change in public sentiment, and the 63 percent of blacks (and 43 percent of whites) who did not approve of Goetz's actions were marginalized and depicted as being out of touch as the image of a racial consensus dominated the print media and airwaves.

The Racialization of Fear

Occasionally, the media *did* consider the possibility that race was an important factor in Goetz's support, but when the relevance of race was not dismissed outright, it was generally presented in a matter-of-fact way, with the implicit assumption that fear of young black men is part of common sense, no matter how unfortunate that recognition may be.[32] For example, a *New York Times* editorial that argued emphatically that Goetz's acquittal was *not* due to racism nonetheless suggested that it had the potential to lead to troubling racial outcomes:

> To blacks accustomed to continuing charges of police abuse, the Goetz acquittal might look like part of a pattern. . . . It's not surprising when some voices charge systemic racism. . . . Unsurprising, but also unwarranted. The New York police, under a black commissioner, are working to cope with discipline problems among rapidly recruited young officers. Judges and juries err, if at all, on the side of the defendant, whatever his race. The Goetz jurors found too much reason for doubt about the prosecutor's evidence against a white man. . . . The more immediate reason for black anxiety about the Goetz verdict is its potential for inflaming racial discrimination based on fear of crime.

The article expressed concern about this possibility but nevertheless suggested that fear of crime based on race was perfectly logical:

> There is no denying that race is an element behind such fear: blacks are found to commit robbery at a rate 10 times that of whites. It is widely assumed that young black males are by definition dangerous. Mr. Goetz's defense played off that assumption. He said he shot down four young blacks not because they brandished weapons or assaulted him but because of their body language. The jury had no trouble putting itself in his place.

The *Times* was not comfortable with this situation, as it noted that "accepting assumptions and stereotypes creates another class of victims" and cautioned that "adopting stereotypes of fear is too easy, and too costly," but it did nothing to combat the assumed link between young black men and danger that it mentioned, and so ultimately it reinforced exactly the stereotypes that it warned against, as it suggested that fear of blacks was reasonable.[33]

Thus, when the *Times* acknowledged that race may have played a part in Goetz's actions or in the support he received, it tended to suggest that race was relevant only in a minor, fairly level-headed manner. The logic suggests that we might still find this troubling and would want to make sure that our biases do not get the best of us but that even the most fair-minded of us would have to admit that we would have shared some of Goetz's trepidation. Attention to some of the mail surrounding the case and of Goetz's own statements, as well as of his defense team's strategies, however, shows that racism was not always nearly so subtle in the case.

A rare editorial in the *Times* acknowledged that some of the support for Goetz did, indeed, have something to tell "us about racial hatreds." The editorial printed various pro-Goetz letters that were meant to demonstrate that "[t]he Goetz affair has set powerful feelings in motion in this city. Not all of them are pretty." Among the uglier letters are one that said "Bernhard Hugo Goetz makes me proud, P-R-O-U-D, to be a white, male American! At long last we can hold up our heads again!" and one that asked,

> Why do you conceal the truth and write that merely "a lot of" the crimes in the New York subways are caused by blacks and Hispanics? You know very well that they commit virtually all of the crimes (as well as in the city generally). When are you going to use your column on our behalf and call out "Enough!" Tell them we have had enough of their cold, murderous ways.[34]

The most virulently racist letters, however, never made it into the papers. Shirley Cabey, Darrell Cabey's mother, showed Lillian Rubin some of the hate mail that she received after her son was shot and his identity was revealed. These are letters that "[say] that it's too bad her son has *only* been paralyzed, that express regret that the others will walk again, that threaten to do them violence of one kind or another." These letters include explicit racial epithets and suggest that any and all black men are legitimate targets.[35]

There is some debate about the degree of Goetz's own racism, but it seems clear that his views about race are relevant in determining the basis for his actions.[36] In his videotaped confession, Goetz discussed an earlier instance in which he had been mugged by a black man, and he said that the man's "eyes were shiny."[37] Some of Goetz's defenders argued that the statement may not have been a racial reference, but this seems implausible given what else is known about Goetz. For example, Myra

Friedman, a *New York* magazine reporter and one of Goetz's neighbors, claimed that Goetz told an anticrime group in their apartment building that "[t]he only way we're going to clean up this street is to get rid of the spics and niggers,"[38] and months after the shootings, Goetz claimed that "[t]he society has dishonesty and lies at all levels. . . . [But] lying and dishonesty in the black community is more pronounced."[39]

Whatever Goetz's own views, race was clearly an important factor for his legal team. The mainstream media consistently claimed that race did not enter into Goetz's criminal trial. Indeed, the court transcripts almost never mention anyone's race. What was said, however, may ultimately be less important than what was done. At one point in the trial, Goetz's legal team attempted to re-create the crime scene. Part of the re-creation involved having four black men act as "props." The men were volunteers from the Guardian Angels, and Goetz's attorney, Barry Slotnick, had specifically asked the Angels to send black men. From a legal perspective, their race should have been irrelevant. As Fletcher notes,

> There is no doubt that the dramatic power of this re-creation of the crime was enhanced by having four street-clad black kids standing in for the four alleged aggressors. If one were re-creating the incident on the stage, there is no doubt that one would want to cast young blacks in the roles of Canty, Allen, Ramseur, and Cabey. Authenticity demands no less. But the purpose of the demonstration was solely to clarify . . . claims about possible inferences from the established paths of the bullets. There was, therefore, no legal warrant for Slotnick's calling black youths . . . in order to illustrate points about bullets' passing through human bodies. The witness was not authorized to speak about the rational inference of danger from being surrounded by four young black toughs. But Slotnick designed the dramatic scene so that the implicit message of menace and fear would be so strong that testimony would not be needed.[40]

And there were other moments in the trial when Slotnick relied on implicit assumptions about race:

> Indirectly and covertly, the defense played on the racial factor. Slotnick's strategy of relentlessly attacking the "gang of four," "the predators" on society, calling them "vultures" and "savages," carried undeniable racial undertones. These verbal attacks signaled a perception of the four youths as representing something more than four individuals committing an act of aggression against a defendant. That "something more" requires extrapolation from their characteristics to

the class of individuals for which they stand. There is no doubt that one of the characteristics that figures in this implicit extrapolation is their blackness.[41]

It may well be that Goetz benefited from the fact that racial biases were appealed to covertly rather than directly, since this meant that they never became the subject of open debate. It also made it easier for the media to maintain its claim that the case was about fear rather than race. But analysis of Slotnick's courtroom activities should be enough to demonstrate that the case was about fear that was thoroughly racialized.

Black Fear after the Verdict

Perhaps the best evidence that fear is raced comes not from Goetz's supporters but from some of his most vocal detractors. I have already noted that in March 1985, 37 percent of African Americans who were surveyed, along with 57 percent of whites surveyed, supported Goetz and presumably agreed that he acted upon what they saw as a reasonable basis for fear. A very different kind of fear is hinted at when considering the kinds of hate mail received by the families of Goetz's victims. In the wake of the first grand jury's failure to indict Goetz on anything but weapons charges and in light of the verdict in the criminal trial, it was not whites who were given new reasons to fear for their safety. Black fear of vigilante violence was allotted very little room in the mainstream media's coverage of the case (though this was a prime issue in New York's African American press), but it was occasionally discussed as a side issue or on the letters pages. An article that addressed the reactions to the verdict in Goetz's criminal trial among black politicians noted that Goetz's actions and treatment by the legal system had been a cause for concern within the black community. Then–Manhattan Borough president (and future New York City mayor) Dinkins was quoted as saying that he was "shaken and dismayed by the verdict [which is] a clear and open invitation to vigilantism," while the Black and Puerto Rican Legislative Caucus in Albany called the decision "frightening [because] it sanctions dangerous vigilante actions on the part of misguided citizens." This position was echoed by a variety of black political figures. Wilbert Tatum, the editor-in-chief and chairman of the African American newspaper the *New York Amsterdam News*, said that the verdict was "a tragic miscarriage of justice, not so much in terms of the young men [who were shot] but in terms of the fear it has engendered in all of us . . . [now that] there is no question that there is now license for an open season." And Harriet R. Michel, the president of the New York Urban League, said that the verdict, "which allows people to act with less impunity on their own personal fears, is very anxiety-producing for black people, especially for young black men."[42]

I have taken the time to discuss black fear of racist vigilantism in light of Goetz's acquittal partly because of how easy it might be to ignore given the tremendous amount of ink that was spilled sympathizing with Goetz's plight and suggesting that the kind of fear that he experienced was ubiquitous. Black fear also points to Goetz's shootings as another legacy of lynching. By heightening a climate of racial terror, Goetz's actions, and their public and legal reception, can be seen as one more event on the same continuum of racial violence as lynching, and at the same time, memories of lynching surely made black fear of vigilante justice following the criminal verdict both more reasonable and more potent. But the more important reason that I have discussed black fear of vigilantism here is to help establish that at least as far as violent crime is concerned, there are clear links between race and fear. While this may seem an obvious point, it needs to be made explicitly, because, as I have shown, it is consistently denied by the mainstream media. It was also denied at Goetz's trial and in the courtroom as various parties attempted to determine whether the shootings were motivated by race *or* by fear.

The Stakes: Race, Fear, and Self-Defense

For Goetz, there were high stakes associated with the clear separation of race and fear. His justification for shooting the four young men was that he was acting in self-defense. Goetz's defense hinged on the idea that his belief that he was in imminent danger was reasonable, despite the lack of more traditional evidence of this danger (there were no threats, drawn or visible weapons, or explicit demands for money). But it was not clear exactly what was meant by "reasonable," and there was a protracted dispute about the legal standard that should be used. The prosecutor for the second grand jury argued that the standard should be "whether the defendant's conduct was that of a reasonable man in the defendant's situation." In other words, if Goetz's fear and subsequent actions made sense to a "reasonable man," the self-defense claim could work. If, however, the "reasonable man" standard suggested that Goetz's fear was *not* reasonable, self-defense would not be a viable defense. The trial judge and the appellate division court argued that this standard was too exacting. The only concern should be whether Goetz's actions were reasonable to *him*. If his fear of imminent violence was real to him, self-defense might justify the shootings. This decision was eventually overturned by Chief Judge Sol Wachtler on the New York State Court of Appeals, who argued that the standard proposed by the lower courts "puts too much emphasis on subjective belief and not enough on reason" and that

[w]e cannot lightly impart to the Legislature an intent to fundamentally alter the principles of justification to allow the perpetrator of a serious crime to go free simply because that person believed his actions were reasonable and necessary to prevent some perceived harm. To completely exonerate such an individual, no matter how aberrational or bizarre his thought patterns, would allow citizens to set their own standards for the permissible use of force. It would also allow a legally competent defendant suffering from delusions to kill or perform acts of violence contrary to fundamental principles of justice and criminal law.[43]

Wachtler's decision was praised by the *New York Times*, and arguably for good reason.[44] The standard proposed by the lower courts would have allowed anyone's fear, no matter how idiosyncratic, to become a justification for extreme violence. Wachtler may have even had in mind the possibility that a racist fanatic could justify a shooting spree by citing absurd racist fears. It is likely that the intent of the ruling was to exclude the possibility of racism as an excuse for extreme violence, and the ruling was certainly intended to limit Goetz's defense by disallowing the possibility of a self-defense justification in the event that his fear was not reasonable.

The problem with this logic comes when we consider the systematic nature of racism and of racial fears. Of course it makes no legal sense to allow raving lunatics to go around shooting anyone they are afraid of, so Wachtler was right to strike down the lower courts' standards. But racism is neither "aberrational" nor "bizarre," and its prevalence makes it virtually impossible to argue that someone who kills because he is afraid of black men is acting on the basis of irrational fears. As I noted above, the *Times* occasionally goes so far as to argue that fear of black men is perfectly rational, if unfortunate.

The problem is foreshadowed in other portions of Wachtler's opinion. Wachtler noted that

[a] determination of reasonableness with regard to the defense of justification . . . must be based on the "circumstances" facing a defendant or his "situation." Such terms encompass more than the physical movements of the potential assailant. These terms include any relevant knowledge the defendant had about that person. They also necessarily bring in the physical attributes of all persons involved, including the

defendant. Furthermore, the defendant's circumstances encompass any prior experiences he had which could provide a reasonable basis for a belief that another person's intentions were to injure or rob him or that the use of deadly force was necessary under the circumstances.[45]

"Relevant knowledge" is never defined in Wachtler's opinion, and no mention is made of which "physical attributes" should be taken into consideration. But at the very least, there is nothing in this language to preclude consideration of race. If, on the contrary, Goetz felt that he *knew* that blacks were likely to be criminals and if this "knowledge" was bolstered by "prior experiences" (he has discussed having been mugged by a black man), then his fear becomes more reasonable. While we might want to criticize the basis of his "knowledge" by pointing out that the vast majority of blacks are *not* criminals, it would be difficult to argue that there was no reasonable basis for his fear, given the ubiquity of what Katheryn Russell calls the *"criminalblackman"* throughout the national media.[46] The presence of this image suggests that Goetz was surrounded by a culture that insisted that his fear *was* reasonable.

Concluding Remarks: Race as Self-Defense

For many observers who were critical of Goetz's actions and of the reception those actions received within the mass media and the legal system, the case conjures up some of the most troubling images of racist violence in a national collective memory. The Goetz case marks a departure from the traditional lynching scenario (the cheering mob came *after* the shootings, no one was killed, and so on), but in important ways, it relies upon and extends some of the logic that was central for the dynamics of lynching. After all, lynchings firmly established the links between fear of black men and racist terrorism that were in play in the events surrounding Goetz's criminal trial. Once again, blacks were given reason to fear vigilante violence, while the figure of the black criminal stood in for the myth of the black rapist as shootings were justified as self-defense. Collective memories of earlier racial fears certainly provided the Goetz case with an alarming kind of historical resonance.

If Wachtler's goal *was* to eliminate racism as a valid defense for violence, then his decision ultimately suffers from the same conceptual problem that I have argued occurs throughout the mainstream media's coverage of the Goetz case. Consideration of race and fear as discrete categories makes it impossible to recognize the ways these concepts are interrelated. The question of whether Goetz's actions were based on race or fear precludes attention to the possibility that they were based on both simultaneously, since fear is raced. Near the end of his book on Goetz's criminal trial, Fletcher argues that

> [t]he question [of] whether a reasonable person considers race in as-
> sessing the danger that four youths on the subway might represent
> goes to the heart of what the law demands of us. The statistically ordi-
> nary New Yorker would be more apprehensive of the "kind of people"
> who mugged him once, and it is difficult to expect the ordinary person
> in our time not to perceive race as one—just one—of the factors defin-
> ing the "kind" of person who poses a danger. The law, however, may
> demand that we surmount racially based intuitions of danger. Though
> the question was not resolved in the Goetz case and there is no settled
> law on this issue, the standard of reasonableness may require us to be
> better than we really are.[47]

That may be. But perhaps the real lesson to take away from the Goetz trials is that if fear is socially constructed in a racist manner, there is a problem allowing it legal sanction as a justification for violence. It is quite clear that we are expected to envision the "kind of people" who mugged the "statistically ordinary New Yorker" in the above example as nonwhite. The fact that the passage is not race-neutral is highlighted if one considers Dorothy Gilliam's challenge to "just try to imagine wheth-er a pistol-toting black man would have had such a sweeping vindication had he shot four white teenagers."[48] The notion that race can be an ac-ceptable criterion for determining the likelihood of criminal activity is clearly, then, a one-way street in which race-neutral language masks the continuing association between black men and criminality.[49]

Cheryl Harris writes that before abolition in the United States, "[w]hite identity and whiteness were sources of privilege and protection; their absence meant being the object of property," and she argues that in that context, whiteness should itself be understood as a form of property if "by 'property' one means all of a person's legal rights."[50] The Goetz case suggests that in the contemporary United States, whiteness con-tinues to function as a similar type of property, except that its absence now entails being the object not of property but of heightened suspicion by the criminal justice system and of legally sanctioned violence.[51] The legal standard of reasonableness, which requires us to be, as Fletcher says, "better than we really are," plays a crucial role in maintaining the property value of whiteness. In order to reduce what George Lipsitz refers to as "the possessive investment in whiteness"[52] and to elimi-nate racism as a valid defense in criminal trials, it is imperative that we

develop a better standard for self-defense, one that does not acknowledge the legitimacy of racially based fears, reasonable or not.

Of course, the courtroom was only one arena where Goetz was able
to gain mileage from racially based fears. It is more difficult to suggest
ways to curb the influence of stereotypes of black criminality within popular culture and the mass media. Indeed, as the cases that I discuss in the
next section show, myths of black monstrosity are still powerful enough
to provide ready scapegoats for murder while justifying manhunts for
black men.

Charles Stuart and Susan Smith

On October 23, 1989, a thirty-year-old white woman named Carol Stuart, who was seven months pregnant and on her way back from a child-
birth class near the racially mixed area of Mission Hill in Boston, was
shot to death in her car. Her husband, Charles Stuart, was shot through
the abdomen and sustained serious injuries. Their child, Christopher,
was delivered before Carol Stuart's death by an emergency Caesarean
section and died seventeen days later.[53] Charles Stuart's frantic call from
his car phone to the police was broadcast on national media. The emergency crew that arrived on the scene happened to be carrying a crew
for a reality-based TV show called *Rescue 911*. An episode of that show
used footage from the crime scene, including images of Carol Stuart's
dead body, to garner impressive ratings soon after the shootings. Charles
Stuart identified the killer as a black man wearing a running suit with
red stripes who had tried to rob them and had then mistaken Mr. Stuart
for a police officer. Less than three months later, on January 3, 1990,
Charles's brother, Matthew, told police that he had been involved in
the incident (which was supposed to have been an insurance scam) and
that Charles Stuart had killed his own wife. The following day, Charles
Stuart apparently committed suicide by leaping off of the Tobin Bridge
into Boston Harbor.

Almost exactly five years after Carol Stuart's murder, on October 25,
1994, a white woman named Susan Smith told the police in Union,
South Carolina, that her two sons, three-year-old Michael and fourteen-
month-old Alexander, had been abducted. She claimed, "This black man
jumped in my car and put a gun to my head and told me to drive. I asked
him why he was doing this. He told me to shut up, or he'd kill me."[54]
She said that once they were six miles outside of town, the gunman ordered her out of the car. When she pleaded for her kids, the carjacker
was supposed to have said, "I don't have time" before speeding away,
leaving Smith at the side of the highway. Smith described the gunman as

"black, 20 to 30 years old, from 5 feet 9 inches to 6 feet tall, and wearing a dark blue ski cap, blue jeans and a blue jacket."[55] Nine days later, on November 3, 1994, Smith confessed that there had been no gunman and that she had driven her car, with her two sons in it, into a lake. Smith had escaped from the car in the last moments, leaving the children to drown. On July 30, 1995, Smith was sentenced to life imprisonment for the murders of her sons.

If this were all there was to the stories, the narratives that Stuart and Smith provided to the police would still present us with powerful evidence of the strength of contemporary stereotypes of black male brutality and criminality, since the choice of scapegoats was probably based on an assessment of community beliefs. Clearly, Stuart and Smith thought that their narratives would be more credible if they featured black gunmen. The stereotypes seem even stronger, then, when considering that Stuart and Smith were correct in thinking that their stories would be believed. In the days after Carol Stuart's murder, then-mayor of Boston Raymond Flynn "ordered all available detectives to work on the case," and "hundreds of men in Mission Hill whose only connection to the case was that they were young and black were stopped and frisked" in a manhunt that went on for weeks.[56] Eventually, the police moved to indict a thirty-nine-year-old black man named William Bennett for the shootings.[57] Similarly, in the days between Smith's initial allegations and her confession, there was a nationwide manhunt for her children and their abductor. As many as thirty-one black men were questioned in the case in Union and surrounding communities,[58] while some reports indicate that young black men were interrogated in areas as far away as New York City.[59] People with tips called in from around the nation after a police sketch of the alleged carjacker was circulated throughout the mass media.[60] In both cases, the mass media initially accepted at face value the claim that a black man was the culprit, showing no indication of skepticism.

The Killers Revealed: Race, Tragedy, and Hoaxes in the Mass Media

The coverage of the cases changed dramatically once the true killers were revealed. In both cases, the mainstream media were forced to question how the police, the public, and the media themselves could be so easily deceived. And in both cases, the media pointed to the durability of racist stereotypes as a partial explanation. For example, in coverage about the Stuart case, an article in *Time* magazine that explained that there had been numerous inconsistencies in Charles Stuart's story from the beginning noted that he had "tapped into assumptions about race and crime so powerful that they overwhelmed skepticism about his tale,"[61] while an op-ed piece in the *New York Times* by Derrick Bell noted that "Mr. Stuart's story stands as the latest in a long line of instances in which a negative report about blacks was accepted without scrutiny because it reinforced deeply held stereotypes about black behavior."[62] Coverage of the Smith case after her confession often referenced the Stuart case as having provided a precedent for Smith's use of racist stereotypes. One article about the effect of Smith's allegations on African Americans noted that "as racial hoaxes go, the lies Susan Smith told . . . were not novel or new, but they shot around the world anyway as the gospel truth spoken by a grieving mother" and quoted a thirty-eight-year-old black man as saying that "I guess she figured if she said a black man did it people would believe her no matter what kind of story she came up with. . . . That's what hurts. As long as it's allegedly a black man involved, America will fall for anything."[63] An op-ed piece in the *Los Angeles Times* noted that Smith's tale had a disturbing kind of historical resonance and that when her "story unraveled, that . . . struck a chord, but only in black house-holds. Black experience has taught that black men can be accused of— sometimes executed for—crimes they did not commit."[64] And an article in the *New York Times* echoed this sentiment, quoting Aldon Morris, the chair of the Sociology Department at Northwestern University, as say-ing that

> [t]his case demonstrates once again the stereotypical view of black men in America, that they are other, that they are dangerous, that they should be imprisoned. . . . And this view, of course, is nothing new. It was the same view that guided lynch mobs during the days of segregation in the South. It is the same view that causes black men to be stopped, searched and harassed on a routine basis by the police.[65]

Concern over racism was, however, only one of the issues that capti-vated the mainstream media once the true killer was revealed in each of these cases.

After Charles Stuart's suicide, there was a seemingly endless series of questions that needed to be addressed. It was revealed that Stuart had jumped off the bridge only after his brother had turned himself over to the police and had provided them with information to make Charles the primary suspect. But there was tremendous speculation over the mo-tive for his suicide. Matthew Stuart claimed that he had been helping Charles in an insurance scam, but it was not clear what kind of policies were out on Carol Stuart's life. A lot of the coverage of the case was devoted to tracking down and verifying a variety of policies that Charles had taken out on Carol's life.[66] The media also investigated Matthew Stuart's precise role in the murders. What exactly did he do? Would he be charged? Had he seen the body, and when did he become aware of the murder? Most important, the media sought to address how Charles Stuart, a man who had seemingly embodied the American dream (he came from the blue-collar community of Revere and wound up living in an affluent suburb, in a house with a swimming pool and a Jacuzzi) and who had managed to gain national sympathies so easily, could be such a cold-blooded murderer.[67]

As in the Stuart case, a central concern after Smith's confession and subsequent arrest was with determining her motivations. Her crime was seen not only as monstrous but even as unnatural, and it needed to be explained.[68] An article about her trial noted, for example, that Smith's defense team

> presented a host of mitigating circumstances familiar to those search-
> ing for a social source of evil. Smith's father had committed suicide
> when she was 6. A decade later her stepfather . . . had sexually mo-
> lested her. At the time of the murders, Smith, who was in the midst of
> a divorce from husband David, was also distraught over being dumped
> by Tom Findlay, her boyfriend. If those factors did not explain, much
> less justify, her actions—the prosecution argued that she saw her sons
> as an impediment to her romantic life—the jury was still moved by
> her plight.[69]

But if Smith's suffering did not provide an adequate explanation for the murders she committed, it was the best the media could do. As the media scoured every corner of Smith's personal life to try to determine how a mother could kill her children, the question of why a mother who killed her children would choose to blame a black man was clearly of secondary priority.

In fact, Smith's imaginary black carjacker was mentioned most often not in an attempt to understand her use of racism but in an effort to explain the harm that she had done to the community. An article in *Time* magazine about the reaction to Smith's trial in Union, South Carolina, discussed the "rage at Susan Smith's actions" in the town and elaborated by noting that people "are still outraged at the ease with which she convinced the world that she was the grieving victim of a dark-skinned stranger."[70] *Newsweek* picked up on the same sense of anger when it noted that "during nine suspenseful days last October, [Smith] hoodwinked the town and the national news media with a lurid fabrication seemingly drawn from tabloid crime reports—that her children had been abducted by a black carjacker."⁷¹ There were very few articles that suggested that the anger directed against Smith was based on a concern with racism or with the way her charges had affected African Americans or race relations. Instead, aside from killing her children, her biggest crime seems to have been that she played local and national audiences for fools.⁷²

The Black Press and the Continuing Relevance of Racial Terror
Mainstream media coverage stands in marked contrast with coverage of the cases in the African American press. While the mainstream media did note that Stuart and Smith relied upon ages-old racial stereotypes, their analysis of racism tended to stop there. The African American press, on the other hand, attempted to place the Stuart and Smith narratives within the larger context of a racist system, and at the same time, it attempted to assess the damage that these narratives had done to contemporary race relations and African American communities.

An article in the *Michigan Chronicle* opened in a manner similar to mainstream news articles about the use of race in the Smith and Stuart cases by noting that

> [t]he recent killings of the two young children in South Carolina by their mother, Susan Smith, like Charles Stuart of Boston who killed his pregnant wife in 1989, reminds us: Both felt they could escape justice by simply blaming the murders of their family members on America's number one suspect—"The Black Man."⁷³

But the article goes on to place this tradition of racist scapegoating within a broader history of racism that is not limited to stereotypes. It presents Stuart's and Smith's allegations as part of a continuum that includes slavery and lynching, and it claimed that

> history has shown that there are two Americas, one White and one Black, and two American dreams, the American dream of wealth, prosperity, democracy for Whites and the American nightmare of poverty, racism and caste system for African Americans.⁷⁴

Other articles in the African American press provide similar analyses that seek to link stereotypes with economic and political modes of power and oppression and that at the same time critique the basis of those stereotypes. For example, an article in the Cleveland *Call and Post* considered "how frequently in this nation the fountain of evil is perceived as flowing from the veins of all Blacks" and then noted that

Most crime in this nation is intra-racial—perpetuated by persons of the same race against each other. According to 1990 crime statistics, almost two-thirds of all robberies are committed by whites against whites or Blacks against Blacks; only one-third are by Blacks against whites. About 90 percent of all rapes are intra-racial—and of those, two-thirds are committed by whites against whites.[75]

The fact that the author specifically chose to report statistics about rape is, perhaps, an indication of a concern that Stuart's and Smith's imaginary gunmen are really not all that far removed from the mythical black rapists that were used to justify lynching.

In fact, lynching is a primary reference point for many of the articles about Stuart and Smith in the African American press. But unlike the mainstream media, the black papers discussed lynching as more than history, as they considered contemporary uses of, and possibilities for, racial terrorism. Virtually the only published accounts of the extent of the manhunts in the Stuart and Smith cases appeared in the African American press. The mainstream media occasionally noted that there had been national manhunts, but they said very little about the actual African American men who were hunted. In addition to presenting raw numbers of men who were arrested or questioned, black papers and magazines often quoted individual black men who had been made to feel like potential suspects and targets. One article quoted a textile worker in Union as saying that in the days before Smith's confession, "We all felt the tension from the white community" and quoted another resident of Union, who had been told that the police sketch of the kidnapper looked like him, as saying, "It really bothered me, made me feel uncomfortable."[76] Some articles considered the racial tension that was generated as a result of Stuart's and Smith's allegations in the context of lynching and suggested, particularly in Smith's case, that racial violence had been narrowly averted when the true culprit was revealed. One article noted that a man named Frederick Douglass Smith had been interrogated at least twice in the Smith case, and asked, "Was Black F. D. Smith lucky that she confessed?" The article's answer was that "in bygone years, Southern white police have found Black scapegoats for the guilty white females, [and] generated mob violence and lynchings of the accused Black men."[77] An article in the *New York Amsterdam News* noted that before Smith's confession, "South Carolinians were strapping on their guns with a grim look on their faces."[78] The possibility of a lynching was presented not as solely a matter of history but as a troubling facet of contemporary reality.

Racial Hoaxes, Black Gunmen, and Collective Memory

Collective memories of lynching thus served several functions in the Stuart and Smith cases. In order to deflect from their own guilt and to gain sympathy from the media, police, and various national audiences, Stuart and Smith both relied upon a stereotype of black male criminality that gained power and resonance from earlier invocations of the mythical black male rapist. Once the real murderers had been revealed, the mainstream media contextualized the killings by noting that the Stuart and Smith narratives were rooted in stereotypes of black male criminality that had been used to justify lynchings. Unlike the mass media, the black press tended to connect memories of lynching to historical and contemporary systems of oppression while arguing that racial terror is not confined to the past. Ultimately, while the mainstream media and the black press considered the past in very different ways and with varying degrees of depth, they both relied upon collective memories of mob violence in order to determine how to assess and understand these newest manifestations of racism.

In chapter 2, I considered the possibility that lynching has become a "hanging signifier." The haste with which Stuart's and Smith's allegations were accepted provides compelling evidence that the political power of the metaphor of lynching remains largely out of reach for some social actors. References to histories of lynching might have provided a useful note of caution early on in each of these cases, but the mass media turned a deaf ear when the issue was raised by the black press. While the black press certainly provided an important alternative voice as the events in these cases unfolded, its ability to mobilize collective memories of lynching was severely limited by the potency of stereotypes of black criminality.

Invocations of monstrous actions by innocent or nonexistent black men are the most common type of racial hoaxes, and they tap into the most powerful fears that surrounded lynchings. Throughout this book, however, I have argued that racial categories and collective memories are always contested. While lynchings helped to enable the myth of the black rapist and to imbue other stereotypes of black criminality with rhetorical power, there was a flip side of the coin, since lynching's opponents worked to expose lynching as racist spectacle and as an exercise of white supremacist power. My analysis of the Tawana Brawley case examines a very different kind of an apparent racial "hoax," one that relied upon collective memories that resonated with antiracist struggles.

Collective Memory, Credibility Structures, and the Case of Tawana Brawley

On November 28, 1987, in the small town of Wappingers Falls, New York, a fifteen-year-old black girl was found crawling near a garbage bag. She was at the brink of consciousness, apparently having been beaten and possibly raped, and her hair had been chopped off or pulled out. Feces were smeared over her, and the words "KKK" and "nigger" had been scrawled on her body. In the days that followed, it was reported that Tawana Brawley claimed that she had been abducted and sexually abused by six white men. On October 6 of the following year, a New York State grand jury released a report that said, in effect, that Brawley's tale was a hoax. The question of what, if anything, really happened to Tawana Brawley became one of the most hotly contested and visible issues in American racial politics in the 1980s.[79] Recently, the Tawana Brawley case was in the news again, as a defamation suit filed by Steven Pagones, a former assistant district attorney who was accused of being one of Brawley's abductors, came to trial. (Brawley and her advisers were ordered to pay a total of $530,000 in the case, which was at most a minor victory for Pagones, considering that he originally sought $395 million.)[80] The Brawley case is probably the single most spectacularized instance of a black woman's (or, really, a black girl's) claims of sexual (and racial) victimization in recent memory, with the notable exception of Anita Hill's allegations of sexual harassment by Clarence Thomas. The representations of Brawley's claims in the mass media and in the black press say quite a bit about contemporary understandings of race, justice, and gender.

Initial coverage tended to accept Brawley's allegations at face value. For example, Mary Murphy reported for WCBS-TV that Brawley was "recovering from an ordeal of sexual torture and racial abuse" and gave Brawley the opportunity to tell a mass audience that a police officer was involved.[81] But in its earliest stages, the story was mostly covered as a local issue. Local papers, including the *Poughkeepsie Journal*, the *Newburgh Evening News*, and the *Times Herald-Record* of Middletown, New York, reported the story early on, and consistently, but the New York City papers, including the *Daily News*, the *New York Post*, and the *New York Times*, as well as the rest of the national press, largely ignored the story at first. The first *New York Times* report of Brawley's allegations did not come until December 14, 1987, in the wake of a rally during which over one thousand protesters had demanded the appointment of a special prosecutor in the case. For the most part, this article accepted Brawley's story, noting that according to the police, she had been "found . . . in a fetal position inside a plastic bag" and that she "had been beaten. 'Nigger' and 'KKK' had been written in charcoal or marker on her torso, feces had been smeared across her body and her hair had been chopped off." Still, there was some skepticism in the article, which noted that "[l]ocal law-enforcement officials have questioned the truthfulness of the girl's statements."[82] More important, Brawley's allegations were reported as a matter of relatively minor importance. Her story was covered as only one of three Hudson Valley incidents that had prompted the rally, and the article appeared in the Metro section of the paper.

A book about the Brawley case, *Outrage: The Story behind the Tawana Brawley Hoax* (1990), which was written by the *New York Times* reporters who were assigned to cover the story, argues that the *Times* was reluctant to cover the case in its early stages because there was too much uncertainty about the events in question and because the *Times* had run into difficulties reporting on the Howard Beach case the previous year. As a result of the Howard Beach case, the paper had adopted a more reactive posture when it came to racial politics, generally reporting events only after civil rights activists or political officials had deemed them newsworthy.[83] It is reasonable to assume that other national media outlets ignored the story for similar reasons. Still, it bears noting that the story only became major news once Brawley's allegations started to be seen as a "hoax." That the story of a black girl's extreme racial and sexual victimization was not by itself sufficiently newsworthy for the mainstream press became an important bone of contention in later coverage by some of the black press.

It did not take long, however, before Brawley's allegations were subjected to serious scrutiny as various problems with her story came to light. The evidence that suggested that Brawley's tale had been fabricated seemed exhaustive. For example: It turned out that the neighbor who had reported seeing Brawley near the garbage bag had actually reported seeing her crawl *into* the bag, not out of it. Her hospital report noted that there was little if any evidence of anything having happened to her physically; there were no signs of rape, no injuries other than a small scratch and what looked like an old bruise, and no signs that she had suffered from exposure in a cold November. Various witnesses claimed to have seen Brawley in her old apartment and at basketball courts during the days that she was said to have been missing. Ultimately, the evidence against Brawley's story was gathered together in a 170-page report by a grand jury, which noted that "based on all the evidence that has been presented to the grand jury, we conclude that Tawana Brawley was not the victim of a forcible sexual assault by multiple assailants over a four-day period. . . . There is no evidence that any sexual assault occurred."[84]

The mainstream media accepted the grand jury report as the final word on the matter. The *New York Times*, for example, referred to the grand jury's reliance upon a "mountain of evidence . . . that Ms. Brawley had concocted her story"[85] and repeatedly emphasized the breadth of the investigation, calling it "exhaustive."[86] The *Times* noted that there were "180 witnesses who testified during the seven-month" investigation[87] and that these witnesses included "medical and scientific experts as well as eyewitnesses."[88]

Cast of Characters

But to say that there had been a hoax was not enough. For at least a short time, many people throughout the nation were led to believe that a black girl had been the victim of particularly horrific forms of sexual and racial victimization. The media had to address how this had happened and why. Aside from Tawana Brawley herself, attention focused on Glenda Brawley (Tawana's mother), Ralph King (the man who was living with Glenda Brawley), and the "team" of C. Vernon Mason, Alton Maddox, and the Reverend Al Sharpton, who were Brawley's advisers.

If this incident *was* a hoax, the most pressing question was, Why? What would anyone have had to gain from it? Ralph King seemed to provide the key to the answer. The *New York Times* reporters who covered the Brawley case devote large portions of *Outrage* to descriptions of King's various run-ins with the legal system. Most important is the fact that in one incident, he repeatedly stabbed his former wife, and in a later attack, he shot her to death. King was convicted of second-degree assault and first-degree manslaughter for the attack and the killing and ultimately served seven years in prison for the crimes.[89] *Outrage* argues that King's propensity for violence resurfaced in the Brawley home, where he started to beat Glenda Brawley. *Outrage* claims that King and Glenda Brawley may have both been responsible for beating Tawana on at least one occasion and states that Tawana had told her friends that King was a "filthy pervert" and that he was interested in her sexually. Eventually, she apparently confided to her friends that she was pregnant and that King was the father. (According to this story, she had an abortion.)[90] *Outrage* explains the "hoax" as an attempt to avoid further brutality by King.

According to this version of events (which was supplied, in part, by Daryl T. Rodriguez, who had been Tawana's boyfriend before her disappearance), Tawana ran away from home one night after being beaten by

King. (This beating also explains the only signs of physical damage that were found when she was taken to the hospital; apparently King had hit her behind the left ear. This was the bruise that was found during Tawana's examination.) By the time Tawana decided that she might want to return home, King had become aware of her absence and was furious. Glenda Brawley wanted her to come home but was afraid of King's rage. In order to avoid any repercussions from King, Tawana and Glenda together concocted the "hoax." According to Rodriguez, the idea was that if Tawana had been raped, "Ralph would [take] her back into the house and feel sorry for her, and everything would be normal. He wouldn't hit her anymore, and he would treat her a little better. So she thought up the idea of putting the feces on her, pulling her hairpiece out to make it look like a real rape."[91] Or, as *Outrage* puts it, "King's anger would melt to sympathy, clearing her way to return home."[92]

It was conceivable that if the hoax really was the result of a desperate plan to avoid King's brutality, Glenda Brawley might have been portrayed as a caring mother who was doing what she needed to in order to protect her daughter. Instead, the dominant narrative emphasized the efforts she went to in order to maintain her lies. Early in *Outrage*, the authors (who later discuss Glenda Brawley's role in manufacturing the story of Tawana's abduction) discuss her efforts to "dutifully [spread] the word of her daughter's disappearance," noting, however, that she had earlier been content to stay home for days while her sister and King searched for Tawana. The book goes on to describe the scene at the Brawleys' apartment after Tawana had been taken to the hospital. Police officers had asked Glenda Brawley's permission to visit in order to show Glenda and King a picture of Tawana and confirm that this was, indeed, Glenda's daughter. While they were there, Glenda's sister called from the hospital to tell her about Tawana's condition. The account in *Outrage* notes that "Glenda Brawley's impassive face hardened into a mask of anguish, and she shrieked."[93] The emphasis throughout the book on Glenda's role in manufacturing the abduction story renders the word "mask" superfluous here, since we know that there are no grounds for her to have experienced genuine anguish. Still, this passage does set the stage for the unfolding portrayal of Glenda as supremely manipulative and emotionally duplicitous.

Despite this portrayal, Glenda Brawley's manipulation was seen as minor league in comparison to that of Tawana Brawley's advisers, C. Vernon Mason, Alton Maddox, and the Reverend Al Sharpton. Ultimately, Glenda Brawley's motivations prevent her complete demonization. At the same time, her sights were set low (her goal in continuing to perpetrate the "hoax" would have been primarily to save her family's reputation). In contrast, the three advisers are presented as having been either out for self-aggrandizement or engaged in a racial holy war or both. More important, these three men are presented as being dangerous in a way that Glenda Brawley could never have been because they made credible claims to represent large portions of the black community and therefore were able to gain access to the media, which would have been well beyond Glenda Brawley's reach had she been acting alone.

Maddox had a long history of trying racially explosive cases. He had achieved a high degree of visibility in the case of Michael Stewart, the black graffiti artist who was strangled to death by white transit police in New York City. *Outrage* notes that "Maddox showed how the case was badly mishandled by the police, the medical examiner, and the Manhattan district attorney's office."[94] But not all of his cases were so clear-cut. He had lost a case in 1986 when the white model Marla Hanson accused a black man of slashing her face with a razor. *Outrage* discusses Maddox's tactics in this case:

> In a brutal cross-examination, Maddox tried to show that the victim's charges were tainted by racism.
>
> "When you saw two black men walking in a civilized manner down Dyer Avenue, it ran across your mind that you were about to be raped—isn't that correct?" he asked Miss Hanson.
>
> "Yes," she admitted, "that thought ran through my mind."
>
> It was that way in all his defenses: racism, not his client, was on trial.[95]

The image of Maddox as a racial crusader less concerned with the particulars of any given case than with broader issues of racial justice dominates the way he has been portrayed throughout his legal career. *Outrage* notes, for instance, that along with Mason and Sharpton, Maddox had been partly responsible for the convictions in the trials following the death of Michael Griffith in Howard Beach a year earlier. But far from crediting Maddox with the convictions in the case, *Outrage* argues that Maddox's need for a high-stakes trial was responsible for letting some of the offenders off the hook. Maddox's client, Cedric Sandiford, had survived the attack and was the state's key witness. Maddox would not allow him to testify before a grand jury, and without his testimony, the state was compelled to dismiss the charges against some of the defendants. The "Maddox-Mason-Sharpton triumvirate"[96] *did* manage to apply enough political pressure to force then-governor Mario Cuomo to appoint a special prosecutor to the case, and the special prosecutor was able to secure some convictions. Thus, "the case made Maddox one of the best-known lawyers in New York," but *Outrage* argues that "he cared little for fame. He cared more about the answer to one question: what would it take to get justice?"[97] But the justice that he was concerned with was never simply for the people directly involved in one particular case; rather, it was for an entire race: "The answer seemed somehow to lie not in battering the white faces filled with hate, but in retrying the Dred Scott decision of 1857."[98]

Thus, it is not surprising that Maddox is presented as not particularly concerned with allegations that Tawana Brawley's case was a fabrication. Describing his first visit to the Brawley household, *Outrage* notes that

> he came in like a revolutionary with a satchel of explosives, and when he took off his coat and started talking, it was clear that this was an implacable zealot: it was in the unflinching eyes, the orator's voice, the compact fighter's body. He might have been a maniac or a messiah—either way it was his agenda that mattered. To Maddox, it was brutally simple: the white mob had struck again. [The book earlier notes that Maddox had grown up in a segregated town that had a history of lynchings.] So he did not ask Glenda Brawley and Ralph King any troublesome questions about Tawana; the facts could wait. He explained his mission: to prove to the world that Tawana Brawley had been molested and that the police had been involved all the way and were engaged in a cover-up. The whole criminal justice system was corrupt in its treatment of black Americans, he said. He wanted justice, nothing less.[99]

The idea here that Maddox's "agenda" was all that mattered to him helps to explain why he would so readily accept Brawley's story. His zeal and his background had blinded him to the particulars of any case. After all, there was no point in getting bogged down with the particulars of any one case as long as racism as a whole was on trial.

Like Maddox, Mason is portrayed as a racial crusader, but one with political aspirations and a need for media attention. *Outrage* notes that Mason came from a civil rights background and that the clients in his private practice included victims of housing or employment discrimination and of police brutality, but that "Whenever possible, Mason sought publicity to broaden [his] cases, to raise wider issues. 'The game is to try to impact the structure,' he liked to say, 'because with many of the smaller individual cases you're just putting your finger in the dike.'"[100] Mason's concern with tackling "the structure" was not always to the benefit of his clients: "It was a full agenda, and some clients complained that their cases languished while Mason focused on higher-profile causes."[101] The highest-profile case until now had been the Howard Beach case, and, as I have discussed above, *Outrage* accuses the three Brawley advisers of racial grandstanding in that case, at the expense of possible convictions. *Outrage* also discusses Mason's political aspirations and clout, noting that he ran in an unsuccessful bid to unseat Manhattan District Attorney Robert M. Morgenthau in the 1985 election but that he nonetheless managed to receive one-third of the vote. *Outrage* notes that Mason's prominence increased after that election because of the Howard Beach case and because of his role in representing the young black men who were shot in the New York subway by Bernhard Goetz. *Outrage*, therefore, presents the Brawley case as one more opportunity for Mason to step into a national racial spotlight and to increase his visibility and political power.

Although Maddox and Mason were concerned with the political stakes in, and the spectacular nature of, the Brawley case, they did also serve as Brawley's lawyers and therefore had an ostensible function that was not explicitly linked to the media or any forum outside of the courtroom. This was not the case for Sharpton. Sharpton's primary role had to do with community outreach and the cameras. He was

> the whole circus—part lion, part clown, and part Houdini. He loved to roar and bellow, mug for laughs, juggle fact with fancy, and delight crowds with slick illusions and vanishing acts. Just when exasperated critics thought they had him bound and gagged, padlocked in a steamer trunk at the bottom of a water tank, he would pop up again, waving to his fans, not even wet.
>
> The rotund preacher with the semiautomatic mouth straddled the worlds of news and entertainment, promotion and boxing, religion and community activism, the media and the mob.[102]

The imagery here might be a bit misleading, since it suggests that Sharpton is a relatively harmless figure; he might be "the whole circus," but everything in the passage suggests that he performs as sideshow entertainment. *Outrage* is quick to note, however, that there is another side to Sharpton's outward performances. When discussing his background, for example, the book mentions that "Sharpton was drawn into an underworld of mob investors and FBI undercover agents. In one venture in the early 1980s, Sharpton sought to buy into the Mafia-dominated New York–area carting industry, ostensibly as a way of creating job opportunities for blacks."[103] The possibility that Sharpton was tied to organized crime was raised during the trial of Matthew Ianniello, who was charged with using mob influence in the private garbage-collection industry. While the account does note that "Sharpton was not accused of any wrongdoing," there is a clear suggestion that Sharpton's efforts to "help" blacks are not all that straightforward and may conceal ulterior motives. This suggestion is furthered as the book goes on to discuss Sharpton's role as an informant for the FBI. The FBI claimed to have videotape of Sharpton involved in a drug deal and asked him to let them tap his phone as a way to avoid further legal problems. Sharpton complied.[104] *Outrage* states that Sharpton's entire involvement with the FBI was "murky" and that there was no proof of any illegal activity or of any betrayal of the civil rights movement, but it still notes that "[t]he most striking question was why he had agreed so readily to secret arrangements with the FBI, which had long regarded black activism—indeed, all activism—as subversive. What did the feds really have on him?"[105]

Discussions of Sharpton's possible criminal connections are particularly important because the trial for Pagones's civil suit started during an election year in which Sharpton came in second in the Democratic mayoral primary for New York City. Sharpton was considering another bid for mayor in the 2001 election, and many of the articles about Pagones's suit addressed Sharpton's political aspirations, noting, for example, that he was "haunted" by the case that had "crept back into the public consciousness."[106] Thus, collective memory of Brawley's allegations and Sharpton's role as one of her advisers are cited as potentially damaging to Sharpton's political career. Sharpton's future in New York politics is, however, merely a peripheral issue in the Brawley saga. Ultimately, the most enigmatic and compelling figure in the case was Tawana Brawley herself.

Initial press reports about Tawana Brawley raised some minor questions about her account but were generally very sympathetic and tended to portray her as the victim of a horrific crime. As the case progressed, however, and more problems with her story came to light, sympathetic portrayals started to drop away, to be replaced with more sinister imagery.[107] This evolution was far from inevitable. After all, if Brawley *had* made up the story to avoid further brutality at King's hands, it would still have made sense to see her as a victim worthy of sympathy. In fact, it is reasonable to suggest that Brawley's fear and the kinds of suffering that she must have gone through must have been truly staggering if they were enough to force her to resort to cutting her hair, covering herself in feces, and crawling into a garbage bag.

This position had little support in the mainstream press.[108] The grand jury's report, which is consistently lauded for its comprehensiveness and its sheer size ("170 pages" appears constantly in the newspapers' accounts), offers not a single word of explanation as to *why* Brawley would concoct such a tale and be willing to engage in such devastating self-defilement. As I have mentioned, the media *did* make some effort to explain the reasons for the "hoax," but their primary concern was always with the specific machinations that made up the hoax and with the evidence establishing that it *was* a hoax. Very little attention was focused on examining Brawley's emotional state prior to her disappearance. I would suggest that this absence would be inconceivable if the "hoaxter" had been white. If a fifteen-year-old white girl had been accused of having chopped off her hair, scrawling racial epithets over her body, and covering herself with feces, it does not seem plausible to suggest that there would not have been widespread speculation and national hand-wringing over why this had happened. Nor does it make sense to suggest that a national audience would have been satisfied with the explanation that this was a ruse to avoid further exposure to domestic abuse. Instead, it seems fairly certain that there would have been *some* attempt to determine why this *particular* theatrical display was chosen. The fact that there was not requires explanation.

In his analysis of Clarence Thomas's use of imagery associated with dirt and defilement during the Hill–Thomas hearings, Kendall Thomas expands upon Joel Kovel's idea that

> "the blackness of black skin (even if it is really brown)" has been fused with the idea of dirt, and more generally, with the image of anything that can pass out of the body, such as feces. In Kovel's view, the notion that blacks are "an essentially dirty and smelly people" is the generative substrate of the racial fantasies that provide the psychosymbolic framework of white racism. . . . What bears remarking here is his claim that the "nuclear experience" of white racism "is a sense of disgust about the body of the black person based upon a very primitive fantasy: that it contains an essence—dirt—that smells and may rub off onto the body of the racist."[109]

Thomas goes beyond Kovel, drawing upon Frantz Fanon's work to suggest that "the primal fantasy of white racism insinuates itself into the psychic structure of those against whom it is directed and becomes inscribed in the 'mind [and] very skin' of its victims."[110] Thomas uses this observation to explain Clarence Thomas's symbolic separation from "the fact of his blackness" (he argues that Thomas "was chiefly represented as . . . 'a Republican judicial conservative who opposes quotas, and also happens to be black'"), but this argument about the nature and the power of internalized oppression may also be relevant in providing an explanation for Brawley's actions.[111] If so, it would provide a truly horrifying portrait of the strength of contemporary racism. Regardless of whether or not Brawley's drama was an outward manifestation of an internalized racist projection, the broader point is that the association of blackness with dirt in the racist imagination helps to explain why there was so little attention devoted to the theatrical choices Brawley made. In this analysis, it becomes plausible to suggest that the mainstream media were incapable of registering shock at the idea that a black girl would cover herself with shit. Whatever the reasons, the fact that the media *did not* feel the need to speculate about Brawley's suffering cleared the way to highlight her role at the center of a hoax that threatened to do irreparable harm to racial relations.

Outrage suggests that Brawley's story is less surprising, given her background. It mentions that she was a good student who was described by friends as "intelligent, sweet, and friendly," but this image is undercut with the information that she had been arrested "for hitting another girl during an argument and for pulling a knife and making threats."[112] Even her intelligence works against her, for we are told that she "loved to read" and was particularly attracted to the kinds of stories that appealed to "pubescent adolescents with vivid imaginations, drawing upon elements of gothic horror and greed, rape and revenge, brother-sister incest, and the fairy-tale agonies of children locked away by wicked adults."[113] In another context this information might have been seen as praise. Here, we are all too aware of the eventual uses of this imagination.

The portrayal of Brawley's adolescence is not limited to a discussion of her literary interests. *Outrage* notes that she went to parties "usually with older teens" and quotes her peers as saying that "she liked attention from guys" and "had a posse of boyfriends." Other "acquaintances" are said to have called her "a tease," "fast," "wild," "aggressive," and "flirtatious."[114] Ordinarily, it would be considered highly inappropriate for *New York Times* reporters to reveal this kind of information about an alleged rape victim, but in this case, the charges are seen as fair game since the goal is to explain the actions of a dangerous hoaxter. Once Brawley is cast in the stereotypical role of the sexually available black woman, it becomes more difficult to see her as the potential subject of sexual victimization, and at the same time, it becomes more plausible to think that she would have chosen a sexually based hoax.

The same paragraph that discusses Brawley's sex life refers to friends who "said she did not use drugs, but had a tendency to exaggerate, even to lie," and quotes one friend in particular as saying that "[s]he didn't get into drugs or anything like that that I knew of. . . . The only thing about her is she used to lie sometimes. She'd stretch the truth." Of course, this friend's credibility is not questioned when it comes to Brawley's lies, but his claims about Brawley's lack of drug use are challenged by other friends, who noted that "there were at least two occasions in the spring of 1987 when, they said, she smoked marijuana."[115] The most damning evidence presented as contributing to the genesis of Brawley's story is that she and her friends knew about another girl, who was also named Tawana, who had "tried to conceal a late-night escapade with a boy" by telling the police that she had been abducted by two white men in a green car who had driven her into the woods and raped her. We are told that when the police investigated Tawana Ward Dempsey's story, *her* hoax was easily revealed.[116] Brawley's active imagination presumably left her in a better position to create a more convincing hoax.

African American Support for Brawley: Credibility versus Reason according to the *Times*

The picture that I have just outlined of Brawley's tale seems fairly damning and would, at first glance, lead one to think that there should be no more to the story. After all, given the mountain of evidence against her and given the unsavory characters who were involved in creating and spreading the tale, including a brutal black man, a manipulative mother, a sexually duplicitous teenage girl, and a host of opportunistically racist demagogues, there seems to be no question that Brawley's allegations were a hoax. The fact that a sizable percentage of the black population *did* believe Brawley therefore raises troubling questions for the mainstream media. The *New York Times* and WCBS-TV conducted a telephone poll in late 1988 (in the wake of the grand jury report) in which 18 percent of African Americans in New York City (compared with 3 percent of whites) said that they believed that Brawley had told the truth about what had happened to her.[117] Those numbers tell only part of the story, however, since follow-up stories and reports that surfaced during Pagones's defamation suit consistently suggest that there is a highly vocal part of the black community that supports Brawley and that there is a clear divide between black and white opinion about the case. For example, a 1998 article about public reactions to the case claimed that "people seem mostly to think now what they always thought of the case" and then quoted a white woman as saying, "It's obvious he [Pagones] didn't do it" and a black man as saying, "Everyone in the black community knows he did it."[118] The media's attempts to account for this apparently race-based gap in public perceptions are centrally concerned with differences in collective memory and racially constructed understandings of common sense.

Early on in *Outrage*, there is a discussion of the recent history of racism in the area of New York State that Brawley lived in:

> If educated, well-dressed, middle-class blacks in Dutchess and neighboring counties experienced racism only in its subtler forms, the poorer blacks in the area had a litany of complaints, ranging from job discrimination to rent gouging, from being patronized by white social workers to being eyed with suspicion by white store clerks. Many of these wounds, real or perceived, were nursed in private or aired mainly in the security of black churches and clubs. The official forums remained all but closed to blacks.[119]

The account goes on to note that a black man named Jimmy Lee Bruce Jr. was killed in the nearby town of Wallkill by two off-duty white police officers in 1986 and that the case, along with the killings in New York City of Michael Griffith, Michael Stewart, and Eleanor Bumpurs, had sparked a revival of the region's civil rights movement.[120] Finally, *Outrage* notes that

> the ordinary black people of the Hudson Valley were more than ready to voice their outrage when . . . three white men brandishing bats and pipes tried to attack a black Peekskill man named Alphonso Smith. And they were ready again, later that month, when a black teenaged girl from Wappingers Falls was found in a garbage bag, smeared with excrement and racial slurs.[121]

The suggestion here is that history and a collective memory of racism has prepared blacks to accept Brawley's allegations more readily than would whites. This idea is expressed in its clearest form when *Outrage* claims that "in the poisonous atmosphere left by Howard Beach and other racial cases, many blacks were willing to believe any black's account of abuse by whites; and no account by a white, especially by a white police officer or public official, could shake them."[122]

Clearly, I would agree with the *Times* reporters that there are differentially constructed collective memories for people of various races and that our understandings of the past influence how we understand the present. And I think that some of the black support for Brawley is related to these differences in collective memory. But the claim that collective memory has conditioned "many blacks" to believe "any black's account" of white abuse, with complete disregard for anything any white person might say, suggests that blacks' collective memory has rendered (at least many of) them irrational and that past racism has had the effect of blinding them to the particulars of contemporary reality.[123]

This point is made explicitly in an op-ed piece by Bob Herbert about a rally in support of Brawley at the Bethany Baptist Church in the Bedford-Stuyvesant section of Brooklyn in 1997. Herbert refers to the rally, which occurred during Pagones's defamation suit, as "a revival of the festival of ignorance and hate" that originated when Brawley first made her allegations. He goes on to say that "covering the [original] story was a nightmare. There was nothing real to report," but he claims that did not matter at the rally, since "there was no room for reality at Bethany Baptist." At best, black people are presented here as insane or as out of touch with reality. At worst, they are seen as unwilling to give up their "cherished beliefs about the wickedness of white people." This scenario, too, presents blacks as fundamentally irrational because "reasonable individuals would hope" that Brawley had lied, since that "would mean that she hadn't been raped."[124] But the idea that blacks have a stake in believing unwarranted claims of racism adds an especially troubling component to the charge of irrationality, since it reproduces the logic behind some contemporary efforts to abolish affirmative action and welfare. The claim is that people who support affirmative action and welfare are using their belief in racism as a crutch and are therefore looking for government handouts instead of taking responsibility for their own lives. With stakes so high, these beliefs must be "cherished" indeed.

A more sinister explanation for black support of Brawley is that Brawley's supporters *knew* that the story was a hoax but appreciated the irony in the idea that, for once, it would be white men who were made to suffer from unjust accusations of sexual brutality. In this scenario, the history of lynching is reversed, as a black woman conjures up a series of mythical white rapists and a black crowd demands mob justice. An article in the *New Republic* presents this possibility:

> [E]ven the likelihood that her story was a hoax was made to echo an equally venerable archetype of suffering: for centuries, whites had falsely accused blacks of raping white women. That whites themselves would now taste victimization by lie seemed to give any number of otherwise intelligent people a certain satisfaction.[125]

An editorial by Stanley Diamond in *The Nation* that is meant to be sympathetic to Brawley and her supporters makes a similar point when it claims that

> [i]n cultural perspective, if not in fact, it doesn't matter whether the crime occurred or not. Tawana Brawley's handlers . . . must know this. They simply reversed the predicament black Americans find all too

familiar: the use of false charges to rationalize the maiming and murder of countless blacks in the United States; the mass creation of victims.

The article concludes by saying that

> [a]lthough oppressors have imprisoned and murdered designated victims throughout history—rationalizing their acts with false charges, fake trials and manufactured evidence—the Brawley case is the opposite and is rare if not unique. It may be asking too much of the white community to excuse the Brawley deceit; but they misunderstand it at their peril.[126]

Diamond's claim that Brawley's handlers "simply reversed" the lynching scenario is undercut by his observation that the case is "rare if not unique." As I have argued throughout this book, there is nothing "simple" about this kind of reversal, since configurations of race, gender, and justice are interrelated in highly complex ways. My larger concern, however, is with the idea that blacks would find the reversal of the lynching scenario either appealing or compelling. The suggestion that we can only understand Brawley's support within the black community if we recognize that there is a strong desire for racial vengeance that takes precedence over rational examinations of evidence is disturbing, to say the least.

Brawley's Support: Another Explanation

If African Americans who support Brawley are neither blinded by historical racism nor motivated by vengeance, then it is worth speculating about other reasons for this support.[127] And again, I agree that history and collective memory hold some of the answers. My objection to the mainstream media's reliance upon collective memory as an explanation is the suggestion that Brawley's supporters are so obsessed with history that they are incapable of judging the evidence in the present on a case-by-case basis. I would argue, instead, that it is likely that their understandings of the past have helped to determine the methods that Brawley's supporters (and her detractors too, for that matter) use to weigh evidence and to evaluate its relevance.

Certainly, Brawley's advisers called upon history in order to gather support for their cause. During a radio call-in show, Mason told then-governor Mario Cuomo that New York State "enjoys the peculiar distinction of being about where Alabama and Arkansas and Mississippi and all those states down there were about thirty years ago,"[128] and he argued in court that

> [f]our hundred years of oppression is riding on this case, and we have reached a point when the African nation in this country, and particu-

larly those Africans in New York, are thoroughly disgusted with the way justice is administered and they are thoroughly disgusted with black victims of racial crimes being told by a grand jury that they are hallucinating and that what happened to them amounts to a hoax. I hope that from this day forward we can wipe clean those four hundred years of injustices and begin to proceed into the twenty-first century like intelligent and civilized men and women.[129]

While Mason's comments focused on a generalized history of racism, Sharpton and Louis Farrakhan addressed the specific history of racism against black women within the legal system. Sharpton claimed that "[i]n the history of the state of New York, a white man has never been convicted for raping a black woman,"[130] and Farrakhan claimed that "[i]f Tawana was white, there would be no question about it. . . . But they don't think black women can be raped. This is why the media tries to portray her as a temptress and a seductress."[131] While both of these comments may be exaggerations, they both tap into the very real history of a legal system that has been unable or unwilling to treat black women's sexual victimization, particularly at the hands of white men, seriously.

Mason, Farrakhan, and Sharpton thus worked not only to inform their constituencies of this history (if they were not already aware of it) but also to invoke it as the appropriate lens through which to view Brawley's charges. But while the *Times* presents this lens as working to obscure contemporary reality, I would suggest instead that it provided different ways to see and different things to focus on. Brawley's advisers were attempting to invoke an African American common sense in which, as Stuart Hall might argue, the "'taken-for-granted' terrain . . . which new conceptions of the world must take into account, contest and transform"[132] included a collective memory of racism that would guide any interpretations of the present.

The African American press provided an important source of alternative information about the Brawley case. Throughout the Brawley case, circulation of black newspapers increased tremendously among African Americans, especially in New York.[133] While there was no unanimity in coverage or perspective among black newspapers,[134] on the whole the black press was much more likely to endorse Brawley's version of events than was the mainstream press. Two of the most prominent African American papers in New York, the *Amsterdam News* and the *Beacon*, generally support Brawley to this day. But neither paper saw the case as a *simple* matter of racism. Neither paper presented her case as true for the sole reason that it "seemed familiar enough to suggest that something had happened to the teenager."[135] Instead, both papers presented reasons to doubt the medical testimony that the grand jury relied upon, to question the credibility of the mainstream press, and to see the case within a larger historical context in which black women's sexual victimization was routinely ignored or endorsed by the legal system.

The *Beacon* reported that the grand jury had relied upon medical testimony from outside experts and suggested that financial interests had tainted the findings of those experts. It quoted Mason as saying that "[r]ather than having those physicians, those nurses, those medical labs who examined and treated Tawana Brawley, he [then–state attorney general Robert Abrams] flew in experts from all over the country and paid them hundreds of thousands of dollars,"[136] while the *Amsterdam News* presented a lengthy article discussing the findings of four black physicians who "examined Tawana Brawley's complete medical and psychiatric records for the purpose of further evaluating" the grand jury's findings. The article summarized the grand jury report by saying that it "essentially concluded that a 15-year-old Black girl who had been found unconscious, in subfreezing weather, in a garbage bag, her hair shorn, her body covered from head to toe with dog feces, racial epithets scrawled on her body, had done these things to herself." The paper quickly dismissed this finding: "As common sense might tell you, the physicians concluded that Abrams' report is not compatible with the medical record."[137] The article discussed a series of apparent inconsistencies and problems with the medical evidence that was presented to the grand jury, but for the present discussion, the most interesting thing about the piece is the way it distinguished between the African American doctors who reviewed the evidence for the current article and Abrams's "hired-guns" who testified in front of the grand jury. The consistent references to the race of the African American physicians, coupled with the information that *these* doctors were "working for free," made it abundantly clear that medical authority is not seen as an objective, race-neutral fact but, rather, as a highly contested political arena where race is every bit as salient as it is in the broader society.[138]

Another article about the medical evidence in the *Amsterdam News* indicted the mainstream press for its inability and unwillingness to adequately discuss the evidence in the case. An editorial note at the beginning of the article says that the article was offered

> so that our readers will have the opportunity to weigh this version against a version culled from tabloids in New York City whose writers had little knowledge of medicine or rape for that matter—writers who

offered themselves up as authorities. The versions of the tabloids, by the way, are the versions that have been generally accepted by those who did not wish to believe that five white men could have raped a Black child.[139]

The desire not to believe Brawley was presented as part of a larger pattern in which black women's claims of sexual victimization are routinely subjected to far greater scrutiny than are white women's. The paper noted that the grand jury was told about various facets of Brawley's life and argued that

> Tawana's condition and the personal lives of her family members were not the proper subjects at a Grand Jury investigation into her rape in the first place. With white victims, an allegation, a presentation and clinical signs like those contained on the first five pages of her 110 pages of medical records would have established that a rape had occurred.[140]

An article in the *Beacon* suggested that the mainstream media's unquestioning acceptance of the grand jury report is par for the course, since unfair treatment "is customary in cases involving African American victims and white defendants." The article elaborated by claiming that

> [w]hite men are sometimes convicted for crimes against white women, Black men are usually convicted and punished for crimes against Black women. White men [are] never punished for crimes against Black women, while Black men are usually lynched or executed for their crimes against White women.[141]

This is certainly an exaggeration, but it nevertheless attempts to contextualize Brawley's allegations by pointing to specific aspects of collective memory and historical racism that are all but ignored by the mainstream media.

It is, I suspect, precisely because the *New York Times* and other mainstream media sources failed to address historically racist treatments of black sexuality with any complexity that so many of Brawley's potential supporters (black and white) turned elsewhere for information. People with any awareness of this history would have been likely to be suspicious of so pat and decisive a dismissal of yet another claim of black female victimization, especially since that dismissal seemed to be based upon racist stereotypes that were central to that history. To the extent that the black press acknowledged a collective memory of racial terror that often silenced black women, it filled a void and was therefore in a better position to attempt to mobilize support based upon an otherwise neglected history.

Support for Brawley did not come without a price. Brawley's advisers, along with the *Amsterdam News*, the *Beacon*, and much of the rest of the African American press, helped to keep the case in a national spotlight and thus added to the spectacle. One result is that because one of the few highly visible instances of black female victimization has been widely discredited as a hoax, similar claims are likely to be regarded with even greater skepticism in the future, and stereotypes of sexually available black women are likely to be reinforced.[142] Surely, this is only an issue because of the failure of the mainstream press to have addressed the victimization of black women in the past and because of its decision that this was the *one* case of black female pain that was worth covering in detail. Still, if Brawley's allegations *were* fabricated, her advisers and supporters within the African American press are partly responsible for making the spectacle possible.

Memory, Credibility, and Common Sense

By failing to treat Brawley's allegations as especially newsworthy until considerable doubt had arisen about their reliability and by choosing to depict the case as a story full of stereotypical figures, including dangerous black men and sexually duplicitous and available black women, the mainstream media relied upon and continued processes of racial formation that were central to the dynamics of lynching. The more interesting use of collective memory in this case is, however, as an explanation for the nature of black beliefs and common sense. I have argued that the suggestion that a history of black victimization has predisposed a large segment of the African American population to believe that *any* claim of racism is itself racist, since it presupposes an inability and a disinclination to understand or evaluate evidence in the present and ultimately suggests that a collective memory of racism has produced widespread irrationality. At the same time, I have argued that a more nuanced sense of collective memory suggests that past injustices do not blind people to contemporary reality; instead, history helps structure the patterns that people look for when attempting to understand the present. Brawley's advisers placed the story within a historical context that addressed the specificity of racism within the legal system, science, and the mass media. By acknowledging the very concrete ways in which Brawley's story fit into larger historical patterns, Brawley's advisers and much of the African American press filled a void left by mainstream news outlets and appealed to an otherwise unacknowledged racialized common sense that held that these patterns were essential parts of the explanation for Brawley's saga.

Concluding Remarks

In this chapter, I have argued that collective memories of lynching have provided ways to understand contemporary instances of racialized violence. They have provided alarming resonance to black fears of vigilante violence in the wake of Goetz's actions and Stuart's and Smith's allegations, and at the same time, they have provided a lens through which to view popular and legal support for those same actions and allegations. I have also argued that representations of race and violence have relied upon or critiqued variations of racial stereotypes that were central to the dynamics of lynching and that decisions to either acknowledge or neglect these dynamics have had important repercussions upon various audiences' notions of credibility and common sense. In chapter 4, I move from a discussion of fairly localized instances of racialized violence that have become national spectacles to a discussion of an explicitly political drama of truly national proportions as I examine the role of collective memories of lynching in the Hill–Thomas hearings.

CHAPTER 4

The Hill–Thomas Hearings and the
Meaning of a "High-Tech Lynching"

From my standpoint, as a black American, as far as I am concerned,
it is a high-tech lynching for uppity blacks who in any way deign to
think for themselves, to do for themselves, to have different ideas, and
it is a message that, unless you kow-tow to an old order, this is what
will happen to you, you will be lynched, destroyed, caricatured by a
committee of the U.S. Senate, rather than hung from a tree.

—*Clarence Thomas*

T
he portion of Clarence Thomas's confirmation hearings devoted
to an examination of Anita Hill's allegations of sexual harrassment
was one of the most watched political events in television history.
More than 27 million households tuned in to the first day of testimony
about the allegations on October 11, 1991,[1] and in the following days,
coverage and discussions of the hearings dominated the mass media.[2]
All around the country, people were glued to their television sets and
talking about the hearings. In the years since, Anita Hill and Clarence
Thomas have become iconic figures on the American cultural landscape.
The elections of 1992, which have been dubbed "the year of the woman"
by many (and which ushered in four new female U.S. senators, including
the first African American woman senator, Carol Moseley-Braun), have
been largely attributed to a revitalized awareness of, and concern with,
the Senate's insensitivity to the needs of women in the wake of the Hill–
Thomas hearings. Sexual harassment laws and sexual harassment policies
at many public and private institutions have changed considerably since,
and because of, the hearings.[3] The Hill–Thomas hearings have become
a prism through which to see all other issues of sexual harassment,

alleged harassment, or even alleged sexual improprieties. Most notable in this regard, are, of course, the political/sexual "scandals" involving President Bill Clinton and Paula Jones and Monica Lewinsky. Hill herself was asked to help with Jones's lawsuit and is regularly sought out by the media to offer commentary on the more spectacular cases involving the possibility of sexual harassment. And of course, the hearings concluded with the appointment of one of the most conservative Supreme Court justices on the Rhenquist court.[4] This was, then, one of the most important political spectacles in recent memory, and the lynching metaphor was at its core. The Hill–Thomas hearings offer an excellent chance for sustained attention to the power and the possible uses of this metaphor.

The quote that I have used to introduce this chapter represents perhaps the single most powerful rhetorical moment of the hearings.[5] Thomas's charge that he was the victim of a "high-tech lynching" was a highly self-conscious use of language that drew explicit attention to the role of lynching as metaphor. Thomas was well aware that this was not a "real" lynching; he did not claim that anyone was being killed.[6] But neither did he seem to suggest that his victimization was any less important than what happened to those victims of old-fashioned lynchings of the past.[7] "High-tech" is not a phrase that suggests mitigation, and Thomas clearly wanted to establish his status as a victim, claiming that "I am a victim of this process and my name has been harmed, my integrity has been harmed, my character has been harmed, my family has been harmed, my friends have been harmed. There is nothing this committee, this body or this country can do to give me my good name back, nothing."[8] But if lynching as metaphor no longer requires a dead body (and because lynching as language and "caricature" requires no physical victimization at all), then it is important to ask, Just what is the nature of Thomas's charge? How are we to make sense of the lynching metaphor? What kind of victimization is Thomas claiming to have suffered? What is the relationship between "high-tech" and older, more mundane, varieties of lynchings?

In order to gauge the power and meaning of Thomas's metaphoric invocation of lynching, I first address the importance of the physical, embodied nature of lynching as a material practice and then consider the question of what it means to claim to be the subject of a lynching without claiming any sort of physical victimization. This analysis closely examines Thomas's rhetoric, the symbolic significance of torture, and the politics of fear.

The fact that Anita Hill is African American considerably complicates any discussion of the power or the appropriateness of Thomas's metaphor, since black men were seldom lynched on the basis of black women's claims of sexual victimization. Despite any question of historical accuracy, I would suggest that Thomas's metaphor was actually dependent upon Hill's race (the metaphor might still have had rhetorical power had Hill been white, but it would have worked very differently). For this reason, I argue that an examination of the role of black women in lynch narratives is crucially important for an understanding of the full complexity of the hearings. In this chapter, I reconsider the importance of lynching as a method of social control aimed at black women, one that worked to reinforce and consolidate stereotypes of black female sexuality that were very much in play during the hearings. Legacies of lynching can be identified, for example, in the mass media's rapid circulation of allegations that Hill was a victim of "erotomania" or in the earlier representations of Thomas's sister Emma Mae Martin as a "welfare queen."

While I argue that racist stereotypes were enlisted in an effort to discredit Hill, I also suggest that they explain only a part of Hill's troubles. In later parts of the chapter, I address strategic difficulties facing Hill's supporters and consider the consequences of discussing Hill as a victim of sexual harassment without addressing the relevance of her race. Perhaps more important, I argue that the power of sexual harassment law and rhetoric is indebted to a troubling history of racism within early feminist struggles, and I suggest that Thomas's metaphor tapped into this history and pitted antisexist discourse in a contest against antiracist discourse. My examination of this contest suggests that apparently counterhegemonic rhetoric cannot easily escape its own history and that problematic political affinities of the past can resurface and create important vulnerabilities for social movements in the present.

For a variety of reasons, it is safe to say that Hill faced an uphill battle no matter how she decided to press her case. Still, it is worth considering Hill's strategic choices and options during the hearings. To this end, I speculate upon what would have happened if *she* had been the one to claim to be the victim of a lynching. While pursuing this speculation, I refer back to the antilynching struggles addressed in chapter 1, and I argue that while the antilynching movement generated a powerful source of visual and linguistic resources that can be tapped into by contemporary political actors, it is possible that these resources may be gendered in such a way as to be functionally unavailable to African American women. The possibilities for political struggle are, however, fluid. And while it is true that Thomas's use of the lynching metaphor placed Hill in a very difficult situation, Hill has nevertheless found ways to resist Thomas's efforts to control the debate. I conclude the chapter by considering Hill's recent attempts to challenge Thomas's metaphor by resituating lynching as a central part of her own familial history.

Lynching, Terror, and the Body

In the preceding chapters, I have argued that by now, the myth of the black rapist is widely recognized as a racist invention. When asked to elaborate about what he sees as "stereotyped language" in the hearings, Thomas calls upon this recognition by reminding the senators of "language about the sexual prowess of black men, language about the sex organs of black men and the sizes, etc.," by noting that "that kind of language has been used about black men as long as I've been on the face of this earth," and by arguing that "this plays into the most bigoted, racist stereotypes that any black man will face." Thomas goes on to explain his charge of lynching:

> Senator, in the 1970's, I became very interested in the issue of lynching. And if you want to track through this country in the 19th and 20th century the lynchings of black men, you will see that there is invariably, or in many instances, a relationship with sex, and an accusation that that person cannot shake off. That is the point that I'm trying to make, and that is the point that I was making last night, that this is a high-tech lynching. I cannot shake off these accusations, because they play to the worst stereotypes we have about black men in this country.[9]

Thomas's suggestion that we understand lynching as a racist crime based on sexualized stereotypes of black men is perfectly in line with the work of antilynching crusaders from Ida Wells-Barnett on. Thomas's rhetoric here is, however, worth careful consideration. By claiming that he "became very interested in the issue of lynching" in the 1970s, Thomas is setting himself up as a relative expert who is about to teach the Senate something about lynching's history. This move suggests that the racism to which he refers is relatively unknown, something that is only discovered by those who develop and take the time to pursue a special interest. Thomas furthers this suggestion by going on to claim that he "cannot shake off these accusations," since they play into enduring stereotypes.

While the "high-tech lynching" metaphor itself directed Thomas's audiences to understand his plight in terms of past histories of racialized violence, Thomas's extended historical narrative directs our attention to a very specific historical understanding of this violence by pointing toward a pool of images of black men who have been victimized because of highly sexualized racist stereotypes. In effect, Thomas is denying a discursive shift and suggesting that stereotypes of black men have remained static since the turn of the century. He is merely the newest victim of ages-old ways of thinking.

But again, the phrase "high-tech" suggests that Thomas is acutely aware that there is something new here. Presumably, that "something" is the heightened sense of spectacle due to new media technologies, especially television, that were unavailable during the peak years of lynching.[10] And certainly, Thomas is right to note that the media has played a central role in the dynamics of lynching. Newspapers often supported community demands for lynchings after allegations of crime or praised lynch mobs after a lynching had taken place. Occasionally, they contributed to lynchings by announcing the location and dates of lynchings that had already been scheduled.[11] As I noted in chapter 1, the antilynching movement devoted a considerable amount of its resources to challenging the national media's role in heightening the spectacle surrounding lynching and in creating a national audience as an extension of the mob. Pat Ward Williams's *Accused/Blowtorch/Padlock* (Figure 14) demonstrates that this critique has been carried forward in contemporary antiracist cultural activism.[12] Thomas's focus on the mass-mediated aspects of lynching serves, however, to equate spectacle and punishment. What is lost in all of this is a focus on the body as anything other than image. While this may seem like a relatively unimportant distinction (after all, Thomas's words were clearly meant only metaphorically), physical punishment was not only the form that lynching took, it was central to lynching's underlying logic.

Because lynch mobs were so varied, ranging in size from small groups operating under cloak of darkness to massive spectacles involving thousands of participants, and because lynchings themselves took so many different forms, "it is a mistake" to see all lynchings as the same sort of communal rituals, with the same underlying meanings.[13] Most lynchings, however, had common features. In general, lynch mobs were not concerned with evidence of their victims' guilt or innocence, and their actions found community support, which could be expressed in open praise for lynchings or in silent complicity through a lack of meaningful law enforcement. Lynchings were not only meant to mete out individual punishment but were also intended to be a method of enforcing white supremacist social codes.[14] Finally, many lynchings involved highly ritualized forms of torture. Many lynchings involved castration, and the sexual aspects of torture in lynching have been analyzed in detail by Robyn Wiegman and Martha Hodes, among others. Some of the forms

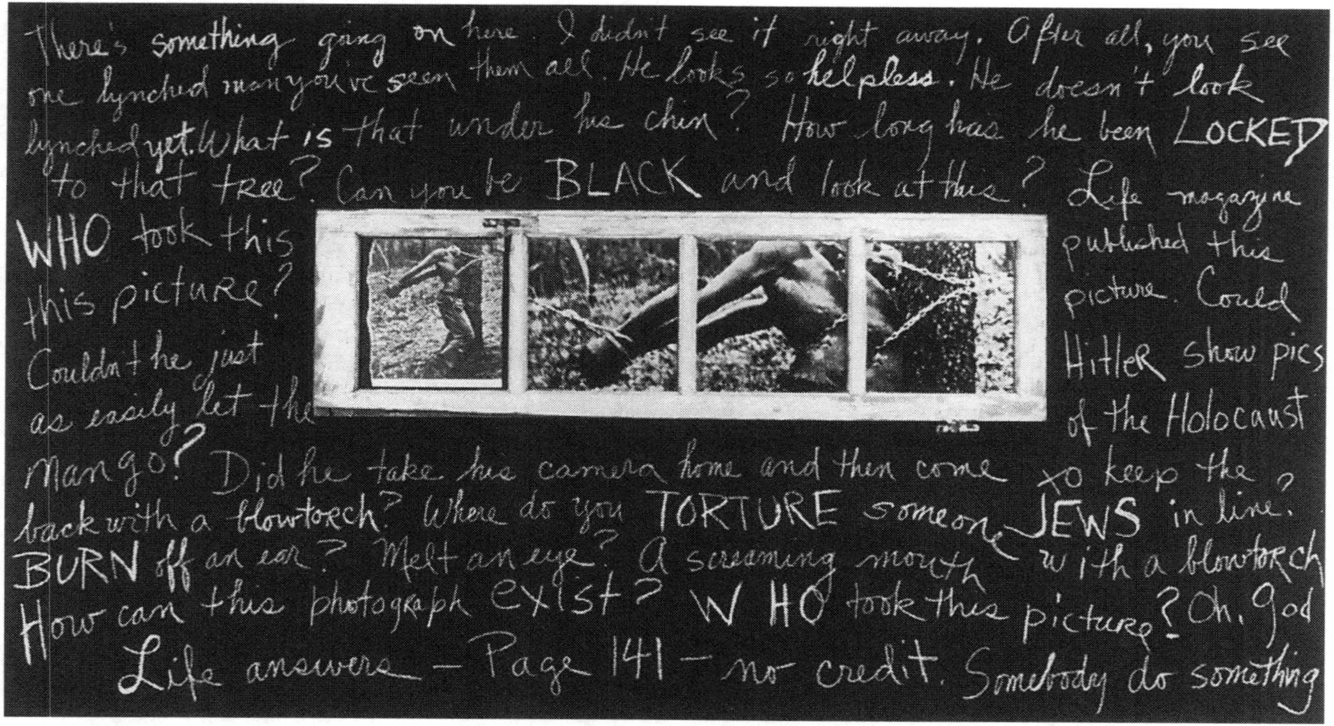

Figure 14. Pat Ward Williams, *Accused/Blowtorch/Padlock*, 1986. Wood, tar paper, gelatin silver prints, film positive, paper, pastel, and metal. Collection of the artist. Used with permission.

that torture took during lynchings were not, however, explicitly sexual,[15] and for an understanding of the importance of a more generalized form of torture as an element in public executions, I turn to Foucault's work.

Foucault opens *Discipline and Punish* with a consideration of "the disappearance of torture as a public spectacle,"[16] and he argues that "at the beginning of the nineteenth century . . . the great spectacle of physical punishment disappeared; the tortured body was avoided; the theatrical representation of pain was excluded from punishment."[17] Foucault is only addressing legal punishment and does not claim that his discussion is applicable to extralegal violence.[18] Moreover, he notes that "there were delays" in this process and that elements of torture "haunt" contemporary legal systems.[19] Foucault's explanation of the importance and the decline of torture and public execution can shed important light upon the dynamics of lynching. Foucault argues that

> torture forms part of a ritual. It is an element in the liturgy of punishment and meets two demands. It must mark the victim: it is intended, either by the scar it leaves on the body, or by the spectacle that accompanies it, to brand the victim with infamy. . . . men will remember public exhibition, the pillory, torture and pain duly observed. And, from the point of view of the law that imposes it, public torture and execution must be spectacular, it must be seen by all almost as its triumph. The very excess of the violence employed is one of the elements of its glory: the fact that the guilty man should moan and cry out under the blows is not a shameful side-effect, it is the very ceremonial of justice being expressed in all its force. . . . Justice pursues the body beyond all possible pain.[20]

The excess of violence is precisely the point of torture, since the point of the spectacle is to deploy

> before all eyes an invincible force. Its aim is not so much to re-establish a balance as to bring into play, as its extreme point, the dissymmetry between the subject who has dared to violate the law and the all-powerful sovereign who displays his strength. . . . the punishment is carried out in such a way as to give a spectacle not of measure, but of imbalance and excess. . . . The ceremony of punishment, then, is an exercise of "terror." . . . [The goal is] to make everyone aware, through the body of the criminal, of the unrestrained presence of the sovereign.[21]

One of the most important effects of lynchings was to create a collective memory of terror among blacks in order to fully emphasize not only the superiority of white power but also the consequences of challenging that power, and extreme uses of violence were absolutely essential to achieve this end. But this does not yet explain why the peak years of lynching (approximately 1880–1930) occurred nearly one hundred years after Foucault suggests that public torture and execution had begun to decline.

Foucault argues that torture began to give way to punishment and discipline in the late eighteenth century as the object of "criminal justice" shifted from the body to "the soul"[22] and that the guillotine was accepted as a method of punishment in France because it perfectly expressed this shift:

> The guillotine takes life almost without touching the body, just as prison deprives of liberty or a fine reduces wealth. It is intended to apply the law not so much to a real body capable of feeling pain as to a juridical subject, the possessor, among other rights, of the right to exist. It had to have the abstraction of the law itself.[23]

That is, torture declined as punishment became understood increasingly as a juridical method of regulating an individual's soul. The decline of torture, therefore, represented not a more humanitarian ethic but an expanded understanding of the offender's placement within "a whole set of assessing, diagnostic, prognostic, normative judgements"[24] in which punishment "assumed as its principal object loss of wealth or rights."[25]

Such a shift is only possible, however, for juridical subjects who are understood as having the abstract rights of citizens. African Americans did not begin to gain the rights of citizenship until emancipation, and lynching assumed its role as an instrument of racial terrorism in response to this new development. Wiegman writes that "it was precisely the imposition of an extreme corporeality" that separated African American men from "the privileged ranks of citizenry." Emancipation threatened to undo the work of the slave system, which had defined African Americans within the roles of bodies and property, and lynching functioned as a method to "reclaim and reassert the centrality of black male corporeality, deterring the now theoretically possible move toward citizenry and disembodied abstraction."[26]

The insistence upon seeing blacks as, above all, fully embodied was nothing new in the late 1800s. Popular justifications of slavery relied upon representations of blacks as "heathens and savages" who did not have the intellectual capacity to allow them to "ris[e] above their violent passions," and this belief in the lack of black intellectual capacity enabled whites to "punish blacks ruthlessly without suffering attacks of conscience."[27] But during Reconstruction and its aftermath, this insistence on black corporeality was threatened as blacks attempted to participate in political affairs and to benefit from education.[28] Lynching was the most dramatic method of limiting black social and economic mobility while at the same time reasserting the equation between blackness and embodiedness.

Toni Morrison has argued that this equation was in play from the very beginning of Thomas's confirmation hearings. She notes that Thomas "was introduced by his sponsor with a reference to the nominee's laugh," and she quotes Senator John Danforth as saying that Thomas's laugh "is the loudest laugh I have ever heard. It comes from deep inside, and it shakes his body."[29] Moreover, "[t]he *New York Times* found it interesting to include in that paper's initial story on the president's nominee a curious spotlight on his body. Weight lifting was among his accomplishments, said the *Times*." Morrison mentions several other instances where the press, as well as politicians, focused on Thomas's body, and she argues that "a reference to a black person's body is de rigueur in white discourse" and that "[w]hat would have been extraordinary would have been to ignore Thomas's body, for in ignoring it, the articles would have had to discuss in some detail that aspect of him more difficult to appraise—his mind."[30]

The media's focus on Thomas's body rather than his mind was, however, far from a form of punishment. Instead, it actually furthered the plans of Thomas's supporters. According to Jane Mayer and Jill Abramson, President Bush made a mistake during his nomination speech for Thomas, misreading the part of the speech that called Thomas "the best man" for the job and instead referring to him as "the best qualified" person.[31] This mistake threatened to draw attention away from Thomas's character and to direct it toward his professional accomplishments, which were rather unimpressive. Thomas had been a judge for less than two years, had not practiced law for more than a decade, had never argued a case before a jury, and had not issued any substantive constitutional opinions.[32] Moreover, the American Bar Association gave Thomas the lowest rating that any Supreme Court nominee has received in modern times.[33] Thomas's handlers, including Kenneth Duberstein, the lobbyist that Bush and John Sununu had asked to manage and promote Thomas's confirmation, and a Justice Department lobbyist named John Mackey, were convinced that the lack of a distinguished legal track record, coupled with what was seen as politically extremist and potentially divisive views on Thomas's part, meant that "a campaign of ideas wouldn't do."[34] In order to shift attention away from Thomas's qualifications and political ideas, they decided to focus on Thomas's personal biography—to "tell the Pin Point story."[35]

Thomas's narrative about growing up in, and escaping from, the poverty in the rural town of Pin Point, Georgia, stressed his hard work and his ability to become a success story despite hardships. Mayer and Abramson note that Thomas had been making "moving autobiographical speeches and interviews describing the searing pain he had suffered growing up poor and black in the South" long before his Supreme Court confirmation hearings and that "his emphasis on his deprived background gained him attention and set him apart" during his early employment in the Reagan and Bush administrations.[36] The decision during the confirmation hearings to maintain this focus on Thomas's life story rather than his political views made it possible to present Thomas as a symbol of "making it on one's own; of searing poverty turned to economic privilege; of self-reliance over hand-outs."[37]

Thomas's efforts to present himself as a self-made success story were, of course, also a repudiation of affirmative action programs and the welfare state. Despite the fact that Thomas had attended Yale Law School as an affirmative action student, he referred to affirmative action programs as "quotas" and presented them as something that only helped the black middle classes. He argued that "the masses" of African Americans "are just where they were before any of these policies,"[38] and he claimed, "We [blacks in the South] learned to fend for ourselves in a hostile environment . . . not only without the assistance of government, but with its opposition."[39] His anti–affirmative action stance was a big part of what made him so appealing to the Bush administration, but it was also one of his most controversial political positions and was probably the most important factor leading to the NAACP's "reluctant" decision to oppose his nomination.[40] Thomas's claim that he was being punished for refusing to "kow-tow to an old order" can be read as an indictment of a black civil rights establishment that refused to tolerate dissent,[41] and of an all-white Senate Judiciary Committee that resented Thomas's rise from poverty and was attempting to knock down this modern-day, black Horatio Alger.[42] The lynching metaphor made this resentment seem all the more predictable, since a successful confirmation hearing would provide the clearest possible repudiation of any attempt to limit Thomas to the corporeal; as a Supreme Court justice, Thomas would become one of the nine most important arbiters of the abstract.[43] Thomas was correct to suggest that sustained attention to his ideas made some senators uncomfortable and that they focused on his embodiment to the exclusion of his intellect. (By referring to his personal struggles they were indirectly addressing his race instead of his judicial philosophy.) But again, they followed his lead in their estimation that the best way to *secure* his confirmation was to address his character rather than his qualifications.

Tokenism and Legitimation

The best evidence that Thomas's charges of a high-tech lynching come at a time when racial discourse has shifted dramatically from that of the turn of the century is the fact that Thomas's race not only presented no obstacle to his nomination but was, arguably, a prerequisite. From the moment that Thurgood Marshall announced his decision to retire from the Supreme Court, there was widespread speculation that President Bush would appoint a black justice to fill his position. Then–attorney general Richard Thornburgh made this speculation all the more plausible when he announced, on *Meet the Press*, that the prospective nominees included "qualified women, blacks, Hispanics, persons with disabilities and the like" and that "certainly, the President wants a court—Supreme Court and other courts that reflect the diversity of our society."[44] Thomas was ideally suited for the strategic needs of the Bush administration because his race and background could provide a shield against charges that the Republican Party was hostile to the needs of people of color and could force civil rights leaders and liberals into difficult debates over race and public policy.[45] While Bush would later deny the importance of race to the nomination, his insistence that "the fact that [Thomas] is black and a minority had nothing to do with [the nomination] in the sense that [Thomas] is the best qualified at this time" and that he did not "feel that [he] had to nominate a black American at this time for the court"[46] was clearly disingenuous in light of Thomas's meager qualifications. The White House had publicly opposed affirmative action, but it had only considered minority candidates to fill Marshall's seat.[47] Senator Joseph Biden acknowledged in the wake of the hearings that "[h]ad Thomas been white, he never would have been nominated. The only reason he is on the Court is because he is black."[48]

While Thomas's race was particularly important to the Bush administration because of the ways it could distract attention from a larger political agenda hostile to racial minorities, the presence of an African American on the Supreme Court had been important ever since Thurgood Marshall's confirmation. From the moment that Thomas's nomination was announced, the media made constant references to the importance of the man he would be replacing. These references pointed to the need to present the Supreme Court, and by extension the government as a whole, as antiracist. They were an integral part of a state legitimation strategy that relied on tokenism to provide a sense of racial inclusion (if not balance) in the highest levels of government. A more important legitimation strategy than tokenism, however, is the presentation, for years, of Marshall's consistent advocacy of civil rights legislation (most notably his role in *Brown v. Board of Education* of 1954) as "evidence" that the government had a clear concern with racism.[49] The fact that so many of his judicial battles were successful has been taken as evidence that the nation's racist history has been addressed.[50] The Bush administration had certainly been uncomfortable with Marshall's politics, but not because of his race.[51] On the contrary, it was in the adminstration's interest to elevate an African American to the highest position of abstract citizenry, as long as he could be counted upon to fulfill the administration's ideological needs.

Emma Mae Martin, Erotomania, and Jezebel: Black Women and Lynching

The glowing references to Marshall's legacy, coupled with the Democratic senators' reluctance to question Thomas in the face of his charges of racism, demonstrate a need for the government to be seen as antiracist and a governmental consensus that there is a need to appear appalled by racist stereotypes of black men. The hearings provided ample evidence, however, that there is no clear corresponding consensus when it comes to stereotypes of black women.

As I noted earlier, when asked to elaborate on his charge of a high-tech lynching and on what he saw as racism in the hearings, Thomas referred to a variety of stereotypes about black men. But, as discussed in chapter 1, while the black rapist might have been the most popular trope associated with lynching, lynching also reinforced stereotypes of sexually insatiable black women that had been part of U.S. racial imaginary since the inception of the nation. Notable politicians of the eighteenth century, such as Thomas Jefferson, argued that black women had limited intellectual abilities and a bestial sexuality.[52] During the antebellum period, this belief was codified in legal statutes that, especially in slave states, defined rape as a crime against white women only. Black men were sometimes executed for even the attempted rape of a white woman, even when the woman herself did not claim any form of victimization. But there was no punishment for the rape or attempted rape of a black woman.[53]

Because legal definitions of rape only addressed white women's victimization, white slaveholders were in effect granted virtually indiscriminate sexual access to their black slaves. Hypersexualized images of the "bad-black-girl, or Jezebel," were used to justify these relationships, as slave owners who coerced their female slaves into having sexual relationships with them then "attributed these liasons to the hypersexuality of the female slave who was purported to be the aggressor or seducer."[54]

K. Sue Jewell considers a variety of newer images of African American women that have had wide circulation but ultimately argues that "when changes have occurred they have been slight modifications in physical characteristics, while changes in emotional make-up have been extremely slow to surface" and that for the most part, "the cultural images of African American women have changed only minimally."[55] Indeed, stereotypes of sexually dangerous black women were central to Thomas's confirmation hearings, and they had surfaced long before Anita Hill took the stage.

In order to establish himself as a self-made man, Thomas needed to establish that his hard work and ambition were what had saved him and were what separated him from others who were unable to rise from a life of hardship. For Thomas to really be seen as heroic, it was important to make the point that some people fail to pull themselves up by their own bootstraps. Perhaps the starkest contrast to the figure of a modern-day, black Horatio Alger is the "welfare queen," and as Wahneema Lubiano points out, Thomas called upon that figure in the very first weeks of the hearings as he launched a powerful verbal assault against his sister, Emma Mae Martin. Despite having taken advantage of a variety of opportunities that were not offered to Emma Mae Martin because of her gender,[56] Thomas criticized Martin for failing to make it out of "the same" conditions that he had been born into and for subsequently "falling into" welfare dependency.[57] Lubiano argues that the U.S. welfare system is often seen as the root of the nation's "decline" and that black women are represented as having primary responsibility for the problem. She points out that Thomas accused Martin not only of welfare dependency but of passing that dependency on to her children, who are conditioned to "wait for the check." Thus, Martin is seen as "the mother of welfare."[58] Lubiano argues that the figure of "the welfare-dependent single mother is finally the synecdoche, the shortest possible shorthand, for the pathology of poor, urban, black culture."[59] This figure suggests that black women's unrestrained sexuality is at the root of America's problems, and by positioning himself as both the alternative (he managed to escape Martin's fate) and the cure (he was opposed to state welfare policies) to the problems posed by the welfare queen, Thomas created a compelling rationale for his advancement.[60]

The figure of the hypersexualized black woman was invoked much more directly when Anita Hill took the stand than it had been in discussions of Emma Mae Martin. One of the most prevalent tactics used in an attempt to discredit Hill was to portray her as "a woman scorned."[61] The idea that Hill was acting out of vengeance because Thomas refused

to return her affections came up as a result of the initial efforts to counter Hill's allegations. In an interview with the *New York Times*, one of
Thomas's witnesses, Phyllis Berry-Meyers, said,

> Did she have a crush on the chairman? Yeah. My impression was that
> Anita wished to have a greater relationship with the chairman than just
> a professional one. Professor Hill was hurt because he treated her just
> like he treated everyone else on the staff.[62]

Berry never said (and was never asked) how she arrived at this conclusion, and Hill later testified that she barely knew Berry and that Berry
was certainly never in a position to know about her feelings about anyone. Despite Hill's testimony about this point and Berry's admission
that she did not "remember them having anything at any time that was
more than professional, cordial, and friendly,"[63] the possibility that
Hill's allegations were the product of a romantic rebuff became a constant theme in the hearings, as Berry's *New York Times* interview and her
later testimony helped to draw attention away from Thomas's alleged
sexual improprieties and toward Hill's sexual behavior and character.

The focus on Hill's sexuality was intensified as John Doggett's testimony was introduced. Doggett was a Texas lawyer and businessman who
had become friends with Thomas at Yale Law School and who had been
introduced to Hill by a mutual friend from Yale. Doggett claimed that
Hill saw him at a party and told him, "I'm very disappointed in you. You
really shouldn't lead women on, or lead on women and then let them
down." Hill denied ever having made this statement, but it is the basis
for Doggett's claim that

> [i]t is my opinion that Ms. Hill's fantasies about my sexual interest in her
> were an indication of the fact that she was having a problem with "being
> rejected" by men she was attracted to. Her statements and actions in
> my presence during the time when she alleges that Clarence Thomas
> harassed her were totally inconsistent with her current descriptions and
> are, in my opinion, yet another example of her ability to fabricate the
> idea that someone was interested in her when in fact no such interest
> existed.[64]

Even though Doggett offered no further evidence for his speculation
about Hill's fantasies, the committee took the possibility that she was
delusional very seriously.[65] Senator Arlen Specter in particular introduced portions of Doggett's testimony quite early in the hearings and
supplemented them with a statement made by Charles Kothe, a man
who claimed to know Thomas and Hill both very well but who claimed

no psychological expertise. Kothe said that "I find the references to the alleged sexual harassment not only unbelievable but preposterous. I am convinced that such are the product of fantasy."[66] Behind the scenes, Thomas's supporters, including President Bush's nephew Jamie Bush and Senator Danforth, attempted to find psychologists who could offer testimony that would suggest that Hill was insane.[67] The media took up the question of Hill's possible insanity as one of the most important ways of assessing her credibility. In the *New York Times*, William Safire claimed that Thomas was "the victim of a late hit by a self-deluded person,"[68] while Ellen Goodman argued against the confirmation in the *Boston Globe* by claiming that "to accept Anita Hill's story, you had to believe only that Clarence Thomas would lie to salvage his honor in front of the country and his family. To accept Thomas's denial, you had to believe that Hill was a psychopath."[69]

Thomas's supporters introduced the possibility that Hill was insane at a crucial moment, shortly after Hill had passed a lie-detector test. Rather than seriously trying to refute the findings of the test (which were ruled inadmissible in the hearings but which might have had considerable impact in popular culture), Senator Simpson read a statement by Thomas's friend Larry Thompson, who was a former U.S. attorney in Georgia. Thompson's statement claimed that "if a person suffers from a delusional disorder he or she may pass a polygraph test. Therefore, a polygraph examination in this context has absolutely no bearing on whether the events at issue are true or untrue."[70] The idea that Hill was insane was thus an integral part of Thomas's defense because it made the necessity of refuting her specific allegations or of determining a motive for her supposed lies less urgent.

Doggett's and Kothe's testimonies, which were presented without any collaborating evidence or corresponding expert testimony from a psychologist, were the only evidence that suggested the possibility that Hill was insane. As David Wilkins notes, "not a single witness who claims to know Hill well . . . provided any support for the claim that she suffers from delusions or is otherwise unfit."[71] The fact that this possibility was taken seriously despite the dearth of evidence prompted "several leading experts in the psychology of women (including the editor of the leading journal, the heads of the two major professional organizations in the field, and the Chair of the National Coalition for Women's Mental Health)" to issue a statement noting, in part, that

> [t]here is no evidentiary basis for concluding that Professor Anita Hill
> is suffering from a delusional disorder; furthermore, her description

of her experiences and reactions are completely consistent with those documented in the psychological literature on sexual harassment. As behavioral scientists who are experts in the psychology of women, we are extremely concerned at this casual and frivolous misuse of psychiatric terminology for political purposes. It is critical that, if questions of mental disorder are to be raised, they are addressed with the seriousness that they deserve.[72]

Wilkins remarks that there is as much reason to suspect Thomas of being insane as there is to think that of Hill. He asks,

Why is it that the claim that Judge Thomas would have to be crazy to make these advances to Professor Hill automatically counts as an argument *in favor* of his telling the truth, instead of a potential explanation of why his denial is so convincing even in the face of contrary evidence?[73]

Wilkins's answer is that "the reason that we have not heard these allegations is that men are not generally regarded to be prone to delusions or fantasies."[74] The argument here, that the idea of insanity is gendered in such a way that it will be disproportionately applied to women, makes sense in light of important feminist critiques of psychiatric labeling practices. Jane Usher in particular argues that the idea of "mental illness" has regularly been applied to women as a mechanism of social control and an expression of misogyny.[75] But while Wilkins's suggestion that presumptions of insanity are gendered is important here, he fails to note that these presumptions are also raced. The specific form of insanity that Hill is accused of having is a subtype of delusional disorder commonly referred to as "erotomania." The clinical definition of this disorder was clearly inapplicable to Hill's case: "The central theme of the delusion is that another person is in love with the individual . . . [and] the delusion often concerns idealized romantic love and spiritual union rather than sexual attraction,"[76] but Hill never claimed that Thomas loved her. As Louise Fitzgerald says, "On the contrary, she testified that Judge Thomas persisted in describing pornographic scenes of rape and women having sex with animals; her descriptions were of sexual exploitation, not romantic love."[77] Still, the clinical definition was largely beside the point, since it was not discussed in the hearings or in the mass media. "Erotomania" is, however, a term that firmly links insanity to sexuality, and the facts that it was so widely circulated and that there was so much attention focused on the possibility of Hill's sexual delusions fit in quite well with stereotypes defining black women in terms of sexual excess and insatiability.

I have noted that one of the ways lynching worked to enable stereotypes of black women was to prevent them from complaining about their sexual victimization. The fact that Hill was almost prevented from testifying resonates strongly with this aspect of lynching's legacy. Hill first spoke to the FBI about her experiences with Thomas in September 1991. Her answers to a series of questions about sexual harassment were then submitted to the Senate Judiciary Committee, which decided that the allegations were not important enough to merit any further investigation or to delay the confirmation vote. Then, on October 5, 1991, just days before the scheduled vote, Nina Totenberg reported the allegations on National Public Radio, while Timothy Phelps reported the story in *Newsday*. Throughout the hearings, some Republican staffers tried to turn the fact that the FBI report was "leaked" into a major scandal.[78] The immediate scandal, however, was that the Senate had seemingly decided that charges of sexual harassment were not a serious enough matter to affect decisions about whether or not to confirm the appointment of an associate justice to the U.S. Supreme Court.

The scandal resulted in widespread outrage and protest. Among the most notable examples of protest: "[T]housands of voters called Senators, demanding a delay of the confirmation vote in order to allow for an investigation,"[79] seven congresswomen marched to the Senate to demand a delay and were denied entrance,[80] and two letters, one signed by 120 women law professors and another signed by an additional 170 law professors, were sent to the Judiciary Committee, also demanding a delay in the vote.[81] Ultimately, the political pressure made Thomas and his Senate sponsor, Senator Danforth, nervous. They thought that the public response might cost Thomas too many Senate votes, so they asked for, and were granted, a delay.[82]

This background information is important for a number of reasons. First, it gives some sense of how lightly the Senate took Hill's allegations. Without strong political pressure, the issue would have been ignored.[83] Second, as the *New York Times* argued,

> the decision [to delay] . . . reflected the growing power of women and of issues of importance to women in American politics. Once the allegations had been made public, any "rush to judgement" . . . would surely be taken . . . to mean that the Senate considered the questions at stake trivial.[84]

The risk of being seen as discounting women's interests was one that the Senate (or Thomas) could not afford. In Judith Resnick's words, this moment "denotes the limits and the power of women's concerns."[85] The extent of that power is shown in the fact that the committee, the Senate, and Thomas were embarrassed enough that they felt the need to delay the vote until Hill's allegations could be heard more thoroughly. Resnick points to procedural problems within the hearings (including their brevity and the fact that, unlike Thomas, Hill had no clear advocate on the committee) as indications of the limits of that power.

Still, political pressure did force the Senate to respond to the charge that by ignoring Hill's allegations, they had trivialized the issue of sexual harassment. As the *New York Times* wrote, "The Senate still operates like a men's club, mostly taking the white male viewpoint as the universal norm, and it is therefore highly vulnerable to suggestions of insensitivity."[86] Or, as Senator Specter put it, "the Senate itself [was] on trial,"[87] and its legitimacy regarding "women's concerns" was at stake. One purpose of the hearings, then, was to reestablish the Senate's credibility. This could only be done by ensuring the integrity of the process as well as that of the soon-to-be-confirmed nominee, and the way to do this was to at least appear to give the allegations of sexual harassment a fair hearing.

Some of the problems in the hearings might be due to the fact that sexual harassment is a relatively new concept in American jurisprudence. As Deborah Rhode notes, it was not until 1964 that Congress passed a civil rights law banning sexual discrimination, and it was not until the mid-1970s that "an alliance of legal scholars, attorneys, and working women's organizations manage[d] to begin exposing harassment as a form of unlawful discrimination."[88] This might help to explain some of the ignorance of the committee members regarding sexual harassment. For example, Senator Orrin Hatch's comment that he "[did not] know why anybody would put up with [incidents of sexual harassment] or why anybody would respect or work with another person who would do that"[89] suggests that he was unaware of the research on sexual harassment that shows that there are many reasons (including, among other things, fear of retaliation and lack of meaningful grievance procedures) why victims of harassment "put up with it."[90] This ignorance might also help to explain some of the evidence that was admitted into the hearings. For example, members of the committee supported Thomas's suggestion that

> I think that if you want to be really fair, you parade every single one
> [of the women he had worked with] before you, and you ask them in
> their relationships with me whether or not any of this nonsense, this

garbage, this trash, that you siphoned out of the sewers against me, whether any of it is true. Ask them. They've worked with me. Ask my chief of staff, my former chief of staff. She worked shoulder to shoulder with me.[91]

Women whom he worked with were asked precisely these sorts of questions, despite the fact that the sexual harassment literature reveals that some harassers will, apparently, harass only one person and in other respects may live "exemplary lives." Because there is no clear pattern that describes the type of person who becomes a sexual harasser and because one incident is enough to constitute harassment, the "character witnesses" that Thomas called for should have been irrelevant. Whether the senators' ignorance was genuine or calculated, the facts that expert testimony about harassment was excluded from the hearings and that Thomas's witnesses were called provide clear evidence of the relative lack of impact that sexual harassment researchers and victims' advocates have had within national political processes.

Thus, a general lack of recognition of sexual harassment as a serious concern made it easier to trivialize Hill's allegations. It may have been difficult to gain a sympathetic hearing of Hill's allegations, however, even if sexual harrassment had been much more widely recognized, since the history and deployment of the very concept of sexual harassment present additional pitfalls when confronting allegations of racism. The consistent construction of Hill's allegations as indicative of "women's concerns" more broadly elides the differential treatment accorded women of various races who have been sexually victimized. Moreover, the construction of sexual harassment as purely a crime of gender, and therefore not one of race, also glosses over the very different kinds of attention accorded to sexual crimes based on the race of the accused perpetrator. Charles R. Lawrence III calls attention to the fact that "the system has always been willing to believe rape survivors *some* of the time. When black men have raped white women, and often when they haven't, women have been believed. When poor men have raped rich women, women have been believed." Lawrence goes on to say that we "would do well to ask whether the *some* of the time that women are believed is evidence of the continuing vitality of patriarchy rather than of its demise."[92] Lawrence's comments about rape are applicable to other forms of sexual victimization, and they point to some of the reasons that people who are concerned with racism in U.S. history might be skeptical about an investigation by an all-white Senate committee into allegations of sexual misconduct by an African American man.

Thomas's lynching metaphor is important here not only because white mobs were all too ready to believe some claims of rape at the hands of black men but also because of white women's complicity in creating and perpetuating the myth of the black rapist. In the earliest antilynching pamphlets, Ida B. Wells documented cases in which white women falsely claimed to have been raped by black men, and she argued that these accusations were used not only to justify lynchings but also to shore up white supremacist ideology.[93] Angela Davis examines the evidence of this legacy in some of the key texts in contemporary antirape movements that "do not hesitate to argue that men of color are especially prone to commit sexual violence against women."[94] In particular, she notes that Susan Brownmiller's book *Against Our Will* (1975) presented Emmet Till "as a guilty sexist—almost as guilty as his racist murderers."[95] Ultimately, Davis concludes that various texts at the core of the antirape movement "have facilitated the resurrection of the timeworn myth of the Black rapist."[96] The fact that sexual harassment legislation was born out of the same feminist movements that Davis indicts makes it easier to see why allegations of sexual harassment lodged against a black man and pursued by a white committee might be seen as racially suspect. Thomas's metaphor is fundamentally inaccurate, since black men were seldom lynched at the behest of *black* women, but it owes part of its rhetorical potency to the fact that the criteria for determining which claims of sexual victimization to take seriously have been so thoroughly intertwined with white supremacist notions of justice. In this sense, Hill's race drops out, as she is presented as a surrogate for "feminism" or feminist discourse, which in turn stands in for the white woman making false accusations of rape. Elsa Barkley Brown sees Hill's supporters as partly responsible for helping enable Thomas to discount Hill's race because they relied upon an "analysis of sexual harassment in which race and class were not central issues" and because they had "constructed Hill as a generic or universal woman with no race or class (or with race or class being unimportant to her experience)" and were therefore "unable to deal with the racialized and class specific discussion when it emerged."[97]

The elision of Hill's race had consequences in the realm of public opinion. Reflecting upon the widespread assertion that Hill was being manipulated by white feminists, Emma Coleman Jordan suggests that the high-tech lynching metaphor invoked memories of white women's role in the lynching of black men and that it therefore "set up an opposition between black and white women."[98] That made Hill's position as a black woman receiving the backing of white feminists untenable for many black women. Thus, they were open to Thomas's "characterization that Hill was not acting for herself but as the delusional, unwitting pawn of clever and politically sophisticated white feminists who opposed his presumed position on abortion."[99] Thomas's metaphor was an extremely effective method of pinpointing the elements of racism in the history of mainstream white feminism and of suggesting that the forces animating Hill's discourse could not be separated from this legacy.

But Thomas's surreptitious attack upon white feminist discourse does not mean that he was unconcerned with sexual victimization. Some of the most widely circulated lynching narratives and images of lynchings include representations of sexual mutilation and castration. Lynching "must be seen as both a racial and sexual crime. In effect, Thomas covertly suggested that he was being subjected to a form of sexual harassment more gruesome and brutal than any verbal harassment could ever be."[100] Various commentators who have argued that Thomas's metaphor was an attempt to shift the terrain to a discussion of racial rather than sexual victimization fail, therefore, to acknowledge the ways that the lynching metaphor references both kinds of suffering.[101] Again, lynching was often defined precisely by an excess of violence, and sexual harassment is necessarily a weaker claim because it is contained within this excess as one of its components.

One of the effects of the extremity of the violence of lynching, coupled with its role as a site for the construction and elaboration of the black rapist myth, is that black women who have been sexually victimized by black men have had to face the possibility that naming their victimization would have repercussions on, and bring them into conflict with, their larger communities. Emma Coleman Jordan suggests that Hill was faced with a typical "Hobbesian choice" facing black women who have been sexually victimized by black men. She writes that a woman in this situation can choose between "claiming individual protection as a member of her gender and race or contributing to the collective stigma upon her race if she decides to report the sexual misdeeds of a black man to white authority figures."[102] Indeed, Hill's awareness of this dilemma might help to account for the fact that she did not come forward earlier, since "a young Hill . . . may have recognized that speaking of the particularities of Thomas's harassment had the potential to restigmatize the whole black community."[103]

In her short story "Advancing Luna—and Ida B. Wells," Alice Walker addresses the difficulty that black women have when they have to decide whether to discuss sexual crimes committed by black men. The black female narrator of the story has to decide what to do with her knowledge that a black man has raped a white woman. The narrator thinks to herself that "whenever interracial rape is mentioned, a black woman's first thought is to protect the lives of her brothers, her father, her sons, her lover. A history of lynching has bred this reflex in her," and she goes on to imagine a conversation with Ida B. Wells in which Wells advises her to "write nothing. Nothing at all. It will be used against black men and therefore against all of us. . . . say nothing. And to your dying breath!"[104] The stakes in the story are higher than in the hearings, since violent retaliation was reserved almost exclusively for the alleged sexual victimization of *white* women, but Walker captures the sense that black women are made aware that allegations of a black man's sexual misconduct have repercussions beyond the specific man who is accused of the crime.[105]

Angela Davis writes that when Hill finally did come forward, she paid a price, since "African American women who challenge African American male supremacy . . . [are defined] as collaborators in racist attacks on African American men," and thus Hill was "defined as a traitor, as the enemy."[106] Jordan echoes this sentiment, writing that "Hill . . . stood accused of violating one of the most powerful taboos of African American survival."[107] Thomas's claim that he "cannot shake off these accusations, because they play to the worst stereotypes we have about black men in this country" forces an acknowledgment of Hill's parallel to the white woman making a false accusation of rape. It suggests that the historical weight of racism gives her an unfair advantage, since she is relying upon stereotypes against which there is no possible defense.

There are indications that Hill is acutely aware of these dynamics of the hearings. In "Moon's Paradox," an essay about a case of domestic abuse involving a black couple, Felicia Moon and her husband, the famous football player, Warren Moon, Hill writes,

> Not only would Felicia Moon's testimony about domestic violence at the hands of her husband have had no positive community value, it would have threatened the community. It would have been used by the enemy to destroy the image of one of its prized members. She lacked both the historical images of Black women being lynched and the modern-day images of Black women being wrongly accused that might have moved the community to embrace her. And without jeopardizing a Black man, she could not present a picture of a battered and beaten Black woman that might have moved the community to embrace a story of domestic violence.[108]

Hill elaborates by noting that

> [a]lthough the public might have assumed that her choice was between portraying Warren Moon as a hero versus a wife beater, it is perhaps

more likely that Felicia Moon felt she had to choose between stick-
ing to her story or contributing to another instance of discriminatory
prosecution of a Black man. Whereas some segments viewed hers as an
opportunity to become a cause célèbre in the war against domestic violence, she saw the possibility of alienating a community in which she
was rooted. . . . she saw it as a choice between her own well-being, on
the one hand, and the well-being of the husband, children, marriage,
and community, on the other hand.[109]

"Moon's Paradox" was also Hill's paradox. Despite all of the ways that
Thomas's metaphor involved "manipulations of history"[110] and was a
"tool of conspiratorial amnesia"[111] because of its erasure of the role of
black women in the lynching scenario, Hill was confronted with the fact
that one aspect of the metaphor was appropriate. As long as the myth of
the black rapist lingers, it is impossible to fully separate allegations of
sexual misconduct by a black man from larger issues of racism and community struggle.

Conclusion

Hill's claim that Felicia Moon lacked images of black women's suffering
hints at a powerful argument about the stakes involved in struggles over
collective memory. As I argued in the Introduction to this book, it is
fairly obvious that the configurations of racism have shifted in important
ways from the time when lynching was at its peak. Thomas's use of the
lynching metaphor relies upon common sense understandings of race
and collective memories of racial terror that are indebted to the antilynching movement and that have been further elaborated throughout
struggles over the terrain of popular culture. While Thomas's metaphor
draws its rhetorical force from antiracist struggles, Hill's analysis of
Felicia Moon's plight suggests that whatever rhetorical resources were
made available by these struggles were gendered in such a way as to have
rendered them functionally unavailable to black women.

Hazel Carby suggests that the specific forms of victimization that
black women have faced have not been as powerfully institutionalized
within collective memory as have the kinds of victimization facing black
men. Thus, "the institutionalized rape of black women has never been as
powerful a symbol of black oppression as the spectacle of lynching."[112]
Elsa Barkley Brown expands upon this idea and discusses a "masculine
construct of collective memory and African American identity . . . which
allows us to forget the female fruit hanging from Southern trees, fend-
ing off unwanted advances, and organizing to 'uplift the race.'"[113] Brown
wonders why it is that

people don't remember the lynching of Black women and the brutality of that experience. Why it is that the other experiences of violence that have so permeated the history of Black women in the United States—the rape, the sexual and other forms of physical abuse as employees in white homes, the contemporary domestic and public sexual and other physical violence—are not as vividly and importantly retained in our memory. Why it is that lynching (and the notion of it as a masculine experience) is not just remembered but is in fact central to how we understand the history of African American men, and indeed the African American experience in general. But violence against women—lynching, rape, and other forms of violence—is not.[114]

Chapter 1 provides some tentative answers to these questions, since it argues that the antilynching movement devoted a disproportionate amount of its resources to addressing black men's victimization and racist stereotypes of black masculinity.[115] While stereotypes of black male criminality are still widely circulated, they remain the only racist stereotypes of African Americans that have received the sustained attention of a mass movement. The failure to develop a widely recognized and shared collective memory of violence that has been used against black women meant that Hill did not have access to visual or rhetorical resources that would have provided her allegations of sexual victimization with historical resonance and power.

However, the passage I have just quoted from Brown contains an important qualification to this claim. Brown's claim that images of violence against black women are not "vividly and importantly retained in our memory" suggests that the problem is not that a collective memory of black women's victimization does not exist but that it is relatively weak. Certainly Brown's own work, as well as that of Carby, Davis, Wiegman, and others, shows that there are some people who remember black women's suffering quite well and who are attempting to introduce those memories to a wider audience.

Hill herself has taken an active role in this process. The widespread use of racist stereotypes of black women in the hearings makes it interesting to speculate about the possible outcome had Hill been the one to have charged racism.[116] Hill's analysis of Felicia Moon's plight suggests that any claims that Hill might have made to this effect would have fallen upon deaf ears or upon ears that had been historically underprepared to hear and recognize those claims. While this may help to explain Hill's decision not to challenge Thomas's use of the lynching metaphor during the hearings, in the years since the hearings, she has been less willing to allow Thomas sole access to a history of racism and antiracist struggle. In *Speaking Truth to Power*, Hill's 1997 book that uses autobiographical and historical detail to provide her memoirs of the hearings, Hill places lynching at the center of her own familial history.[117]

Hill notes that in 1913, her maternal grandparents, who were living in Arkansas, were approached by a white neighbor who wanted her grandmother to work for him. When Hill's grandfather explained that his wife was too busy with work at home, the neighbor asked if he "had forgotten who [he was] talking to" and said, "I'll be around to see you tonight."[118] Hill discusses the rates of lynching in Arkansas and notes that the kinds of threats that the neighbor had made needed to be taken seriously. Following this confrontation, Hill's grandparents decided to try to avoid future threats, and so they moved to Oklahoma. Hill notes, though, that Oklahoma was far from a safe haven. She discusses the lynching rates there and notes that of the 122 lynchings of blacks from 1882 to 1968 in Oklahoma, "at least two . . . were of women." Hill discusses racial violence in some detail, but the only victims that she mentions by name in this section of the book are those two black women who were killed by lynch mobs—Laura Nelson and Marie Scott.[119] She provides some details about these two cases, noting, for example, that "[m]embers of the mob raped Miss Nelson before hanging her."[120] Thus, by providing information that suggests that lynching was central to her own personal history (Hill's parents would not have met if her grandparents had not fled Arkansas) and that specifically addresses the history of black women and lynching, Hill contests her erasure in Thomas's use of the lynching metaphor and suggests that racism is as important to her life as it is to Thomas's.

As I have shown, Thomas's charge of a "high-tech lynching" was meant to invoke only a small part of the complex history of lynching. Hill's memoirs can be seen as an attempt to challenge Thomas's metaphor by elaborating a collective memory attentive to the relevance of racism to black women's lives. But neither Hill nor Thomas started with a blank slate. While they were active participants in the ongoing construction of a collective memory of racism and lynching, I hope to have demonstrated that they also drew upon larger "cultural repertoires"[121] that shape how we understand race and gender and that have been forged by the mass media, popular culture, and political struggles.

Not Just Memory

O n January 14, 2000, an extraordinary exhibit opened at the Roth Horowitz Gallery in New York City. Originally entitled *Witness*, the show was a collection of photographic postcards of lynchings along with some newspaper clippings and antilynching pamphlets. In the middle of a cold New York winter, people waited in lines down the block to get into the exhibit; it was soon moved to the larger New York Historical Society, and it eventually toured to the Warhol Museum in Pittsburgh. The exhibit drew record crowds at each of these venues and was the subject of numerous stories in local and national media outlets. In May 2002, the exhibit had its first southern showing at the Martin Luther King National Historical Site in Atlanta, Georgia. The exhibition, now titled *Without Sanctuary: Lynching Photography in America*, was initially timed to correspond with the publication of a coffee-table book, also titled *Without Sanctuary*, containing many of the same images. By March 2002, the book, published by a small art house named Twin Palms Publishers, was in its fourth printing, already one of the press's all-time best sellers.

Part of the Allen-Littlefield Collection on deposit in the Robert W.

Woodruff Library at Emory University, the postcards were originally intended as celebratory reminders of vigilante violence that often had the full support of the leading citizens of the cities and towns in which the lynchings occurred. Their circulation worked to strengthen the bonds of white supremacy and extend the surveillance and terrorist functions of the mob. Their reappearance in this new context, partly contained within the institutional walls of museums but spilling out onto the Internet and into news reports, provides an important occasion to reconsider the stakes and processes involved in constructing collective memories of lynching.

James Allen, who spent nearly twenty years collecting the images for the exhibit and book, decided upon the title *Without Sanctuary* because the postcards were so worn with the marks of circulation that he had the sense that the victims "were being continually relynched and that they never had a refuge, even in death."[1] Allen has not said very much publicly about his motivations in deciding to collect or exhibit the postcards, but if one of the functions of the photographs in the past was to continue the lynchings and deny refuge to the victims, then it is worth asking whether displaying the images in a gallery can finally provide the sanctuary that had so long been elusive. The victims of the mob haunt this exhibit as they haunt this book and as they haunt any project that seeks to enlist the memories of their deaths for contemporary purposes. What exactly is to be gained by dwelling upon lynching and dragging such a terrifying part of our past into the present? What are the perils involved in such an undertaking?

Most of the people who have written about *Without Sanctuary* have found it horrific but crucially important. Press accounts are filled with truisms about the power of memory and with George Santayana's warning that "those who cannot remember the past are condemned to repeat it."[2] For many commentators, the photographs provide a lens into racial dynamics of the past and present. For example, Roberta Smith writes in the *New York Times* that the postcards "give one a far deeper and far sadder understanding of what it has meant to be white and to be black in America. And what it still means."[3] Many of these critics draw connections between lynchings and other forms of racism. Roane Carey sees "echoes" of lynching in the murder of James Byrd Jr., the torture of Abner Louima, sentencing disparities between whites and blacks, and the popularity of Charles Murray and Richard Herrnstein's book *The Bell Curve*.[4] Louima is referred to frequently, as are other victims of police violence, including Amadou Diallo and Patrick Dorismond. For all of these writers, lynching functions metaphorically in much the same way as the antilynching movement intended: It stands as a glaring symbol of systemic racial injustice. The Web site devoted to *Without Sanctuary* has a discussion board where some visitors have extended the metaphor beyond matters that are closely defined in terms of race: The murder of Matthew Shepard, colonial violence perpetrated by the French in Algeria, and suffering in Kosovo are all mentioned as evidence that the images in the photos have recent and contemporary counterparts.[5]

While some of these connections are quite powerful and appropriate, there is a danger that if lynching becomes too elastic a metaphor, it will be stretched too thin, losing its specificity and much of its meaning. These photos have always circulated as part of larger political projects. Participants in lynch mobs thought of the postcards as a way to brag about their accomplishments and used the photos to reinforce messages about the strength and necessity of white supremacy. Much of the power of the antilynching movement was based upon its ability to turn these messages on their head, and antilynching activists enlisted some of the same images in their efforts to mobilize resistance to a racist social order. The challenge posed by the antilynching movement to recognize the moral imperative of acting against racist social practices seems very likely to become blunted as visitors to the *Without Sanctuary* galleries and Web site gaze at images of lynching only to see examples of "man's inhumanity to man."

In her analysis of photographs of the Holocaust, Barbie Zelizer discusses the ways that images of Nazi atrocities have resurfaced and provided the template for stories about Bosnia, Cambodia, and Rwanda. Zelizer cautions that the "recycling of photos from the past not only dulls our response to them but potentially undermines the immediacy and depth of our response to contemporary instances of brutality, discounting them as somehow already known to us."[6] The difference between including a photograph of a lynching in a flyer for an antilynching fund-raising campaign and including the same photo in an exhibit with nearly a hundred similar photos is stark. In the first instance, the photo is meant to serve as a call to action. In the second, the repetition alone is likely to be not only numbing but also paralyzing.[7] Having seen these images, what are we to do? And how useful is it for visitors to *Without Sanctuary* to draw parallels between the suffering displayed for them in museum galleries and on coffee tables and computer screens, and contemporary suffering in far-flung regions of the world? Will any of that suffering be understood in its full complexity, or will it all be discounted and somehow cheapened as routine and "already known"? The original title of the exhibition, *Witness*, suggests that there is an overriding moral obligation to view and come to terms with these photos. But as Zelizer says, if the act of bearing witness is not closely tied to an effort to take responsibility for the violence on display, it becomes hollow.[8]

There are other dangers, too, in displaying these photographs. In attempting to explain how the viewing experience at the *Without Sanctuary* exhibit differs from the experience of earlier spectators looking at the same photographs, an article in the *New York Times* notes that the postcards had largely disappeared from public view until now and that they "can be made public again only because now we ask them to carry a different meaning than they once did—an outcry against racism rather than a reinforcement of it."[9] This sounds right, except that the symbolic baggage that has been historically attached to these images is too heavy to be easily discarded. I have already suggested that at least some viewers are far more likely to be dumbstruck than to cry out against racism when confronted with these images. But there are a variety of other possible reactions, some of which are more troubling and are hinted at in the visitor logs at the *Without Sanctuary* Web site.

It does not seem likely that these postcards would be capable of working to terrorize African American communities in the same ways they did when they first circulated. Nevertheless, the visitor logs suggest that the images are still potent enough to elicit not only a sense of horror but also considerable pain, anguish, and resentment. One visitor says that "to transmit these photos around over the net stirs up emotions that may never allow black folk to trust or fellowship with white folk. . . . I won't forget what has happened in the past to my people, but I don't need you to reiterate every detail either."[10] Similar sentiments crop up on a fairly regular basis throughout the logs, perhaps most strikingly in the following comment: "I am an African-American female and what I felt as I observed these photos is a soul so tortured I feel a need to run somewhere and hide."[11]

As upsetting as these reactions may be, there is another, more sinister kind of posting that was probably less predictable and is certainly more ominous. For the most part, viewers of *Without Sanctuary* are prepared to see the postcards as an indictment of a racist national past, if not as a lens into continuing racist social dynamics. A few visitors to the Web site, however, understand the photos in much the way they were originally intended to be seen. For example, a white supremacist writes about the Web site as entertainment.[12] And someone identifying himself as "Nathan Bedford Forrest," the name of one of the founders of the Ku Klux Klan, praises lynching. He offers Richard Wright's comment that "the white brutality that I had not seen was a more effective control of my behavior than that which I knew" as evidence that lynching "usually proved an efficient means of intimidation and oppression."[13] Comments like these are rare and are immediately identified as abhorrent by the vast majority of visitors to the site. Still, this type of comment is enough to give one pause and to draw attention to the fact that meaning does not reside within the photographs but is, instead, determined through social interaction. The process of remembering lynching is fraught with difficulties, and even the best-intentioned invocations of lynching can be put to dangerous uses.

The debates surrounding *Without Sanctuary* resonate with earlier struggles over how to remember lynching. Once again, various constituencies understand lynching metaphorically as providing a lens into broader social dynamics while disagreeing about the nature of those dynamics. Metaphors are always incomplete comparisons, and historical metaphors by necessity involve incomplete comparisons with the past. As a material practice, lynching has been embedded within a complex web of social relationships. Contemporary invocations of lynching conjure up some of those relationships while neglecting others, and the metaphor of lynching is therefore never fixed.

Stuart Hall's analysis of popular culture sheds important light upon the relationship between signs and meaning. He uses the swastika to talk about the "profoundly ambiguous" nature of signs:

> Every now and then . . . we find that sign which, above all other signs, ought to be fixed—solidified—in its cultural meaning and connotation forever: the swastika. And yet there it dangles, partly—but not entirely—cut loose from its profound cultural reference in twentieth-century history. What does it mean? What is it signifying? Its signification is rich, and richly ambiguous: certainly unstable. This terrifying sign may delimit a range of meanings but it carries no guarantee of a single meaning within itself. The streets are full of kids who are not "fascist" because they may wear a swastika on a chain. On the other hand, perhaps they *could* be. . . . What the sign means will ultimately depend, in the politics of youth culture, less on the intrinsic cultural symbolism of the thing in itself, and more on the balance of forces between, say, the National Front and the Anti-Nazi League, between White Rock and the Two Tone Sound.[14]

Like the swastika, lynching would seem to be a sign whose meaning should be rock solid and unambiguous. Yet as I argued in chapter 2, it is at times precariously close to becoming what I have called a "hanging signifier," dangling and in danger of being cut loose from its own "profound cultural reference" in nineteenth- and twentieth-century history. But this does not mean that lynching is an infinitely malleable metaphor, available for any use at all. Instead, the range of possible meanings attached to lynching is determined in relation to both the constraining influences of history and the current configurations of power and knowledge.

As I argued in chapter 1, the material practice of lynching was intended as a metaphor for race relations more broadly defined. Yet even when rates of lynching were at their peak, there was no single set of meanings attached to lynching. Instead, antilynching activists and organizations were engaged in heated battles with lynch mobs and public apologists for lynching over how lynching would be understood and remembered. Contemporary collective memories and invocations of lynching have been fundamentally shaped by these battles of the past. If we "remember" or understand lynching as a terrorist practice justified by racist stereotypes of black men, it is largely because of the efforts of the antilynching movement to secure that understanding. Similarly, if we have "memory holes"[15] when it comes to the lynching and rape of black women, the explanation for this historical amnesia can be found, at least in part, in the fact that there has been no movement devoted to securing a memory of the suffering of black women that has been comparable in scope to the antilynching movement.

But lynching has been a recurrent metaphor for race relations, and struggles over how lynching would be understood and remembered were not limited to the turn of the century. Instead, they have been waged continually throughout popular culture and the mass media. I have focused on contemporary Hollywood cinema as an especially potent site for the reconstruction and rearticulation of collective memories of lynching. Hollywood films have always been key sites for struggles over meanings of race, and cinematic representations of lynching and interracial rape have presented those struggles in their starkest terms. Films that have drawn upon and worked to reconfigure collective memories of lynching have intervened in contemporary configurations of racial categories, and at the same time, they have helped to transform the meaning of the lynching metaphor.[16]

Because lynching has functioned as such a widely recognized metaphor for race relations, the rearticulation and deployment of the lynching metaphor is intimately linked to ongoing processes of national racial formation and the construction of collective memories not only of lynching but of race and racism.[17] My analysis, in chapter 3, of recent instances, or alleged instances, of spectacularized racialized violence provides some sense of the highly complex and deeply personal ways our sense of the past helps to structure contemporary possibilities for action and belief. Media representations of the various cases that I examined in that chapter have either relied upon or critiqued variations of racial stereotypes that were central to the dynamics of lynching, and I argued that decisions either to acknowledge or to neglect these dynamics have had important repercussions for various audiences' notions of credibility and common sense. Chapter 3 demonstrates that the lynching metaphor can operate with varying levels of depth. At one level, lynching has been invoked as a synecdoche, or the "shortest possible shorthand" for racism.[18] (For recent examples of this kind of invocation of the collective memory of lynching for antiracist purposes, see Figures 15 and 16.)[19] But at a deeper level, conflicting understandings of the nature of past racialized violence help to explain Susan Smith's and Charles Stuart's successful use of fictional black scapegoats, and at the same time, they illuminate black terror in the wake of Bernhard Goetz's actions and support for Tawana Brawley.

While lynching can be invoked for a wide variety of purposes, it is not infinitely malleable. At first glance, Clarence Thomas's reference to

Figure 15. Noni Olabisi, *Freedom Won't Wait*, 1992. Acrylic mural, Los Angeles, Fifty-fourth Street, west of Western Avenue. This mural was commissioned by the Social and Public Art Resource Center (SPARC) in Venice, California, as a response to the turmoil surrounding the beating of Rodney King and the acquittal of the officers who were responsible. It invokes collective memories of lynching to suggest that the King beating should be understood within a broader historical context of racist violence. Photograph taken by the author.

Figure 16. Noni Olabisi, *To Protect and Serve*, 1995. Acrylic mural. Jefferson Park, California, Eleventh Avenue and Jefferson Boulevard. In its celebration of the Black Panther Party for Self Defense, this mural, also commissioned by the Social and Public Art Resource Center (SPARC), wrests the slogan "to protect and serve" from the Los Angeles Police Department, figured as agents of racist brutality, and suggests that the Panthers are worthy of this description. As in *Freedom Won't Wait*, collective memories of lynching—the ominous presence of two hooded members of the KKK—are invoked to suggest that police violence is only one recent manifestation of much broader histories of racism. Photograph taken by the author.

a "high-tech lynching" might seem to stretch the lynching metaphor to a point beyond recognition. After all, Thomas gained considerable political mileage by referencing lynching, despite the fact that his situation was glaringly different from the suffering faced by victims of more common, "low-tech" lynchings. The most important differences include the facts that black men were seldom lynched at the behest of black women and that Thomas appeared to see the mere *accusation* of sexual harassment as a lynching, whereas, although traditional lynchings were often justified as a response to allegations of rape, the lynchings themselves entailed severe forms of physical punishment. Still, as I have argued in chapter 4, Thomas sought to anchor his use of the lynching metaphor to particular aspects of the history of lynching. He was engaged in a productive use of history that allowed him to create a present in which his status as victim was harder to challenge. This was a present that he was able to construct out of shards of the past, since the selective appropriation of lynching's history fully enabled his status as a victim.

Even so, Thomas's problematically partial invocation of the history of lynching was not entirely without cost. While Thomas was able to reference lynching in order to help shift the terms of public and senatorial debate away from the question of Hill's possible victimization and toward his own, his "high-tech lynching" metaphor has been subject to intense and far-ranging debate. The lynching metaphor seemed to have transformed the debate surrounding Thomas's confirmation in ways entirely beyond Thomas's control, for not only the history of lynching but also Thomas's own record regarding issues of race were subjected to heightened levels of scrutiny. Hill's memoirs are only one among the more recent interventions into a debate on race and power that Thomas inadvertently triggered.

Throughout this book, I have argued that lynching has become a metaphor for racism and that collective memories of lynching have been mobilized and reconstructed in order to understand and either to contest or to further various racial projects. But while collective memories of lynching are strongly associated with conceptions of race and racism, lynching has also been invoked as a lens through which to view a variety of national events in which race was not at center stage. Long before Thomas charged that he was the victim of a "high-tech lynching," supporters of another Supreme Court nominee, Robert Bork (nominated in 1987), claimed that his confirmations were a lynching. The federal judge in the Oklahoma City bombing case warned that a "penalty phase hearing cannot be turned into some kind of lynching."[20] Senator Orrin Hatch referred to opposition to the nomination of Charles Pickering to the Fifth Circuit Court of Appeals as a lynching.[21] And the 1998 murder of Matthew Shepard, a gay college student who was tied to a fence and left to die in Wyoming, has been widely understood as a lynching.[22] While lynching was invoked with varying degrees of seriousness in these cases, each case demonstrates some of the possible ways memories of lynching can be invoked in order to frame contemporary events.[23] I have argued throughout this book that the meaning of lynching is not fixed, and these cases hint at the variety of purposes the lynching metaphor can serve.

Finally, I would like to note that the danger of writing about collective memories of lynching is that a focus on lynching as memory might suggest that the phenomenon of racial terror is solely a thing of the past. While it is true that lynching as a public spectacle had been virtually eliminated by the 1950s, it would be premature to relegate lynching to the dustbins of history, since racist violence is very much a part of contemporary society. The death of Michael Griffith in Howard Beach, Queens, New York;[24] the murders of Yusef K. Hawkins, Christopher Wilson, and James Byrd Jr.;[25]

the police shooting of Amadou Diallo;[26] and the series of anti-Arab hate crimes in the wake of the September 11, 2001, attacks[27] may not all clearly fit into standard definitions of lynching, but they are only a few of the far-too-numerous events that should provide evidence that in today's United States, lynching is not limited to the realm of metaphor or memory.

However, as the mobilization against racist police brutality in the wake of the killing of Diallo suggests, some instances of contemporary racist violence lend themselves to processes of metaphorization in ways that are very similar to the metaphorization of earlier lynchings, since they have been enlisted in antiracist struggles as evidence of broad patterns of systemic racism. Each of the events mentioned above has entered into our national consciousness (with varying degrees of ubiquity, to be sure) as part of an ongoing process of national racial formation. As these events become more distant from us in time and more firmly identified as parts of our collective memories rather than of our contemporary realities, attention to memories and metaphors of lynching can alert us to the stakes and the contests that are involved in the construction of racialized violence as part of our national racial imaginary.

The lynching metaphor, and collective memories of lynching, can be reconstructed and deployed in a wide variety of ways and for a seemingly endless number of purposes, but the meaning that is attached to lynching is never arbitrary. Instead, our understandings of lynching are circumscribed by discursive battles in the past and the present. These battles are of utmost importance for contemporary racial projects that are often enacted as battles over discursive terrain, battles that are also, at least in part, waged over historical resources and collective memory.

Coda: Remembering Terror Post-9/11

As an investigation into the ways we construct and deploy collective memories of terrorism, this project has inevitably taken on a new kind of resonance in the wake of the attacks on the World Trade Center and the Pentagon on September 11, 2001. America, we are told in countless ways, has lost its innocence. No longer can we walk the streets with a naive belief in our safety. Instead, the United States is a nation under siege. We need to be constantly alert, careful about how and where we travel, cautious about our mail, and wary of our neighbors and the strangers among us. Terrorism constrains our movements, shatters our sense of security, and threatens the very core of our national identity. It must be defeated at any cost.

No matter that America has lost its innocence before. That innocence was said to have been a casualty of the bombings at Pearl Harbor. Or in

Oklahoma City. Or of the bullets at Columbine. It died along with the Kennedy brothers and Martin Luther King Jr., though it seems never to have been an issue in thoughts of the assassination of Malcolm X. Our national innocence seems to be simultaneously remarkably fragile and amazingly resilient, for we can count on it to reappear, rising like the phoenix from its ashes, just in time to be newly consumed.[28]

The idea that the events of September 11 have caused us to lose our innocence is, then, contingent upon a very selective sense of our national history, one that is based upon forgetting or downplaying earlier national traumas. More important, the sense that the events of September 11 were *uniquely* terrifying is contingent upon the construction of a national collective memory that has marginalized histories of lynching and other forms of racist violence. But while drawing attention to these histories might have helped to contextualize national fear in the wake of the attacks, the problem here goes beyond collective amnesia. Indeed, the idea that terror is something new makes sense only if we ignore not only the racial dynamics of our past but also the continuing fear experienced within many communities of color on a daily basis. The shootings of James Ramseur, Eleanor Bumpurs, and Amadou Diallo, among countless others, have ensured that for large segments of the population, a sense of security, so taken for granted by most of the mainstream media, has never been firmly established. As collective memories of recent events are constructed and enlisted for a variety of projects, it is crucial to consider the question of whose fears are deemed relevant within national political discourse.

Notes

Introduction

1. Quoted in Ferrell, *Nightmare and Dream*, 198–99. See also *Congressional Record*, 67th Cong., 2d sess., December 1921 and January 1922; Garrett, December 19, 1921, 548; Sisson, January 18, 1922, 1721.

2. Quoted in Miller, *The Complete Transcripts of the Clarence Thomas–Anita Hill Hearings*, 118.

3. Ibid., 157.

4. I discuss these issues at much greater length in chapter 4.

5. Lawrence, "'The Message of the Verdict,'" 112.

6. This is not to say, however, that Thomas's reference to lynching was uncontested. Quite the contrary is true. As I discuss in chapter 4, a variety of commentators called Thomas to task for various historical inaccuracies and elisions. Most notable is that fact that black men were seldom lynched as the result of a *black* woman's charges of sexual victimization. For a discussion of the rare cases where black men *were* lynched as a result of such charges, see Tolnay and Beck, "When Race Didn't Matter."

7. Lubiano, "Black Ladies, Welfare Queens, and State Minstrels," 347.

8. The definition is from "The Changing Character of Lynching." From the Association of Southern Women for the Prevention of Lynching (ASWPL) Papers. For an extended discussion of debates within the antilynching movement over how lynching should be defined, see Waldrep, "War of Words."

9. Burke, *On Symbols and Society*, 247.

10. White, *Tropics of Discourse*, 22.

11. Lakoff and Johnson argue that "[i]n all aspects of life . . . we define our reality in terms of metaphors and then proceed to act on the basis of [them]. We draw inferences, set goals, make commitments, and execute plans, all on the basis of how we . . . structure our experience, consciously and unconsciously, by means of metaphor" (Lakoff and Johnson, *Metaphors We Live By*, 158). In contexts that are explicitly centered around political struggle, if we accept that the basis of comparison implicit in the application of any particular metaphor is valid, our judgments about the appropriateness of particular courses of action are likely to be constrained by that metaphor. For an extended discussion of the political power of metaphors, see Pinchin, "The Misrule of Metaphor."

12. Burke, *On Symbols and Society*, 250.

13. Omi and Winant, *Racial Formation in the United States from the 1960s to the 1990s*, 55.

14. Ibid.

15. Ibid., 69.

16. Hall, "Gramsci's Relevance for the Study of Race and Ethnicity," 431.

17. Ibid.

18. Omi and Winant, *Racial Formation*, 56.

19. Ibid.

20. Halbwachs, *On Collective Memory*, 40.

21. Sturken, *Tangled Memories*, 47.

22. Ibid., 18.

23. Ibid., 52.

24. Sturken uses the term "cultural memory" instead of "collective memory" in order to differentiate her work from Halbwachs's and to focus attention on the relationships of power that are inherent in the construction of both history and memory. I agree with her argument that early conceptions of "collective memory" were inattentive to issues of power, but I do not think that the term should be abandoned for this reason. Instead, I would argue that there is value in retrieving and revitalizing the term by consistently inquiring into the nature of memory's construction, elaboration, and deployment.

25. Zelizer, *Remembering to Forget*, 3.

26. Ana Maria Alonso makes a similar point when she writes that "an inquiry into the construction and dissemination of historical memory, itself a central site for the production of effects of power, is critical for an analysis of hegemony" (Alonso, "Gender, Power, and Historical Memory," 405).

27. Gabriel, "Third Cinema as a Guardian of Popular Memory," 55.

28. Lipsitz, *Time Passages*, 33.

29. Irwin-Zarecka, *Neutralizing Memory*, 104.

30. Schwartz has argued that "the past cannot be literally constructed; it can only be selectively exploited. Moreover, the basis of the exploitation cannot be arbitrary. The events selected for commemoration must have some factual significance to begin with in order to qualify for this purpose" (Schwartz, "The Social Context of Commemoration," 376). Schudson echoes this sentiment when he writes that "the present generation may rewrite history, but it does not do so on a blank page" and that "even though the past is regularly reconstructed this is done within limits, stopped by the hard edges of resistance the past provides" (Schudson, *Watergate in American Memory*, 34, 206). Like Schwartz, Schudson is concerned that "radical social constructionists" might lose sight of the ways in which history constrains the production of collective memory (ibid). He writes that "the notion that we manufacture our own history and rewrite it according to the dictates of power, person, and privilege, that human societies are Oceanias where we remember and forget and reconstruct at will, denies the past any influence whatsoever. In effect, this view denies history" (207). That may be, but Schwartz and Schudson seem to be arguing against straw men, since my review of the collective memory literature has not turned up any of the "radical social constructionists" that Schudson refers to. While Schudson does not mention any of these theorists by name, Schwartz makes much of Halbwachs's argument that "the reality of the past is no longer

in the past," but he says little about Halbwachs's claim that the process of social adaptation of the past starts with "ancient facts" (quoted in Schwartz, "The Social Context," 35).

31. Popular Memory Group, "Popular Memory," 229.

32. This section is not intended to provide a comprehensive overview of the dynamics of lynching. Relevant aspects of the history of lynching are addressed in more detail throughout the remaining chapters of this book. For now, I wish only to provide a broad sketch of that history in order to contextualize the analysis that follows. For a more detailed historical analysis of lynching, see Brundage, *Lynching in the New South;* Tolnay and Beck, *A Festival of Violence;* and Wiegman, *American Anatomies.*

33. Brundage, *Under Sentence of Death,* 4.

34. Ibid., 5.

35. Ibid., 5–6.

36. Ibid., 6.

37. Wiegman, *American Anatomies,* 93. Aside from seeing lynching as a distinctly racist practice, there is a strong history of understanding lynching as a method of "frontier justice." Brundage notes that references to western-style vigilante justice were used as a method of legitimating forms of mob violence in other regions and of dismissing the work of antilynching activists (Brundage, *Under Sentence of Death,* 4). The extent of vigilante violence in the West paled, however, in comparison to rates of lynching in the South after Reconstruction. Still, popular representations of lynching as a method of frontier justice that is somehow distinct from racial lynchings suggest that the metaphor of lynching can be enlisted for an even greater variety of purposes than I address in this project.

38. Brundage, *Under Sentence of Death,* 6.

39. Ibid., 7.

40. Tolnay and Beck, *A Festival of Violence,* ix. Tolnay and Beck actually identify 2,805 lynching victims. There is no way to determine the number of lynching victims with any precision, since many lynchings went unreported and the records of many others were lost. Brundage estimates that 3,220 blacks and 723 whites were lynched in the South between 1880 and 1930 (Brundage, *Lynching in the New South,* 8).

41. Brundage, *Lynching in the New South,* 8.

42. Ibid. There has been relatively little research done into the lynchings of Mexicans, but it has become clear in recent years that while far fewer Mexicans than African Americans were lynched, the true extent of mob violence in the Southwest in the late nineteenth and early twentieth centuries was much greater than has previously been acknowledged (see Rosales, *¡Pobre Raza!* and Vélez-Ibáñez, *Border Visions*). Rosales notes that lynching "dramatically affected Mexicans in California, Arizona, New Mexico, and Texas during the nineteenth century" (118), while Vélez-Ibáñez quotes a contemporary observer

writing that, in Texas from 1836 to 1925 "and beyond," "the killing of Mexicans without provocation is so common as to pass almost unnoticed" (94).

43. Tolnay and Beck, *A Festival of Violence*, 249.

44. Ibid., 250.

45. Ibid., 251.

46. Ibid.

47. Brundage argues that there were "four general categories of [lynch] mobs," including "[s]mall mobs, numbering fewer than fifty persons . . . [which] may be separated into two types. They were either terrorist mobs that made no pretense of upholding the law or private mobs that exacted vengeance for a wide variety of alleged offenses. Posses, the third type . . . ranged in size from a few to hundreds of participants, [and] often overstepped their quasi-legal function and were . . . responsible for mob violence. Finally, mass mobs, numbering from more than fifty to hundreds and even thousands of members, punished alleged criminals with extraordinary ferocity and, on occasion, great ceremony" (Brundage, *Lynching in the New South*, 19). While he cautions against seeing all lynchings as the same kind of ritualized event, he agrees that "virtually all lynchings shared important common elements," including an intent to "enforce social conformity and to punish an individual" and that at the same time, they were a "means of racial repression" (18). He notes that there is a tendency for historians and other observers to ignore the smaller mobs and posses and to treat mass mobs as typical, but he notes that these observers "have not exaggerated [the] significance [of mass mobs]," since mass mobs accounted for more than 34 percent of all lynchings in Georgia and 40 percent of all lynchings in Virginia. He notes that mass mobs often numbered in the hundreds or thousands and that they acted with "widespread local approval . . . [and] they wreaked vengeance for alleged crimes that often had attracted widespread local, and, in many instances regional, attention" (36). Despite the fact that mass mobs were male dominated, "women and even children, by inciting the crowd with cheers, providing fuel for the execution pyre and, scavenging for souvenirs after the lynchings, often figured prominently in the proceedings. This inclusiveness of all ages and both sexes gave the violence of mass mobs power to articulate and, in turn, help perpetuate time-honored cultural preoccupations to a far greater degree than any other form of mob violence" (37–38). Grace Hale takes issue with Brundage's typology, noting that both mass mobs and posses conducted "spectacle lynchings" (Hale, *Making Whiteness*, 201).

48. All quotations about the Neal case are from *The Lynching of Claude Neal* (New York: NAACP, 1934), pamphlet. From NAACP Antilynching Publicity and Investigative Papers. Hale suggests that the NAACP's publicity efforts in the wake of Neal's death mark a turning point in the antilynching movement, and she argues that the attempt to spread knowledge and to generate outrage about the lynching signals that the "lynching spectacle . . . had given way to the growing anti-lynching crusade's attempt to make a spectacle of lynching" (Hale, *Making Whiteness*, 226). While lynchings by mass mobs were rare after

the Neal lynching, Hale argues that by the late 1930s, "southern whites no longer needed to 'dirty' their towns with actual lynchings" because representations of lynchings in a variety of forms, including postcards, a film, an Edison recording, and detailed written narratives, "increasingly did the cultural work of othering southern African Americans," and "worked almost as well as lynchings themselves" (226–27).

49. Hale, *Making Whiteness*, 202.

50. Ibid., 207.

51. Ibid., 206.

52. Harris, *Exorcising Blackness*, x.

53. Hale, *Making Whiteness*, 206.

54. Richard Wright addresses the importance of representations of lynching when he writes that "the things that influenced my conduct as a Negro did not have to happen to me directly; I needed but to hear of them to feel their full effects in the deepest layers of my consciousness. Indeed, the white brutality that I had not seen was a more effective control of my behavior than that which I knew. . . . as long as it remained something terrible and yet remote, something whose horror and blood might descend upon me at any moment, I was compelled to give my entire imagination over to it" (Wright, *Black Boy*, 203).

55. See Hale, *Making Whiteness*, 204–39, for an extended discussion of the standard lynching structure as well as its variations.

56. Wiegman, *American Anatomies*, 83. Wiegman reads castration as an act that "aggressively denies the patriarchal sign and symbol of the masculine, interrupting the privilege of the phallus and thereby reclaiming, through the perversity of dismemberment, the black male's (masculine) potentiality for citizenship" (ibid). Castration's role in the lynching scenario was closely linked to understandings of lynching as a method of punishment for black rapists. I discuss the "myth of the black rapist" and the antilynching movement's response to this myth at length in chapter 1. The current discussion is not meant to provide an exhaustive analysis of the symbolic or gendered dynamics of lynching. For more detailed analyses of these aspects of lynching, see Hale, *Making Whiteness*; Wiegman, *American Anatomies*; Harris, *Exorcising Blackness*; Hall, *Revolt against Chivalry*; and Gunning, *Race, Rape, and Lynching*. I address this work in more detail in the chapters that follow.

57. Hall, *Revolt against Chivalry*, 230.

58. Hale, *Making Whiteness*, 236. Bonds of whiteness were formed not only through racial terrorism but also through narratives that set the boundaries of what was considered appropriate sexuality. Lisa Duggan's analysis of the 1892 murder of Freda Ward by Alice Mitchell, her lover, in Memphis, Tennessee, pairs the "lesbian love murder story" with lynching narratives to demonstrate how both constructed sets of "unfit 'others' . . . who negatively defined the normative characteristics of Americans." Together, both kinds of stories helped to "produce a new form of mass culture and an emerging American modernity at the turn of the century" (Duggan, *Sapphic Slashers*, 60).

59. Tolnay and Beck, *A Festival of Violence*, 252.

60. Brundage, *Lynching in the New South*, 249.

61. Ibid., 250.

62. Ibid., 251. Brundage also notes that the New Deal "set a precedent for greater [federal] intervention to punish lynchers." While federal antilynching legislation never passed, the Department of Justice attempted to appease northern black voters and to express a growing federal commitment to the protection of minority rights by taking "the unprecedented steps of investigating . . . lynchings and pressing charges against mob members" (ibid).

63. Ibid., 257.

64. Zelizer provides a sense of the difficulty of tracking collective memory when she writes that "collective memories are material. They have texture, existing in the world rather than in a person's head. We find memories in objects, narratives about the past, even the routines by which we structure our day. No memory is fully embodied in any of these cultural forms, but instead bounces to and fro among all of them on its way to gaining meaning. Memory's materiality is important, for it helps offset the fluctuations that characterize remembering" (Zelizer, *Remembering to Forget*, 4).

65. Two excellent studies of representations of lynching in literature are Harris, *Exorcising Blackness*, and Gunning, *Race, Rape, and Lynching*.

66. I am referring to *Parade*, which is about the lynching of Leo Frank. Frank's lynching is also the subject of Mamet, *The Old Religion*.

1. Antilynching and the Struggle for Meaning

1. Wells, *A Red Record*, 65.

2. In 1895, Wells married Ferdinand Lee Barnett and changed her name. I refer to her as "Wells" when discussing her writing and activism before her marriage and as "Wells-Barnett" when addressing the time after her marriage or her life as a whole.

3. Harris, *Exorcising Blackness*, x.

4. Hall, "'The Mind That Burns in Each Body,'" 330.

5. Lynchings also provided lessons for their white audiences. As Wiegman argues, as "the most extreme deterritorialization of the body and its subjective boundaries, lynching guaranteed the white mob's privilege of physical and psychic penetration, granted it a definitional authority over social space, and encoded the vigilant and violent system of surveillance that underwrote late-nineteenth- and early-twentieth-century negotiations over race and cultural power" (Wiegman, *American Anatomies*, 94–95). Wiegman explains the importance of death and torture as the forms that lynching took by arguing that "in choosing death and accompanying it with the most extreme practices of corporeal abuse, whiteness enhanced its own significatory lack, filling the absence of meaning that defined it with the fully corporeal presence of a hated, feared, and now conquered blackness. The extremity of punishment in the lynching

and castration scenario thus provided the necessary illusion of returning to the lost moment of slavery's totalized mastery—a moment never actually 'full,' though yearned for, indeed frantically sought after, through the disciplinarity of random mob violence" (100).

6. Quoted in Wells, *Mob Rule in New Orleans*, 14.

7. See note 47 in the Introduction.

8. Some theorists of new social movements (NSMs) suggest that a defining characteristic of NSMs is that they are more concerned with symbolism and public opinion than were older movements. For example, Russell Dalton, Manfred Kuechler, and Wilheim Burklin argue that "[n]ew social movements . . . place greater emphasis on the media as a method of mobilizing public opinion. The media allow social movements to extend their reach to the entire public, and the unconventional actions of the movement are often planned for their media impact. . . . [NSM actions are often] aimed at attracting media attention and mobilizing popular support for an issue" (Dalton, Kuechler, and Burklin, "The Challenge of New Movements," 15). As I demonstrate below, the antilynching movement's consistent focus on the importance of debunking the myth of the black rapist and other racial stereotypes and its enduring insistence that the most important part of the struggle was to change public sentiment about lynching suggest that this is not such a new characteristic of social movements after all.

9. See, for example, Schechter, "Unsettled Business"; Brown, *Eradicating This Evil*; Brundage, "Black Resistance and White Violence in the American South, 1880–1940"; and Hall, *Revolt against Chivalry*.

10. Bederman, *Manliness and Civilization*, 56.

11. See Schechter, "Unsettled Business," 91–104, for an in-depth discussion of Wells's British tours and of the ways she drew upon those tours to further her activism in the United States.

12. Bederman, *Manliness and Civilization*, 68.

13. Ibid., 69.

14. Not that the blueprint was always followed to the letter. Schechter, *Ida B. Wells-Barnett and American Reform, 1880–1930*, provides an important account of the ways that Wells-Barnett was marginalized within the larger antilynching movement in the early twentieth century. Although many of Wells-Barnett's most important arguments about lynching were adopted so thoroughly by the antilynching movement that they became antilynching common sense, her analysis of the gender dynamics surrounding lynching and her calls for self-defense were considered too radical by many of the movement leaders.

15. Zangrando, *The NAACP Crusade against Lynching, 1909–1950*, 46. See Zangrando's book for a more detailed discussion of the NAACP's antilynching finances.

16. Hall, *Revolt against Chivalry*, 165.

17. While the struggle for federal antilynching legislation was ultimately

unsuccessful, there were notable successes at the state level. For example, "[as] early as 1893, Georgia had penalized sheriffs who failed to guard their prisoners against a mob, but the enforcement provisions were inadequate. By 1940, at least thirteen states, six outside the South, had legislated against delinquent officials. In 1896, Ohio enacted a strong antilynching law with a model county-liability provision; nine others utilized the Ohio statute in drafting their own regulations about county liability, and a dozen states, nine of them outside the South, had such measures by 1940" (Zangrando, *The NAACP Crusade*, 20).

18. Brundage, *Lynching in the New South*, 249.

19. Ibid., 234.

20. Ibid., 234–35. The group was originally called the Interracial Commission; it changed its name to the Commission on Interracial Cooperation in 1921 (Ducey, "The Commission on Interracial Cooperation Papers, 1919–1944, and the Association of Southern Women for the Prevention of Lynching Papers, 1930–1942," 1).

21. Hall, *Revolt against Chivalry*, 22.

22. Zangrando, *The NAACP Crusade*, 102.

23. The ASWPL was not the first women's antilynching organization. In 1922, a women's antilynching organization called the Anti-Lynching Crusaders, sponsored by the NAACP, worked to mobilize support for the Dyer Anti-Lynching Bill. The organization was never very large, but it did help pave the way for the ASWPL. See Hall, *Revolt against Chivalry*, 165, and Schechter, *Ida B. Wells-Barnett*, 165–68.

24. Hall, *Revolt against Chivalry*, 171.

25. Ibid., 167.

26. Reed, "An Evaluation of an Anti-Lynching Organization," has argued persuasively that the ASWPL's activities were responsible for a significant part of the decline of lynching in the counties where they were most active and that they were particularly effective at creating a climate where sheriffs felt the need to protect their prisoners. Brundage notes that "in numerous . . . instances [the ASWPL's] timely intercession deterred possible lynchings. The combined tactics of publicity and mobilization of local women activists throughout Georgia and the South were decidedly effective in reducing the numbers of lynchings. In particular, the organization's efforts to prod law officers to uphold the law was notably successful in lessening the proportion of lynchings in which prisoners were taken from custody" (Brundage, *Lynching in the New South*, 248).

27. Wells, *A Red Record*, 101.

28. Bederman, *Manliness and Civilization*, 58.

29. Hall, *Revolt against Chivalry*, 149.

30. "Lynchings and What They Mean: General Findings of the Southern Commission on the Study of Lynching," pamphlet, 63. From CIC Papers.

31. Zangrando, *The NAACP Crusade*, 23. Zangrando notes that the NAACP emerged from the Progressive Era and that the association's attempts to expose

the horrors of lynching to public light reflected the beliefs, aspirations, and techniques of Progressivism (25).

32. See Vendryes, "Hanging on Their Walls," for a discussion of the 1935 antilynching art exhibition in New York City.

33. Zangrando, *The NAACP Crusade*, 33.

34. Antilynching activists and the public defenders of lynching can thus be seen as engaged in a struggle over how lynching would be framed. David A. Snow and Robert D. Benford argue that social "movement organizations and actors [are] actively engaged in the production and maintenance of meaning for constituents, antagonists, and bystanders or observers." Activists are engaged in "signifying work," which Snow and Benford call *"framing,* which denotes an active, process-derived phenomenon that implies agency and contention at the level of reality construction" (Snow and Benford, "Master Frames and Cycles of Protest," 136). Benford and Scott Hunt discuss the political stakes involved in framing as they argue that "social movements can be described as dramas in which protagonists and antagonists compete to affect audiences' interpretations of power relations in a variety of domains. . . . Movement and countermovement activists, targets of change, and the media present divergent interpretations of extant and ideal power relations, desiring some audience to accept and act upon their particular presentation as if it were unquestionably real" (Benford and Hunt, "Dramaturgy and Social Movements," 38). While antilynching activists attempted to challenge the meaning of lynching for a variety of audiences, their efforts to gather support within the black community depended upon what Benford and Hunt call "movement interpretive work," which was meant to stimulate "audiences to redefine their situations as unjust and mutable so that existing power structures can be altered" (48). African Americans probably had no doubts that lynching was unjust, but in order to engage in the antilynching struggle, they needed to be convinced that it was possible to challenge the social support for lynching.

35. Quoted in "Women's Work," internal document for the fund-raising work of the CIC's women's committees. From CIC Papers.

36. It is not clear if this letter was ever published. File on lynching of Claude Neal, from ASWPL Papers.

37. Brundage, *Lynching in the New South*, 58.

38. George W. Chamlee, "Is Lynching Ever Defensible?" *The Forum*, December 1926. From NAACP Antilynching Publicity and Investigative Papers.

39. Jessie Daniel Ames, "Southern Women and Lynching," pamphlet. From ASWPL Papers.

40. Hodes, "The Sexualization of Reconstruction Politics," 63–65.

41. Tillman, "The Black Peril," 182.

42. Quoted in Ferrell, *Nightmare and Dream*, 198–99.

43. Quoted in ibid., 199.

44. From an NAACP organizing letter to Youth Council presidents about

the National Youth Demonstration against Lynching on February 12, 1937. From NAACP Antilynching Publicity and Investigative Papers.

45. The exact percentage of lynch victims charged with rape varies through the years and by region, but it is generally true that by the 1900s, rape was alleged in fewer than one-third of all lynchings. Brundage notes that "during the 1880s and 1890s, alleged 'outrages' did prompt the majority of lynchings by all mobs. As the practice of mob justice persisted into the twentieth century, however, the number of lynchings for alleged outrages declined steadily." Alleged sexual infractions accounted for more than 60 percent of all lynchings in Georgia between 1880 and 1889, but "the percentage of lynchings for sexual transgressions declined to 27 percent" in that state over the next two decades. Brundage provides similar statistics for Virginia (Brundage, *Lynching in the New South*, 68).

While lynching was generally advocated as a punishment for black men who raped white women, some whites thought that lynching did not send a powerful enough message. For example, a doctor named Frank Lydston advocated for castration rather than lynching as punishment for rape because it would create a *stronger* collective memory of terror among African Americans. He claimed that "a hanging or even a burning is soon forgotten; but a negro buck at large amongst the ewes of his flock, minus the elements of manhood, would be a standing terror to those of similar propensities" (quoted in Duggan, *Sapphic Slashers*, 172). The fact that lynchings often involved castration did not challenge the basis of Lydston's argument, since, for him, a *living* victim of castration who remained a member of the black community would be a more powerful continuing reminder of the strength of white supremacy.

46. Statement of Walter White, executive secretary of the NAACP, in U.S. Senate, *Punishment for the Crime of Lynching*.

47. Commission on Interracial Cooperation, "Southern Leaders Impeach Judge Lynch: High Lights from Report of Commission on the Study of Lynching" (1931). From CIC Papers.

48. Statement of Walter White, executive secretary of the NAACP, testimony in U.S. House, *Antilynching*.

49. Quoted in Douglass, "Lynch Law in the South," 4.

50. Wells's own life experiences provide interesting evidence of the place of rape within lynching narratives. After she wrote an editorial, published anonymously, claiming that a lynching in Memphis was motivated by greed, a local paper (which assumed the author was a man) threatened Wells by saying that "it will be the duty of those whom he has attacked to tie the wretch who utters these calumnies to a stake at the intersection of Main and Madison Sts., brand him in the forehead with a hot iron and perform upon him a surgical operation with a pair of tailor's shears" (quoted in Wells, *Southern Horrors*, 4–5). Wells's offense involved speech instead of rape, and thus the suggestion that her lynching should involve castration shows how easily any infraction could be recoded as a sexual transgression. Sandra Gunning argues that the

threat to lynch Wells indicates "the white press's transformation of her into the black beast—indeed, the reduction of all black victims to this one obliterating stereotype" (Gunning, *Race, Rape, and Lynching*, 87).

51. Douglass, "Lynch Law in the South," 19.

52. Wells, *Southern Horrors*, 14. As I have suggested throughout this discussion, Wells's refutation of the idea that lynching was a response to rape was eventually taken up as a standard part of antilynching activism. In the early 1890s, however, many members of African American communities saw her tactics as potentially incendiary or ineffective. In order to maintain good relations with whites, many African American leaders shied away from exposing the myth of the black rapist in favor of stressing the importance of law enforcement as a method of controlling the mob (Schechter, *Ida B. Wells-Barnett*, 106).

53. Wells, *Southern Horrors*, 10.

54. Jessie Daniel Ames, "Can Newspapers Harmonize Their Editorial Policy on Lynching and Their News Stories on Lynching?" Southern Newspaper Publishers' Association, Chattanooga, Tennessee, bulletin no. 645, July 1, 1936. From ASWPL papers.

55. James Weldon Johnson, letter to the editor, *The Forum*, February 1927. From NAACP Antilynching Publicity and Investigative Papers.

56. Wells, *Southern Horrors*, 4–5.

57. Ibid.

58. Wells, *A Red Record*, 11.

59. Wells, *Southern Horrors*, 8.

60. Ibid., 11. Wells's effort to publicize voluntary interracial relationships constituted perhaps the most controversial aspect of her work and was seen as too radical by many antilynching activists in later years. For example, a 1904 antilynching article by Mary Church Terrell drew heavily upon Wells's analysis of lynching but "made no mention of consensual sexual contact across the color line" (Schechter, *Ida B. Wells-Barnett*, 124).

61. Hall, *Revolt against Chivalry*, 155.

62. Ibid., 151.

63. Ibid., 153.

64. Quoted in Aptheker, *Lynching and Rape*, 10.

65. Quoted in the *Baltimore Crisis*, May 1915, 227.

66. Quoted in Hall, *Revolt against Chivalry*, 93.

67. Hall notes that one of the reasons the ASWPL chose to exclude black women was that it wanted to maintain the rhetorical power of the claim that a group of *white* women refused to accept the code of chivalry. The goal was to have "an organization of impeccably respectable white southern women expressing their abhorrence of masculine violence [which would, in Ames's eyes] have an impact on white public opinion that a biracial or black protest movement could not achieve" (Hall, *Revolt against Chivalry*, 181). She notes that Ames's position was controversial and that "black women took strong exception to Ames's statement that she 'frankly' could not see any 'contribution the

Negro race itself could make in the eradication of lynching'" (181–82). Black women did, however, work with the ASWPL and behind the scenes. Hall argues that while the exclusion of black women from official membership roles was "undoubtedly an effective tactic," it also "eliminated the very participants who could have kept the organization accountable to changing black agendas for reform" (182).

68. *High Spots,* the CIC's Department of Woman's Work newsletter, April–June 1933. From CIC Papers.

69. Ames, "Southern Women and Lynching."

70. See Hall, *Revolt against Chivalry,* for the most sustained discussion of the ASWPL's tactics and an analysis of the importance of representational politics.

71. Excerpted in *High Spots.*

72. Statement of Albert E. Barnett, professor of literature and history of the Bible at Scarrit College, Nashville, Tennessee, in U.S. Senate, *Punishment for the Crime of Lynching,* 52.

73. Freedman, "The Manipulation of History at the Clarence Thomas Hearings," 1363. It was not only black men who had cause to fear such a scenario. In 1914 in Wagoner County, Oklahoma, a seventeen-year-old black girl named Marie Scott was lynched after her brother killed one of the white men who had assaulted her. By the time the mob came to lynch her brother, he had fled, and the mob lynched her instead (NAACP, *Thirty Years of Lynching in the United States, 1889–1918,* 23).

74. Freedman, "The Manipulation of History," 1363. Paula Giddings notes that stereotypes that defined black women in terms of sexual excess were actually foundational to the myth of the black rapist: "Black men raped, it was widely believed, because black men's mothers, wives, sisters, and daughters were seen as 'morally obtuse,' 'openly licentious,' and had 'no immorality in doing what nature prompts'" (Giddings, "The Last Taboo," 443–44).

75. Carby, "'On the Threshold of Woman's Era,'" 308–9. This claim is borne out in the words of South Carolina's Senator (soon to be governor) Ben Tillman. Tillman is perhaps best known for the defense of lynching that I quoted earlier, but his thoughts about black women are just as inflammatory: "If you know anything about the Negroes, you know that very few of the women of that race have any idea of virtue at all. . . . It is well understood that when the puberty arouses the passions in the sexes—and those passions are most virulent—Negro girls would take advantage inevitably of white men and boys who had sexual intercourse with them" (quoted in the *Baltimore Crisis,* January 1915, 141).

76. Wells, *Southern Horrors,* 6.

77. Wells, *A Red Record,* 67.

78. Ibid., 68.

79. Ibid., 69.

80. Gunning, *Race, Rape, and Lynching,* 80.

81. Ibid., 86–87.

82. Laura Nelson was lynched in Okemah, Oklahoma, in 1911. She was accused of murdering a deputy sheriff who was in her cabin as part of a posse searching for stolen meat. Weeks before she was lynched, it had been determined that she was innocent and that she had claimed to have shot the deputy in order to protect her fourteen-year-old son, L. W. Nelson. Nelson's husband pled guilty to cattle theft and was sent to the state penitentiary. One night, Laura Nelson and her son were taken from the jail, dragged nearly six miles, and hanged from a bridge (Allen, *Without Sanctuary*, 179–80). According to the NAACP's account, Nelson was raped by members of the mob before being lynched (NAACP, *Thirty Years of Lynching*, 18).

Throughout this book, I include occasional photographs and fairly detailed descriptions of lynchings because I think that they convey powerful information in unique ways. In her discussion of terror and slavery, Saidiya V. Hartman discusses the dangers inherent in this type of decision. She writes that she has chosen not to include Frederick Douglass's account of the beating of his aunt "in order to call attention to the ease with which such scenes are usually reiterated, the casualness with which they are circulated, and the consequences of this routine display of the slave's ravaged body. Rather than inciting indignation, too often they immure us to pain by virtue of their familiarity—the oft-repeated or restored character of these acounts and our distance from them are signaled by the theatrical language usually resorted to in describing these instances—and especially because they reinforce the spectacular character of black suffering. What interests me are the ways we are called upon to participate in such scenes. Are we witnesses who confirm the truth of what happened in the face of the world-destroying capacities of pain, the distortions of torture, the sheer unrepresentability of terror, and the repression of the dominant accounts? Or are we voyeurs fascinated with and repelled by exhibitions of terror and suffering? What does the exposure of the violated body yield? Proof of black sentience or the inhumanity of the 'peculiar institution'? Or does the pain of the other merely provide us with the opportunity for self-reflection? At issue here is the precariousness of empathy and the uncertain line between witness and spectator. Only more obscene than the brutality unleashed at the whipping post is the demand that this suffering be materialized and evidenced by the display of the tortured body or endless recitations of the ghastly and the terrible. In light of this, how does one give expression to these outrages without exacerbating the indifference to suffering that is the consequence of the benumbing spectacle or contend with the narcissistic identification that obliterates the other or the prurience that too often is the response to such displays?" (Hartman, *Scenes of Subjection*, 1–2). There are no easy answers to these questions, so rather than attempting to answer them, I would just note that this caution is well taken.

83. Petition. From "Anti-lynching Measures" subject file, from NAACP Anti-lynching Publicity and Investigative Papers.

84. The most common accusations leveled against black women who were lynched is that they were guilty of some variety of murder or attempted murder. Some black women who were lynched were charged with property crimes, including theft and arson. At least three female lynch victims were accused of "race prejudice" (NAACP, *Thirty Years of Lynching*, 43–105 passim). Women were also lynched for crimes that were attributed to men with whom they were associated, as in the case of Marie Scott, discussed above. Another example is Ballie Crutchfield, who was lynched in Rome, Tennessee, in 1901 after her brother, who had been charged with stealing a purse, escaped from a lynch mob (14).

85. James Weldon Johnson, "Memorandum. Re: Relation between the Crimes of Rape and Lynching," December 20, 1921. From NAACP Antilynching Publicity and Investigative Papers.

86. Bederman, *Manliness and Civilization*, 49. Bederman argues that it was initially easy for whites to ignore Wells's work but that Wells-Barnett compelled their attention by taking her antilynching campaign abroad. Wells-Barnett was able to convince British audiences that lynching was barbaric, and white elites in the United States were forced to respond to international criticism. Wells-Barnett herself noted that "since the crusade against lynching was started . . . governors of states, newspapers, senators and representatives and bishops of churches have all been compelled to take cognizance of the prevalence of [lynching] . . . and to speak in one way or another in the defense of the charge against this barbarism in the United States. This has not been because there was a latent spirit of justice voluntarily asserting itself, especially in those who do the lynching, but because the entire American people now feel, both North and South, that they are objects in the gaze of the civilized world and that for every lynching humanity asks that America render its account to civilization and itself" (Wells, *A Red Record*, 72).

87. Wells, *A Red Record*, 14.

88. CIC, *Mob Murder in America: A Challenge to Every American Citizen* (1920), pamphlet, 3. From CIC Papers.

89. Wells, *A Red Record*, 52–53.

90. Ibid., 55.

91. Antilynching flyer. From "Anti-lynching Measures" subject file, from NAACP Antilynching Publicity and Investigative Papers.

92. Brundage, *Lynching in the New South*, 242–43.

93. Zangrando, *The NAACP Crusade*, 210.

94. Lewis T. Nordyke, in *Survey and Graphic*, November 1939. From newspaper clippings file, from ASWPL Papers.

95. "Annual Lynching Record Shows Improvement," *Christian Century*, February 21, 1924. From CIC Papers.

96. While this claim is valid for the antilynching movement as a whole, the ASWPL was arguably at least as concerned with challenging stereotypes of white women as it was devoted to debunking the myth of the black rapist. The

entire antilynching movement resisted the notion that white women were reliant upon white male protection, but challenging notions of white women's dependency was a keystone of the ASWPL's work. The ASWPL was in line with the rest of the antilynching movement, however, in that it did not devote many of its resources to challenging ideas about black women's sexuality.

2. Cinematic Lynchings

1. The "Gus chase scene" has generally been referred to as a rape scene, despite the facts that there was no rape and that Gus's intentions in the scene are unclear. Earlier in the scene, he proposes marriage to Flora, and before Flora's death, he assures her that he will not harm her. For a discussion of the various interpretations of this scene, see Gaines, *Fire and Desire: Mixed-Race Movies in the Silent Era* 239–41. Thanks to Jane Gaines for alerting me to the importance of this debate.

2. Although *Secrets and Lies* was a British film, it was one of the most successful art house films of recent years in the United States (it was nominated for several academy awards, and Brenda Blethyn was nominated for best supporting actress), so its role in U.S. racial formation cannot be discounted.

3. Sturken, *Tangled Memories*, 8. Sturken uses the term "cultural memory" in order to "define memory that is shared outside the avenues of formal historical discourse yet is entangled with cultural products and imbued with cultural meaning." She prefers "cultural memory" over "collective memory" because she wants to draw attention to the "self-consciousness with which notions of culture are attached" to the objects of memory that she examines (3).

4. Lipsitz, *Time Passages*, 164.

5. Ibid.

6. Guerrero, *Framing Blackness*, 5.

7. Ibid., 3.

8. Shohat and Stam, *Unthinking Eurocentrism*, 183.

9. Burke, *On Symbols and Society*, 247.

10. Shohat and Stam, *Unthinking Eurocentrism*, 183.

11. Shohat and Stam argue that oppressed groups have been particularly sensitive to "stereotypes and distortions" because of "the powerlessness of historically marginalized groups to control their own representation." They note that "[m]inority directors of *all* racial groups constitute less than 3 per cent of the membership of the almost 4,000-member Directors' Guild of America" and that "the most recent report on Hollywood employment practices released by the NAACP reveals that Blacks are underrepresented in 'each and every aspect' of the entertainment industry" (ibid., 184).

12. Shohat and Stam note that the fact that "films are only representations does not prevent them from having real effects in the world; racist films can mobilize for the Ku Klux Klan, or prepare the ground for retrograde social policy. Recognizing the inevitability and the inescapability of representation does not mean, as Stuart Hall has put it, that 'nothing is at stake'" (ibid., 178).

13. *The Birth of a Nation* is probably the most widely discussed film in the history of cinema. As the first full-length feature film, *The Birth of a Nation* helped to inaugurate the studio system, and D. W. Griffith's work as a director supplied some of the most basic elements of cinematic grammar, which are still in use today. Its representations of American racial relations have inspired Ku Klux Klan (KKK) rallies and lynchings and at the same time have galvanized African American opposition and provided the NAACP with some of its most notable early victories, as discussed below. It is no wonder that it has become, according to Ed Guerrero, "the most controversial film ever made in America." For some of the most important discussions of the film, see Guerrero, *Framing Blackness*, 8–17; Lang, *"The Birth of a Nation"*; and Silva, "Introduction."

Other than *The Birth of a Nation*, perhaps the most influential film about lynching is Robert Mulligan's 1962 screen adaptation of Harper Lee's *To Kill a Mockingbird*. Filmed at the height of the civil rights movement, *To Kill a Mockingbird* is centrally concerned with debunking the myth of the black rapist. Its basic structure (a decent white lawyer in a racist town is called upon to make personal and family sacrifices in order to fight for racial justice) provides the blueprint for three of the films that I consider at length in this chapter: *Just Cause*, *Ghosts of Mississippi*, and *A Time to Kill*. Unlike any of these films, though, *Mockingbird* refuses what now seems like a Hollywood imperative for a happy ending, and the innocent black man who was accused of rape is first found guilty by a jury and then lynched. For an excellent discussion of the novel as well as the film, see Johnson, *To Kill a Mockingbird*. Particularly interesting is her discussion of the parallels between *Mockingbird* and the Scottsboro trial.

There are filmed adaptations of several other novels and plays that are, to various degrees, concerned with lynching's dynamics. For a discussion of the 1951 film version of Richard Wright's *Native Son*, see Bogle, *Toms, Coons, Mulattoes, Mammies, and Bucks*, 183–84. For a discussion of lynching and Wright's novel, see Wiegman, *American Anatomies*, 100–103.

14. During the 1990s there was what Guerrero refers to as a "new black film wave" or a "black movie boom" that "has materialized out of a climate of long-muted black frustration and anger over the worsening political and economic conditions that African Americans continue to endure in the nation's decaying urban centers. . . . from the mid-1980s onward, we have witnessed the rise of an insidious, socially fragmenting violence driven by the availability of cheap guns and crack cocaine in the nation's partitioned inner cities. For the most part, black rage has lost its political focus in this violent *apartheid* environment; it has become an internalized form of self-destruction expressed as gang and drug warfare. If such a situation can be said to have positive effects, we can see this rage as an energizing element in much of the new black cultural production, finding expression in a rearticulated criticism of white racism and a resurgent interest in black nationalism among the urban youth inspired by the rap lyrics of Public Enemy, N.W.A., Sister Souljah, and Ice-T, or resonant in the films of Bill Duke, Spike Lee, Matty Rich, and John Single-

ton" (Guerrero, *Framing Blackness*, 158–59). Guerrero goes on to consider a variety of factors that helped to shape representations of African Americans in the 1990s, including, among other things, "such emergent groups within the [black] community finding voices as gays and women" (160); "a sharpening climate of deteriorating race relations, polarization, and outright racial conflict" (161); "sensationalized media events [such as] the Anita Hill–Clarence Thomas Senate hearings, Magic Johnson's retirement, the Mike Tyson rape trial," and the Charles Stuart case (161); and "the intensifying racist tone of mainstream political rhetoric and discourse rooted in the backlash politics of the Reagan years" (161). The black movie boom is largely a result of the fact that during the late 1980s and early 1990s, Hollywood was faced with a desperate economic situation: By the 1992 summer season, "ticket sales were at a fifteen-year low" (165). Guerrero notes that "within this bleak economic context, Hollywood, and the media industry in general, once again turned its attention to the size and consumer power of the mythical, ever-shifting black movie audience, variously estimated at 25 to 30 percent (overrepresenting its 13 percent portion of the population)" (165). Several of the films that I discuss in this chapter, including *Do the Right Thing* and *Rosewood*, are products of this desire to capture black audiences, while films like *Just Cause* and *A Time to Kill* reflect the "intensifying racist tone of mainstream political rhetoric and discourse" that Guerrero refers to.

15. Also, as I have mentioned, the most important of these films, like *The Birth of a Nation* and *To Kill a Mockingbird*, have received extensive consideration elsewhere.

16. Guerrero, *Framing Blackness*, 13.

17. Ibid.

18. Ibid., 14.

19. Ibid.

20. Ibid., 13–14. It is not necessarily the case, however, that all of the attempts to censor the film came from the NAACP or its allies. Instead, it is possible that "the film was banned in many towns not because of its ideological message but because of general white distaste for and paranoia about anything black. In other words, the racism that the NAACP was fighting led not to the support of the film, as one might expect, but to the opposite—the total ban and selective elimination of scenes from the print" (Gaines, *Fire and Desire: Mixed-Race Movies*, 235). Gaines cautions against seeing the NAACP's campaign against *Birth* in too heroic a light, since the censorship of *Birth* was a primary reference point for censors who later had to make decisions about Oscar Micheaux's films, including *Within Our Gates* (1919). Moreover, it is quite possible that the efforts to censor the film may have actually "produced the desire to see it, even encouraged the fascination with its own prohibited status and fantasies of the black bodies deleted from it" (225). More generally, Gaines cautions against seeing cultural products as inherently racist, since meaning does not reside within a text but is instead constructed as an active part of an audience's participation. In this light, Gaines considers film censorship to be an attempt to

fix meaning while at the same time "fixing" texts so that they will not "cause trouble" (232). To highlight the importance of this idea, she asks whether it woud ever "be possible to use an analysis of *The Birth of a Nation* to make an antiracist statement?" and "[h]as showing the film always automatically reproduced racism?" (232). These questions are particularly important when considering imagery surrounding lynching, since they draw attention to the changing contexts of spectatorship and to the question of whether or not it is possible to deploy lynching imagery for antiracist purposes.

21. Quoted in Cripps, "The Making of *The Birth of a Race*," 43.

22. Ibid.

23. Ibid., 45. See also Bogle, *Toms*, 103.

24. Bogle, *Toms*, 103, and Cripps, "The Making of *The Birth of a Race*." Cripps's article presents a detailed overview of the effort to counter Griffith's film and of the financial and ideological concessions that finally resulted in *The Birth of a Race.*

25. Bogle, *Toms*, 110.

26. Pearl Bowser and Louise Spense note, though, that the notion of "survival" is questionable in relation to Micheaux's films, since two of Micheaux's silent films were only discovered in recent years. The following discussion of *Within Our Gates* is based on a print that was repatriated from the National Film Archive of Spain in 1990 and renamed *La Negra*. Bowser and Spense write that "[t]he politics of what is 'lost, stolen, or strayed,' . . . is an important area of research and speculation. What motivates the 'discovery' of a film in an archive? Why only three of at least twenty-five?" ("Identity and Betrayal," 75). Gaines, *Fire and Desire: Mixed-Race Movies*, provides an interesting discussion of the justification for, and problems with, analyzing *La Negra* as if it were the same film that U.S. audiences viewed as *Within Our Gates* in 1919. Among other things, she points out that it does not make sense to discuss *Within* as the "original" because, as it was cut and reedited depending on what censors in various cities would allow, it constantly changed.

27. Reid, *Redefining Black Film*, 12. See also Bowser and Spence, "Identity and Betrayal," 72. Frank was a Jewish man who was lynched after being convicted of the rape and murder of a young white woman. Recently, the Frank case has been the subject of a Broadway musical titled *Parade* and of David Mamet's book *The Old Religion*.

28. Bowser and Spence, "Identity and Betrayal," 57.

29. Pearl Bowser, lecture to National Endowment for the Humanities (NEH) Institute on Black Film, July 1999.

30. Reid, *Redefining Black Film*, 13.

31. Bowser and Spence, "Identity and Betrayal," 57.

32. Reid, *Redefining Black Film*, 13–14. Reid discusses the heroic moment in the film when a black man "annihilates" the Klan members with bricks, and he argues that it is an important precedent for heroes in later "black action films" such as Melvin Van Peebles's *Sweet Sweetback Baadassss Song* (1971).

33. Gaines, "Fire and Desire: Race, Melodrama, and Oscar Micheaux," 56.

34. Jane Gaines discusses the crosscutting at length and argues that it works to solidify the link between the barbarism of the lynching and of the rape ("Fire and Desire: Race, Melodrama," 55–59).

35. Gaines distinguishes between lynching in this film, which she calls "lynching as sensational spectacle," and "lynching as public spectacle, the gruesome ritual that functioned as social control and warning to Blacks." Instead of terrorizing and policing black communities, Micheaux's depiction of lynching was "rhetorically organized to encourage the feeling of righteous indignation in the Black spectator" (Gaines, "Fire and Desire: Race, Melodrama," 55).

36. Quoted in Pearl Bowser's documentary film about "race films," *Midnight Ramble*. Because the initial event that led to the lynchings was Landry's attempt to pay off his debt to Gridlestone, the film also presents economic factors as central to the dynamics of lynching. Landry is able to pay off his debt only because his adopted daughter, Sylvia, has been able to use her education to help them calculate their finances. Thus, the film addresses "the threat that education, high ambition, and achievements posed to the status quo" while suggesting that education "could bring new opportunities for Blacks but could also bring retribution" (Bowser and Spence, *Writing Himself into History*, 138).

37. Bowser and Spence caution against seeing the ending as "tacked on" since the lynching narrative is dependent upon the earlier story of Sylvia Landry's education. If the two narratives were considered as separate stories, Micheaux's argument about the power and pitfalls of education as a source of black empowerment would be lost. On the other hand, considering the film as a whole allows for a reading in which "the film changes from simply self-affirmation to a call for assertive action" (Bowser and Spence, *Writing Himself into History*, 137).

38. It is unclear how many theaters showed "race films" in the 1920s. In 1921, one article in *Billboard* mentioned that there were "800 houses catering to colored audiences," while another article put the number at 600. The head of a black film company claimed that there were only about 120 theaters that might screen his company's films. Aside from black-only theaters, there may have been theaters that had black-only seating sections or that set aside specific days for black audiences. The exact number of venues for black films may be impossible to determine, but it surely pales in comparison to the approximately 22,000 white-only theaters in existence at the time (Bowser and Spence, *Writing Himself into History*, 114). Bowser and Spence write that "it seems clear that the distribution network [for black films] must have been extremely chaotic and decentralized" (115).

39. Gaines, "Fire and Desire: Race, Melodrama," 50.

40. Ibid.

41. Ibid.

42. Guerrero, *Framing Blackness*, 17. A very different tradition of representing lynchings cinematically can be found in westerns, which tend to present

168 Notes to Chapter 2

lynching as a method of "frontier justice" necessitated by the weakness or corruption of the state. The prototypical example is Owen Wister's 1902 novel *The Virginian*, which was made into a film by Victor Fleming in 1929 and remade by Stuart Gilmore in 1946. *The Virginian* distinguishes between frontier and southern lynchings. The character of Judge Henry defends local lynchings by focusing on the fact that unlike lynchings in the South, they do not involve torture and public display of victims. The judge also argues that southern lynchings are unnecessary because the South already has an existing and powerful government that favors the "decent" classes (whites) over the "dangerous" classes (blacks) (Slotkin, *Gunfighter Nation*, 180). Despite the judge's attempts to present western lynching as more legitimate than its southern counterpart, his suggestion that the state cannot be counted on to provide justice in the West is, of course, quite similar to the rationale used by many southern lynch mobs. While the western is perhaps the genre most closely associated with lynching, lynchings in westerns are generally presented in ways that deemphasize racial issues. So while the genre would ultimately make any attempt to pin down a single set of meanings attached to the metaphor of lynching problematic, it is only tangentially relevant for the processes of racial formation that are of concern in this project. Still, an investigation into the ways that westerns have helped to shape collective memories of lynching would no doubt complicate the current discussion in highly provocative ways.

43. Guerrero, *Framing Blackness*, 146. As Mark Reid cautions, though, it is important not to overestimate Lee's importance, since his work did not come out of nowhere. Reid quotes Vincent Canby, writing in the *New York Times*, as saying that Lee is part of "the vanguard" of a "new black cinema, movies that speak with a singularly black voice." This "vanguard" is said to include Robert Townsend and Keenen Ivory Wayans as well as Lee. Reid challenges this claim by putting forward a broader conception of black film, writing that "contrary to Canby's findings, new black cinema includes African-Americans who work for major studios as well as those who work outside the studio system." He mentions films by Warrington Hudlin, Larry Clark, Charles Burnett, and Alonzo Crawford and directs attention to the fact that Lee "borrows from [these films'] cinematic portrayals of urban black life and their use of contemporary black music. In fact, it is in Lee's imitation of these films that he continues the tradition of black filmmaking, and *assists* in the (re)new(al) of African-American cinema" (Reid, *Redefining Black Film*, 106–7).

44. Guerrero notes that "dozens of reviews and articles appeared in national newspapers, including the *New York Times* and the *Village Voice*, and Lee made the covers of *American Film: The Magazine of the Film and Television Arts*, the *National Review*, and *Newsweek*. As well, 'Nightline' and 'The Oprah Winfrey Show' devoted entire programs to the impact the film was projected to have on race relations" (Guerrero, *Framing Blackness*, 146). In fact, much of the coverage was focused on this issue. See especially Joe Klein's suggestion that the film might cause blacks to riot and would therefore threaten David Dinkins's New York

City mayoral campaign ("Spiked? Dinkins and *Do the Right Thing*," *New York*, June 26, 1989). See also Spike Lee's response in the July 17, 1989, issue of *New York*. The film has also been the subject of numerous scholarly articles, but except in bell hooks's *Yearning* and Mark Reid's *Redefining Black Film*, very little has been said about the film's use of lynching imagery.

45. Lee and Jones, *Do the Right Thing*.

46. Buggin' Out's concern with Sal's photos is in sync with some of the lyrics to "Fight the Power," the Public Enemy song that plays throughout the film: "Elvis was a hero to most but he never meant shit to me / Yes he's plain out racist / The sucker was simple and plain / Mother fuck him and John Wayne / 'Cause I'm black and I'm proud. . . . Most of my heroes don't appear on no stamps." Public Enemy and Buggin' Out both seem to define "the powers that be" in terms of cultural representation.

The script mentions Angela Davis as one of the people whose pictures Buggin' Out wants added to the wall, but her name does not make it to the actual film. Whatever the reasons for this omission, it makes sense given the generally passive role that black women play in the film; antiracist struggle is really a male thing here (Lee and Jones, *Do the Right Thing*, 142).

47. Jade is ignored here. Bell hooks sees this as marking the clear limitations of the film, which never articulates any sense of what the "something positive" might be, and she argues that the movie fails to offer any vision of "meaningful resistance to racism and other forms of domination" (hooks, *Yearning*, 183).

48. In his film journal, Lee gives a hint about the importance of Radio Raheem's radio to his identity. He imagines a possible scene "where Raheem's box is slow. He stops to pull out new batteries then he's back in action. Radio Raheem's movement should be sluggish when the batteries are dying. He perks up again with fresh Duracells" (Lee and Jones, *Do the Right Thing*, 41–42).

49. Sal's choice of words is telling. Along with his earlier reaction to Buggin' Out's request for pictures of African Americans, his resistance to Radio Raheem's music suggests that Sal is indeed "disturbed" by African American cultural influences.

50. Reid, *Redefining Black Film*, 102.

51. The stage directions in the script say that "Radio Raheem's prized possession—his box, the only thing he owned of value—his box, the one thing that gave him any sense of worth—has been smashed to bits. (Radio Raheem, like many Black youths, is the victim of materialism and a misplaced sense of values.) Now he doesn't give a fuck anymore. He's gonna make Sal pay with his life" (Lee and Jones, *Do the Right Thing*, 243–44).

52. Spike Lee chose a choke hold as the specific form of police brutality here as a reference to Michael Stewart, a young black graffiti artist who was killed by a choke hold while in the custody of the New York Transit authority (Lee and Jones, *Do the Right Thing*, 59). This case was popularized in the Michelle Shocked song "Graffiti Limbo," in which she explains that no one was convicted for the murder since "the coroner lost the evidence" (Shocked, "Graffiti

Limbo," on *Short, Sharp, Shocked,* Polygram Records, 422-834924-1, 1988). In her live performances, Shocked has noted that the "evidence" of death by strangulation is popped blood vessels in the eyeballs.

53. Eleanor Bumpurs was an elderly black woman who was shotgunned to death by the police as they were attempting to evict her from her apartment in the Bronx.

54. Lee writes of this scene, "Take your pick: Montgomery, Alabama, 1963—or Brooklyn, New York, 1989?" (Lee and Jones, *Do the Right Thing,* photo insert).

55. Lee notes this explicitly: "I'm making an allusion to the Howard Beach incident by using a pizza parlor" (ibid., 24). In 1986, three black men named Cedric Sandiford, Timothy Grimes, and Michael Griffith were driving home to Brooklyn when their car broke down. As they walked through the largely white neighborhood of Howard Beach, Queens, in search of a garage or a telephone, they came across a car full of young white men and one white woman who had been attending a birthday party. After an initial confrontation, the car drove away, and the black men went into a pizza parlor. A little while later (after the police stopped by the pizza parlor to investigate calls about "suspicious-looking black people"), a group of at least a dozen white men from the party, armed with pipes and bats, attacked Sandiford, Grimes, and Griffith as they went outside. Grimes was struck once on the back but managed to escape and hitchhiked home. Griffith and Sandiford were beaten by at least four whites before being able to run away. They were chased on foot and by car, caught, and beaten again. Sandiford pretended to be unconscious until his attackers left, but Griffith managed to break away again. In desperation, he ran onto the highway, where he was struck and killed by a passing car. The incident became the focus for many protests and was part of the inspiration for Spike Lee's film *Do the Right Thing.* Then-mayor Ed Koch was not alone when he compared the event to "the kind of lynching party that took place in the Deep South."

56. Quoted in Mills, "Howard Beach," 480.

57. Mills notes that "[t]he governor linked the timing of his civil rights proposals to Howard Beach. 'This legislation is a belated and modest response to a blatantly serious disease that affects our society,' he announced" (ibid., 484).

58. Hooks, *Yearning,* 176.

59. Harris, *Exorcising Blackness,* 19.

60. This scene is reminiscent of the critique of lynching raised in *Within Our Gates.* Both films position lynching as a target for community protest. While Micheaux's film worked to encourage a sense of outrage and indignation in black audiences, Lee goes a step further by having his characters mirror the kinds of outrage that he works to create in *his* audience.

61. Harris, *Exorcising Blackness,* 19.

62. Lee and Jones, *Do the Right Thing,* 33.

63. Judith Halberstam has made a similar point in her discussion of "imagined violence." She writes that a comparison of the media reactions to "Cop

Killer" and to the videotape of the beating of Rodney King reveals "violence as a one-way street in America: white violence is not only permitted but legally condoned while the mere representation of black-on-white violence is the occasion for censorship and a paranoid retreat to a literal relation between representation and reality" ("Imagined Violence/Queer Violence," 198). The concern surrounding *Do the Right Thing* can be read as an inability or unwillingness to distinguish between representation and reality when it comes to representations that challenge racism. Of course, similar fears had also been expressed decades earlier, with the debut of Micheaux's *Within Our Gates*.

64. That even this minimal resistance was enough to generate so much outrage in the mass media says quite a bit about the strength of contemporary racist paranoia.

65. The movie shows Mister Señor Love Daddy, on the day after the riots, announcing, "Our mayor has commissioned a blue ribboned panel, and I quote, to get to the bottom of last night's disturbance. The City of New York will not let property be destroyed by anyone. End quote."

66. It is possible that the police officer who kills Raheem does so because of a perceived violation of the racial order. After all, Raheem is killed after attacking a white property owner. But while the officer who strangled Raheem seemed to be continually wary of black people, there is little evidence in the film that he killed Raheem because of any sense of racial loyalty.

67. Wiegman, *American Anatomies*, 83.

68. Ibid., 99.

69. Ibid.

70. Lee *does* address the relationship between interracial rape and lynching in his 1991 film, *Jungle Fever*. At one point in that film, the main character's father, played by Ossie Davis, explains why white women and black men are attracted to each other by referencing slavery and noting that the "white man say to his woman, baby, you are the flower of white southern womanhood, too holy and pure to be touched by any man, including me. I'm gonna put you up on a pedestal for the whole world to fall down and worship you. And if any nigger so much as look at you, I'll lynch his ass." Davis's character argues that white women were intrigued by the mystical "big black bucks" that their husbands were so afraid of, while black men longed for the women on the pedestal who were placed out of reach. He suggests that white women bear some responsibility for lynchings because they allowed white men to put them up on the pedestal. He goes on to address the hypocrisy of white men and the sexual victimization of black women when he notes that "[m]eanwhile, the husband no sooner than the sun went down, went down to the slave quarters, grabbing up every piece of black poontang he could get his hands on then running to the gin mill to brag about it." Soon after this speech, the film's interracial couple, Flipper (played by Wesley Snipes) and Angie (played by Annabella Sciorra) are confronted by two white police officers as they are playfully "fighting" on a street in Bensonhurst, Queens (the film is dedicated to Yusef Hawkins, who

was killed in Bensonhurst; see note 25 in the conclusion). The officers are particularly vicious because they were responding to reports that a black man was raping a white woman. As one of the officers throws Flipper against a wall, Angie tries to intervene, saying, "[T]hat's my boyfriend, that's my lover." This was exactly the wrong thing to say, as it seems to further enrage the cops. Flipper attempts to lower the tension by claiming, "I'm not her boyfriend . . . we're just friends." When the officers finally leave, Flipper is terrified and enraged, as he yells at Angie, "What's the matter with you? Huh? What are you doing telling them we're lovers? Are you trying to get me killed?" Lee goes beyond *Do the Right Thing* here, as he suggests that concerns over miscegenation are at the heart of lynching and police brutality, but once again, there is no deeper economic or political analysis here. The officers' brutality was based on an apparently *genuine* concern that a white woman was being raped, and they *left* the scene (albeit reluctantly) once it was clear that this was not a rape. There is no sense here that the charge of rape is often a fabrication that masks other, deeper, reasons for racial animosity and violence.

71. Bell hooks sees Lee as playing into exactly the stereotypes that he is trying to refute: "Conservative folks do not leave this film with the idea deconstructed or challenged that young black men are a menace and a threat. . . . Lee's attempt to challenge the construction of young black men as violent menace by portraying the more deadly police brutality does not work. Raheem's death is predictable. Anticipated, the pathos which should surround his murder is seriously undercut" (hooks, *Yearning*, 179).

72. Such a demonstration was, as I discuss below, one of the central purposes of John Singleton's *Rosewood*.

73. Meeropol wrote under the pen name Lewis Allan. Although a number of singers performed the song, it was popularized by Billie Holiday, who recorded it in 1939. It was one of the few protest songs that she sang. Her recording company thought that it was too inflammatory and, afraid of boycotts, refused to allow her to record it. She was, however, able to convince the company to release her from her contract for one session, and she recorded the song for Commodore Records. The song attracted some attention at the time of its release, but it has only recently been seen as one of her signature songs. By now, the song has become so closely associated with her that it is regularly referred to as "the Billie Holiday song" about lynching. See Davis, *Blues Legacies and Black Feminism*, for a compelling account of the song. Also see Margolick, *Strange Fruit*.

74. The CIC made a special appeal to prevent "legal lynchings" that were a result of mob influence: "Convinced of the terrific price which the community pays for a lynching, it is sometimes felt that lynchings should be prevented by any possible means, even to the point of legal lynching by court sentences. . . . It is . . . a question whether a community is worse off when it has a lynching and defends it, or when it prevents a threatened lynching by prostituting its citizenship and institutions to the demands of the mob" ("The Mob Still Rides:

A Review of the Lynching Record, 1931–1935" (1936), pamphlet, 18–19. From CIC Papers.

75. We might want to see this as a further example of the lynching scenario: Lynching was often carried out for economic and status reasons, and denial of a scholarship seems to be a clear revocation of patriarchal privilege. We soon see, however, that this is only part of the story.

76. Earl's castration suggests that racism is at the heart of his crimes: He was driven to his actions because of that earlier instance of injustice. Monstrosity is thus revealed as a racist production. Richard Wright used a similar strategy in his creation of Bigger Thomas in *Native Son* (1940). An important difference between these two works is that whereas racism is absolutely central throughout *Native Son*, here it is used mainly as a plot device that is largely abandoned.

77. In the wake of the O. J. Simpson criminal trial, the notion that black juries are likely to engage in a process of jury nullification when trying a black defendant has wide currency. This is somewhat ironic, since jury nullification has its origins in cases where all-white juries consistently refused to find white men who had lynched black men guilty of any crime.

78. This portrayal of the NAACP as opportunistic, cynical, and manipulative did not prevent *A Time to Kill* from winning a 1997 NAACP image award.

79. While lynching is understood here as a form of sexual victimization, there is here no attempt to justify it with a charge of rape, so it is not clear why castration is seen as the appropriate form of punishment.

80. This is a reversal of the trial in *Native Son*, in which the body of Bigger's black girlfriend, Betsy, was used as evidence that Bigger had raped and killed Mary Dalton. (The logic was that if he was capable of doing this to "one of his own," he was certainly capable of doing anything to a *white* woman.)

81. As I noted in chapter 1, though, white women were indeed victims of the lynch narrative, and lynchings were used to control their sexuality, specifically by preventing their liaisons with black men.

82. *Mississippi Burning* (directed by Alan Parker, 1988) is a fictionalized account of the investigation into the deaths of civil rights workers James Chaney, Andrew Goodman, and Michael Schwerner. The film is most notable for its attempt to write the FBI into history as the saviors of the civil rights movement rather than as an agency that dedicated many of its resources toward surveilling and disrupting this same movement (two FBI agents are at the center of the film, and they are tirelessly devoted to tracking down the civil rights workers' murderers), and it has been widely criticized for this reason. (*Thunderheart* [1994] received similar criticisms for its representation of the relationship between the FBI and the American Indian Movement.) Blacks are present in the film almost solely as victims or spectators (the FBI investigation angers members of the white community, who respond by terrorizing blacks), and even their victimization is secondary to that of whites (the black civil rights worker rides in the backseat and is the only one of the three lynch victims who does

not get to speak; the streetwise FBI agent, whose anger is the deciding factor pushing him to discover the identity of the killers, only becomes enraged when a white woman is beaten by his deputy). In an otherwise formulaic and one-dimensional detective/adventure film, there is, however, one rather remarkable scene in which the FBI brings in a black agent from out of town to kidnap the mayor and find out what he knows about the killings. We first see the agent wearing a pillowcase over his head, Klan style, and as he removes the hood, he implies that the traditional roles are reversed now, and he is the one in power. He gets the mayor to tell him exactly what happened the night the civil rights workers were killed by asking, "Do you know how much it bleeds when somebody cuts off your balls? . . . Is there something you want to say to me?" This is an important instance of "imagined violence" in which tools of racist terrorism (castration and KKK garb) are reappropriated and used to destablize an important source of institutionalized racism. Of course, this technique is only made viable with the backing of the FBI.

83. See Irwin-Zareka, *Neutralizing Memory*, for a discussion of the term "organized forgetting."

84. The figure of the ex-Klansman-turned-informant is by now a cliché of the genre, having appeared in *Mississippi Burning* and *A Time to Kill*.

85. Freedman, "The Manipulation of History," 1362.

86. This incident is reminiscent of Emmet Till's lynching. Till was abducted from his home and murdered after having been accused of whistling at a white woman. Emmet Till's mother was a member of the studio audience during the episode of *The Oprah Winfrey Show* (February 27, 1997) that was dedicated to *Rosewood*, and she said that the film "brought back a lot of memories . . . the fact that the people knew that the guilty person was not black and they chose to put the blame on that person. They wanted a scapegoat."

87. Mr. Mann is a fictional character created by Singleton. Singleton apparently felt that the massacre needed a heroic black character who fought back. Even though Mr. Mann is not able to prevent the killings, he is instrumental in helping the children to escape from Rosewood.

88. The PBS documentary *The Rosewood Massacre* makes a similar point when a voice-over notes that "there is a story of the 1920s that recorded history does not tell us about. It's a story that shows the America of racial hatred, ignorance, and intolerance. And nowhere was this dark side of America more tangible than in a place called Rosewood, Florida." The voice-over goes on to discuss lynch mobs and to suggest that lynchings generally do not make it into the history books.

89. Wiegman, *American Anatomies*, 84.

3. Lynching as Lens

1. These include the deaths of Yusef Hawkins in Bensonhurst, Brooklyn, New York, in 1989; Michael Griffith in Howard Beach, Queens, New York, in

1986; and James Byrd Jr. in Jasper, Texas, in 1998 (see note 25 in the Conclusion), among others.

2. This is the standard account of the events; see Fletcher, *A Crime of Self-Defense*, for a detailed account of variations and disputed versions of the events in question.

3. On January 25, 1985, a grand jury refused to indict Goetz for attempted murder, but it did indict him for illegal weapons possession. A second grand jury *did* indict him for four counts of attempted murder, one count of reckless endangerment, four counts of assault, and four weapons charges on March 27 of that year. Some of those charges were subsequently dismissed and reinstated in a series of appeals. Finally, on June 16, 1987, Goetz was found innocent of attempted murder, assault, and reckless endangerment but guilty of weapons possession. After appeals, Goetz ultimately served about eight and a half months in prison for weapons charges. See Fletcher, *A Crime*, for an interesting analysis of the legal issues involved in the Goetz case. More recently, on April 23, 1996, Cabey was awarded $43 million in his civil suit against Goetz (see George P. Fletcher, "Justice for All, Twice," *New York Times*, April 24, 1996). Because Goetz cannot afford to pay $43 million, he was ordered to pay Cabey 10 percent of his annual earnings for the rest of his life.

4. The Guardian Angels are a volunteer group devoted to preventing crime; the group has itself been seen in some quarters as a troubling vigilante organization.

5. Marcia Chambers, "Goetz Rejects Offers on Bail from a Stranger and Family," *New York Times*, January 5, 1985. This bail, $50,000, is a remarkably small amount to ask for a man who admits to having shot four men and having then fled the state. Recognizing this, and perhaps suspecting that the amount requested was politically motivated by Goetz's popular support, Judge Leslie Snyder, who presided over Goetz's arraignment, said, "This is a low bail request by the people. I'm surprised. If Western Civilization has taught us anything, it is that we cannot tolerate individuals' taking law and justice into their own hands" (Marcia Chambers, "Goetz Held at Rikers I. in $50,000 Bail in Wounding of Four Teen-Agers on IRT," *New York Times*, January 4, 1985).

6. Suzanne Daley, "Suspect in IRT Shootings Agrees to Return to City to Face Charges," *New York Times*, January 3, 1985.

7. "Gates, Guards, Guns, and Goetz," editorial, *New York Times*, January 27, 1985. The image of Goetz's public support was apparently not lost on Goetz. He announced plans to run for mayor of New York City in the year 2001, saying that he would be a viable candidate. He advocated the death penalty for a criminal's first violent sexual offense, as well as vegetarian lunch options in public schools and a ban on circumcision in the city ("Questions for Bernard [sic] Goetz," *New York Times*, November 1, 1998).

8. Jon Margolis, "Jumping the Gun on 'Hero' Goetz," *Chicago Tribune*, January 21, 1985. Margolis notes that "[g]eneral approval is far from wholehearted

support, much less unabashed hero-worship. The other half were either opposed or confused."

9. Rubin, *Busing and Backlash*, 146. The exact poll results were that 45 percent approved of Goetz's actions, while slightly *more*, 46 percent, disapproved. Rubin argues that "the media fed the belief that the public was of one mind in the case [and that] this gave permission for the kind of unrestrained combination of rage and glee that was so commonly heard, while it also helped to mute the opposition voices" (ibid).

10. Mary McGrory, "The Vigilante Discomfits Officialdom," *Washington Post*, January 13, 1985.

11. *WWWebster Dictionary*, s.v. "vigilante," http://www.m-w.com/ (accessed November 9, 2003).

12. "Why Surrender on the Subway?" editorial, *New York Times*, January 4, 1985.

13. "Gates, Guards, Guns, and Goetz." I rely upon a variety of media sources throughout this chapter, but my most important source for mainstream representations of the Goetz and Brawley cases is the *New York Times*. The New York tabloids, including the *Daily News* and the *Post*, have a higher readership in New York, but the *Times* has a much broader national audience and was arguably more important for determining how the cases will be understood and remembered nationwide. In addition, the tabloid coverage was generally not nearly as interesting as the coverage in the *Times*. Some of the tabloid language and headlines were much more flamboyant than those in the *Times*, but the articles were much more one-dimensional. The tabloids's portrayals closely paralleled those in the *Times*, but the racial stereotypes were even more exaggerated, and the articles tended to omit the few voices that complicated the picture in the *Times*.

14. McGrory, "The Vigilante Discomfits Officialdom."

15. Alfonse D'Amato, letter, *New York Times*, February 9, 1985.

16. There were no grounds for charging Goetz's victims, since not even Goetz claimed that they had actually tried to mug him. (His claim of self-defense was based only on his fear and assumption that they *would* do this.) Nevertheless, District Attorney Robert M. Morgenthau refused to grant any of Goetz's victims immunity before the first grand jury because of the possibility that they would be charged. Goetz's victims were thus unwilling to fully testify before the grand jury, which helps to explain the first grand jury's failure to indict Goetz for anything but illegal weapons possession. For a detailed discussion of the motivations for, and the effects of, Morgenthau's decision, see Rubin, *Quiet Rage*, 130–49.

17. George Fletcher argues that the press focused on Goetz's victims' backgrounds immediately after the shooting because they needed stories and had no information about Goetz himself (Fletcher, *A Crime*, 3–4). This claim may have some basis in fact, but it does not explain why the press continued to focus

on the victims' criminal records after Goetz's identity was revealed or why, as I discuss below, the media continued to circulate false information about sharpened screwdrivers.

18. Rubin, *Quiet Rage*, 6–9. Rubin notes that Goetz's victims claimed that the screwdrivers were used for breaking into video-game machines. This is clearly not a legal use, but it is a far cry from intentionally carrying a deadly weapon.

19. See, for example, the claim that "[o]ne of the Goetz victims has now been convicted of rape; public passions about the case have been stirred once more" ("A 'Reasonable Man' Named Goetz," editorial, *New York Times*, April 29, 1986).

20. Rubin argues that in general, Goetz's victims were dehumanized, whereas Goetz was rendered sympathetically early on. "Goetz becomes a many-faceted, complex human being; they are stereotypes. We know how tall he is, how slight his build, the color of his hair and eyes, what kind of glasses he wears, what clothes he prefers. All things that make him seem life-size, human. But the young men who were shot lie in their hospital beds, the reviled actors in this latest national morality play. We hear nothing about their physical characteristics, about the clothes they wear. . . . We have no idea whether one is better looking, more appealing than another; whether one is shy and another bold. . . . No one tells us, either, that they're all slight of build, more so than Bernie Goetz . . . Without these facts, our imaginations are left to work overtime, as we picture four huge blacks menacing this one small, lone white man" (Rubin, *Quiet Rage*, 56).

21. Quoted in Chambers, "Goetz Rejects Offers on Bail."

22. Joyce Purnick, "Ward Declares Goetz Didn't Shoot in Self-Defense," *New York Times*, February 22, 1985. Ward is far from a civil rights zealot. Just weeks earlier, he had taken issue with a Bronx grand jury that had indicted a police officer in the slaying of Eleanor Bumpurs—an elderly African American woman who was killed by a shotgun blast while the police were attempting to evict her from her apartment. The police claimed that during the course of the eviction, Bumpurs had lunged at them with a butcher knife and that Officer Stephen Sullivan had had no choice but to fire two blasts from his shotgun and kill her. Bumpurs's daughter later claimed that her mother had had arthritis and would have been incapable of acting as the officers described. She also claimed that the family had not received adequate notice of the eviction and that it made sense for her mother to want to defend herself when armed men broke down her door. Officer Sullivan was tried for manslaughter. His trial was accompanied by huge rallies of support by fellow police officers. Sullivan was acquitted of all criminal charges, but the City of New York eventually agreed to pay Bumpurs's family $200,000 to settle the resulting civil case. See Williams, "Spirit-Murdering the Messenger," 3–5, for a discussion of the legal issues surrounding the trial of Officer Sullivan.

23. Esther B. Fein, "Angry Citizens in Many Cities Supporting Goetz," *New York Times*, January 7, 1985.

24. "The Goetz Verdict," editorial, *New York Times*, April 24, 1996.

25. Adam Nossiter, "Race Is Dominant Theme as 2d Goetz Trial Begins," *New York Times*, April 12, 1996. As the headline implies, this article *does* suggest that race was relevant, but only in the second trial, where a predominately black jury found Goetz guilty.

26. "The Other Goetz Jury," editorial, *New York Times*, June 17, 1987.

27. Fletcher, "Justice for All, Twice."

28. John O'Connor, "Review/Television: Goetz Trial as Drama," *New York Times*, May 11, 1988.

29. Rubin, *Quiet Rage*, 197.

30. Ibid.

31. Ibid.

32. The attempt to construct "common sense" in such a way as to include the notion that there are valid reasons to fear young black men is, of course, nothing new. It goes back at least as far as lynching and stereotypes of black male bestiality, and it is an essential part of expansions of the criminal justice system over the past thirty years and the growth of what Angela Davis refers to as the "prison industrial complex." Davis argues that "[f]ear has always been an integral component of racism" and asks "whether and how the increasing fear of crime—this ideologically produced fear of crime—serves to render racism simultaneously more invisible and more virulent." Davis goes on to argue that the "figure of the 'criminal'—the racialized figure of the criminal—has come to represent the most menacing enemy of 'American society'" and that "the prison is the perfect site for the simultaneous production and concealment of racism" (Davis, "Race and Criminalization," 270–71).

33. "The Goetz Case in Black and White," editorial, *New York Times*, June 18, 1987. Ironically, the assumption that there is a reasonable basis for fear of black men tends to surface most explicitly in articles that are intended as correctives to racist stereotypes. For example, an article that opens with the claim that the "crude presumption—that blackness indicates criminality—haunts the trial of Bernard Goetz *[sic]*" goes on to note that "blacks commit robbery at a rate 10 times that of whites." The article notes that "the vast, innocent majority of blacks" suffer because of racist stereotypes but ultimately reinforces the image of a racial divide where only whites are victims when it asks "who . . . is more disadvantaged, the innocent white subjected to crime and fear of crime, or the innocent black forced into humiliating inconvenience and heightened risk of violence from mistaken acts of self defense?" The idea that blacks might have reason to fear forms of violence that are not the result of "mistaken acts of self defense" is noticeably absent here, as is the possibility that whites might, in fact, be criminals ("Fear of Blacks, Fear of Crime," editorial, *New York Times*, December 28, 1986).

34. Sydney H. Schanberg, "The Bernhard Goetz Mailbag," *New York Times*, January 19, 1985. The reference to "Hispanics" points to the fact that, like blacks, Latinos are often stereotyped as criminals. As Katheryn K. Russell notes, "La-

tinos . . . are viewed as stealthy and criminal. They, however, are not perceived as posing the same kind of criminal threat as Blacks. Latinos, like Asians, tend to be viewed as involved in intraracial crimes" (*The Color of Crime*, xiv). Coverage of William Masters's actions in California often referenced the Goetz case. Masters, a white man, confronted two young Latino men who were writing graffiti beneath a highway overpass in Los Angeles. He argued with them and shot them. He killed eighteen-year-old Cesar Arce and claimed that he was acting in self-defense, since his victims had threatened him with a screwdriver and threatened to rob him. The police accepted the claim of self-defense and initially refused to prosecute. Eventually, Masters, like Goetz, was convicted of weapons charges. He served a total of four days in jail and was sentenced to community service and three years of probation. His surviving victim, meanwhile, was sentenced to twenty days in jail, sixty days of graffiti removal, and three years probation for trespassing (Efrain Hernandez Jr., "Valley Man Who Killed Tagger Gets Probation," *Los Angeles Times*, November 9, 1998. Also see Seth Mydans, "A Shooter as Vigilante, and Avenging Angel," *New York Times*, February 10, 1995). Mydans's article notes that Masters was compared to Goetz and to the main character in the film *Falling Down* (1993), which it describes as a film about "a frustrated man [who] rampages through Los Angeles exacting vigilante justice." The article does not mention that—other than a Nazi storekeeper and his own wife—the main character, D-Fens, directs his vigilante violence against a host of racial stereotypes. Most important for the current discussion, D-Fens is menaced by Latino gang members, but when he gets his revenge by shooting one of them, the scene is played for laughs.

35. Rubin, *Quiet Rage*, 104–5.

36. Goetz sued William Kunstler and his publishers, Carol Communications, Inc., because Kunstler had claimed in his autobiography, *My Life as a Radical Lawyer*, that Goetz was, among other things, a racist. The suit was dismissed because Kunstler's book was seen as clearly stating an opinion rather than a matter of fact and because Goetz was a public figure. The court noted, though, that "defendants submit evidence that before the shooting, Goetz stated 'the only way we're going to clean up this street is to get rid of the spics and niggers.'" The court found this statement significant because "[i]n New York, truth is a complete defense to an action for defamation, regardless of the harm done by the statements." In other words, Goetz could not sue for being called a racist if he was in fact a racist (*Goetz v. Kunstler et al.*, 164 Misc. 2d 557; 625 N.Y.S. 2d 447 [1995] N.Y.).

37. " . . . You Have to Think in a Cold-Blooded Way," *New York Times*, April 30, 1987.

38. Quoted in Rubin, *Quiet Rage*, 182. This statement was ruled inadmissible in Goetz's criminal trial. Fletcher defends this decision by arguing that "[i]f this expression of prejudice was relevant at all, it was to demonstrate racial hostility as a motive for the shooting. Allowing the prosecution to bring in evidence of Goetz's racial bias would have invited the defense to produce witness after

witness to testify that Goetz had a sound attitude towards blacks. The trial would have turned into a farcical battle between character witnesses for and against the subway gunman" (Fletcher, *A Crime*, 204). Perhaps, but it would certainly have been possible to impose limits on the number of character witnesses each side could bring forward. In any event, the attempt to proceed as though race was simply irrelevant is at odds with the nonverbal reliance on race in the courtroom that I mention below, as well as with the ways people throughout the city and country understood the case.

39. Quoted in Fletcher, *A Crime*, 204.

40. Ibid., 129–30.

41. Ibid., 206.

42. Quoted in David E. Pitt, "Blacks See Goetz Verdict as Blow to Race Relations," *New York Times*, June 18, 1987.

43. *People v. Goetz*, 116 AD 2d 316; N.Y. (1986).

44. "If You Were Bernhard Goetz . . . ," editorial, *New York Times*, June 9, 1986.

45. *People v. Goetz*.

46. Russell, *The Color of Crime*, 3. Russell claims that there are "at least four related, though distinct, components" of white fear of blacks. These include "the fear of crime, the fear of losing jobs, the fear of cultural demise, and the fear of black revolt" (125). Russell argues that "while it may be commonplace for Whites to fear Blacks, it is not necessarily reasonable," and she notes that a great deal of white fear is based on sensationalistic media stories rather than on a realistic evaluation of the evidence about black crime (127). While I agree that white fear is not *justified* by the statistics on black crime (or on job loss, cultural demise, or the possibility of revolt), I would argue that there is a clear rationale for racist fears, a rationale that is based, as Russell notes, not on the facts but on an understanding and acceptance of prevalent representations of black men. Thus, when I claim that racist fears are reasonable, I mean only that there is a systematically expressed logic behind them. This is a very different sense of "reason" than James Q. Wilson had in mind when he claimed that black crime is responsible for white racism. It is Wilson's sense of the term that Russell is responding to in her critique.

47. Fletcher, *A Crime*, 206.

48. Quoted in Kennedy, *Race, Crime, and the Law*, 424.

49. This association is powerfully borne out not only in the media but also in the criminal justice system. As David Cole notes, "The per capita incarceration rate among blacks is seven times that among whites. African Americans make up about 12 percent of the general population, but more than half of the prison population. They serve longer sentences, have higher arrest and conviction rates, face higher bail amounts, and are more often the victims of police use of deadly force than white citizens. In 1995, one in three young black men between the ages of twenty and twenty-nine was imprisoned or on parole or probation. If incarceration rates continue their current trends, one in four

young black males born today will serve time in prison during his lifetime (meaning that he will be convicted and sentenced to more than one year of incarceration). Nationally, for every one black man who graduates from college, 100 are arrested" (*No Equal Justice*, 4). There are a number of explanations for these statistics, including the economic devastation facing many minority neighborhoods due to deindustrialization, unemployment, and discrimination in housing, education, and hiring (see Lipsitz, *The Possessive Investment in Whiteness*, 10). Added to this is a variety of systematic racial disparities within the criminal justice system itself, including, among many other things, a variety of forms of racial profiling and the fact that "a predominantly white Congress has mandated prison sentences for the possession and distribution of crack cocaine one hundred times more severe than the penalties for powder cocaine. African Americans comprise more than 90 percent of those found guilty of crack cocaine crimes, but only 20 percent of those found guilty of powder cocaine crimes" (Cole, *No Equal Justice*, 8). As Cole notes, "'Consent' searches, pretextual traffic stops, and 'quality of life' policing are all disproportionately used against black citizens" (8).

50. Harris, "Whiteness as Property," 279–80.

51. For an in-depth discussion of the ways the judicial system has legitimated racially based standards of suspicion, see Kennedy, *Race, Crime, and the Law*, 136–67. See also Cole, *No Equal Justice*, 16–62.

52. Lipsitz, *The Possessive Investment in Whiteness*.

53. Constance L. Hays, "Obsession in Boston: Mystery of Couple's Deaths," *New York Times*, January 13, 1990.

54. Steve Dougherty, "The Lost Boys; After a Mysterious Carjacking, Two Small Children Vanish," *People*, November 14, 1994, 50.

55. Rick Bragg, "Town Prays for Tots' Safe Return; Mom Yelled, 'I Love You All,' as Thief Sped Away with Kids," *Houston Chronicle*, October 28, 1994.

56. Margaret Carlson, "Presumed Innocent," *Time*, January 22, 1990, 10+.

57. Two witnesses claimed that Boston police officers had "coerced them to change or falsify their testimony to incriminate Bennett," and a subsequent grand jury investigation found that police engaged in "serious misconduct" but "did not commit criminal violations of federal civil rights statutes." An internal police investigation ultimately concluded that only one officer had violated department rules by swearing at one witness while questioning him. Activists and legal specialists denounced the police report as "flimsy and misleading" (John Ellement and Michael Grunwald, "SJC Tells Police to Share File on Stuart Case Probe," *Boston Globe*, April 6, 1995). Questions were also raised about the information that was relied upon in order to identify two other black men, Timothy Talbert and Alan Swanson, as suspects (Constance Hays, "Official's Handling of Suspects in Boston Killing Prompts Questions," *New York Times*, January 17, 1990).

58. James E. Alsbrook, "Stage Was Set for Lynching, but Cooler Heads Prevailed," *Michigan Citizen*, December 31, 1994.

59. Zamgba J. Brown, "Blacks Reviled by All Facets of Susan Smith Murder Case," *New York Amsterdam News*, November 12, 1994.

60. Robert Davis, "Search for 2 Tots Shifts to Hometown," *USA Today*, October 31, 1994.

61. Carlson, "Presumed Innocent."

62. Derrick Bell, "Stuart's Lie: An American Tradition," *New York Times*, January 14, 1990.

63. Quoted in Don Terry, "A Woman's False Accusation Pains Many Blacks," *New York Times*, November 6, 1994.

64. Cynthia Tucker, "Susan Smith's Bitter Legacy; Race: Prejudice Continues to Fuel Misconceptions about Crime, Criminals, and Victims," *Los Angeles Times*, November 11, 1994.

65. Terry, "A Woman's False Accusation Pains Many Blacks."

66. Charles Stuart was the beneficiary of an $82,000 policy from the Cahners Publishing Company and a $100,000 policy with the Travelers insurance company. The press investigated reports that the Prudential insurance company had issued a $480,000 check to Charles Stuart and that there was at least one other $100,000 policy on Carol Stuart that named her husband as the beneficiary (Fox Butterfield, "New Doubt as Jury Takes Up Stuart Case," *New York Times*, February 4, 1990).

67. See, for example, Fox Butterfield and Constance L. Hays, "A Boston Tragedy: The Stuart Case—A Special Case; Motive Remains a Mystery in Deaths That Haunt a City," *New York Times*, January 15, 1990. The Stuarts' class is an interesting issue in the coverage of the case. It is reasonable to suspect that even if they had not been wealthy, there would have still been a good deal of interest in the case, since Carol Stuart was pregnant when she was shot and because the alleged assailant was black. The portrayal of wealth in this case was, however, central to the portrayal of tragedy, as article after article painted a picture of an otherwise fairy-tale life shattered. It is also worth questioning whether Charles Stuart's motives and psychological makeup would have required such elaborate explanation had he been from a lower class. Again, the consistent concern was with how a man like Stuart could have fallen so far.

68. Halkias, "From Social Butterfly to Modern-Day Medea," notes that there is nothing more monstrous in the public eye than a mother killing her own children.

69. "Susan Smith; Despite a Speedy Conviction, She Remains a Frightening Enigma," *People*, December 25, 1995, 67. Smith was named one of the "25 Most Intriguing People" of 1995 by *People* magazine.

70. Elizabeth Gleick, "Sex, Betrayal, and Murder: As Her Trial Begins, Her Hometown Grapples with the Fallout from Susan Smith's Tangled Emotional History," *Time*, July 17, 1995, 32.

71. Tom Morganthau, Ginny Carrol, and Margaret O'Shea, "Will They Kill Susan Smith?" *Newsweek*, July 31, 1995, 65+.

72. In fact, her choice of scapegoat is occasionally seen as random and dis-

missed as part of a story that she made up "hysterically" (see Bill Hewitt, Gail Cameron Wescott, and Don Sider, "Tears of Hate, Tears of Pity: As Susan Smith's Family Vows Its Love, Her Hometown Is Split on the Punishment for Her Crime," *People*, March 13, 1995, 76). I am not questioning whether or not Smith was hysterical after killing her children. But it is important to note that dismissing her tale as the product of hysteria makes it impossible to analyze the structure of her narrative and her choice of villain.

Although Smith is faulted for having fooled the town and the nation, her various audiences are not generally blamed for having been fooled. Instead, as *Time* magazine claimed, "[W]e are honor bound to believe each tearful young mother" (David Van Biema, "Parents Who Kill," *Time*, November 14, 1994, 50). It is worth speculating whether this is always true. Would *Time*, for example, suggest that we automatically believe a black woman who claimed that a white man had kidnapped her children? The Tawana Brawley case, which I discuss below, provides an illuminating counterstudy.

73. Kenneth Snodgrass, "Yes, I Am Black, and No, I Am Not a Criminal," *Michigan Chronicle*, December 20, 1994.

74. Ibid.

75. Gilbert Price, "Black Man as 'Bogeyman' Seen in Alleged Kidnap," *Cleveland Call and Post*, November 10, 1994.

76. Brown, "Blacks Reviled by All Facets of Susan Smith Murder Case."

77. Alsbrook, "Stage Was Set for Lynching, but Cooler Heads Prevailed."

78. Abiola Sinclair, "But Why Did She Blame a Black Man?" *New York Amsterdam News*, November 12, 1994.

79. Because the question of who believes Brawley and why is so politically charged, I want to make my view clear from the outset. I am not sure what exactly happened to Brawley in November 1987. I do not believe key aspects of her story and am convinced that there is no credible evidence that Steven Pagones was one of her rapists. I am persuaded by some of the medical and eyewitness testimony that suggests Brawley fabricated at least parts of the story. Still, I am not satisfied with accounts of the case in the mainstream press, and I think that whatever did happen to Brawley has not received adequate attention. (As I argue in the text, even if her condition was entirely self-inflicted, it would still require further explanation.) The point of this section, however, is not to weigh in on the debate about whether or not Brawley was telling the truth but to analyze the media representations of the case in order to assess the ways that it plays into a process of national racial formation that draws upon racialized collective memories and common sense.

80. Brawley was ordered to pay $185,000, and her advisers were ordered to pay $345,000 (William Glaberson, "$345,000 Damages Awarded in Brawley Defamation Case," *New York Times*, July 30, 1998; "Tawana Brawley Ordered to Pay $185,000 for False Rape Claim," *Los Angeles Times*, October 10, 1998).

81. Quoted in McFadden et al., *Outrage*, 64. I refer to the charges as "Brawley's allegations" despite the fact that there is considerable debate as to whose

story this was. According to McFadden and his colleagues, a large part of the story that Brawley and her family would later repeat is actually the result of impromptu responses to inappropriately leading questions asked by a black police officer who was not trained to take witness testimony (ibid., 44–48). While this explanation of the genesis of Brawley's charges is plausible, I continue to refer to "Brawley's allegations" because long after that initial questioning, Brawley continued to assert that the narrative of her victimization was true.

82. Ester Iverem, "Bias Cases Fuel Anger of Blacks," *New York Times*, December 14, 1987.

83. McFadden et al., *Outrage*, 143–52. I discuss *Outrage* extensively throughout this section because it is written as an overview of the case by the *New York Times* reporters who were assigned to the story and therefore serves as the most condensed and comprehensive mainstream version of the "final word" on the story. *Outrage* was written before the Pagones case came to trial and before the newest round of press coverage of the Brawley events, but the basic narrative remains the same. There were some notable differences in coverage before and after this trial, and I discuss them later in the text. An earlier book on the case, *Unholy Alliances*, was written by Mike Taibbi and Anna Sims-Phillips, reporters who were assigned to cover the case for WCBS-TV in New York City, and presents a very similar narrative to the one in *Outrage*. Because *Unholy Alliances* was written so close to the events in question, however, there was less time for all of the relevant information to surface, and its tone is therefore less authoritative. More important, the fact that there are fewer authors and that they were never expected to examine the story in the same depth as the *Times* reporters went to means that the version of events in *Unholy Alliances* carries considerably less weight than does that in *Outrage*.

84. James Barron, "Grand Jury Found Nothing to Back Claim," *New York Times*, December 4, 1997.

85. Frank Bruni, "Brawley Adviser Testifies on His Motives," *New York Times*, December 9, 1997.

86. John Goldman, "Rape-Defamation Case Rubs New Salt in Old Wounds; Courts: Tensions about Tawana Brawley Rape Accusations, and from Subsequent Ruling That She Fabricated Story, May Stir Anew with Start of Civil Suit," *New York Times*, November 18, 1997.

87. Evelyn Nieves, "Our Towns: Remembering a Neighbor Called Brawley," *New York Times*, December 7, 1997.

88. Barron, "Grand Jury Found Nothing to Back Claim."

89. *Outrage* raises the possibility that King's light sentencing was due to "reverse racism" and asks, "Did the system regard black life as cheap and treat crimes against blacks less seriously?" (McFadden et al., *Outrage*, 94). The term "reverse racism" is somewhat jarring here, since regarding black life as cheaper than white life seems at first glance like plain, old-fashioned racism. Still, the more striking issue is the *Times* reporters' indictment of a legal system (note the use of colloquial phrasing: "The system" is used in an apparent effort to

position themselves as allies with readers who might not self-identify as part of that system) that (possibly) regards black life as cheaper than white. This charge seems highly ironic, given the almost complete lack of attention paid by the *Times* to the Brawley case in its earliest stages. (The irony emerges more fully when contrasting the coverage of Brawley's initial claims with the coverage of Susan Smith's or Charles Stuart's claims.) A *Newsday* article added to the portrayal of King by noting that he used his van to run a reporter and a photographer off the road and that he had "a seemingly perpetual scowl on his face" (Michael H. Cottman, "Ralph King: A Man Many Feared," *New York Newsday*, April 27, 1989).

90. McFadden et al., *Outrage*, 96–102.

91. Les Payne, "Tawana Made It Up," *New York Newsday*, April 27, 1989.

92. McFadden et al., *Outrage*, 385.

93. Ibid., 25.

94. Ibid., 82.

95. Ibid., 83.

96. Ibid., 163.

97. Ibid., 84.

98. Ibid.

99. Ibid.

100. Ibid., 162.

101. Ibid., 163.

102. Ibid., 107.

103. Ibid., 112.

104. Ibid., 113.

105. Ibid., 114.

106. William Glaberson, "The Case That Haunts Sharpton," *New York Times*, October 24, 1997.

107. It is interesting to note that the *New York Times* often refers to Brawley as a "woman" instead of as a "girl." This makes some sense in the coverage of Pagones's defamation suit, since by the time that case came to trial, Brawley was in her mid-twenties. Even then, though, the phrasing distracts from her youth at the time of her disappearance. (The *Times* notes, for example, that Pagones's suit was meant to challenge the claim that he was "in a gang of white men who abducted and raped Ms. Brawley, a black woman, in November 1987, when she was 15" [Frank Bruni, "Sharpton Reprimanded by Judge after Exchange in Brawley Trial," *New York Times*, February 12, 1998]). But in 1990, when the *Times* referred to the "hoax" perpetrated by "a 15-year-old black woman," the effect is clearly to deny her the presumption of innocence that is generally associated with youth (David J. Garrow, "An Excuse Became a Hoax and Kept Growing," September 9, 1990). This is made explicit in *Outrage*, which discusses Brawley's physical appearance by stating that "[i]nnocence and vulnerability ruled the childlike face, an illusion enhanced by tiny earrings and a little gold necklace" (McFadden et al., *Outrage*, 60). The dismissal of Brawley's

youthful innocence as "an illusion" makes it easier to link her to the chain of stereotypes of black women that I discuss later in the text.

108. Patricia Williams is one of the few commentators to address the lack of attention to the reasons for Brawley's allegations. She argues that to say that "'[s]he lied' is not an answer . . . even if she did it to herself. . . . Surely you don't have to belong to the church that chants 'We believe you Tawana' to think that the mere claim of gang rape from a 15-year-old is a pretty loud signal that something is wrong." Williams argues that the troubles in Brawley's background have to be understood in the context of a society that remains "so protective of minors in the civil sphere, yet otherwise leave[s] them so subject to violence and its consequences" and that is content to make blanket moral judgments about the value of young lives while increasingly subjecting them to the criminal justice system, as they are increasingly sentenced as adults (Patricia Williams, "Through a Glass Darkly," *The Nation*, January 12, 1998).

109. Thomas, "Strange Fruit," 385, quoting Joel Kovel.

110. Ibid.

111. Ibid., 386.

112. McFadden et al., *Outrage*, 98.

113. Ibid.

114. Ibid., 99.

115. Ibid., 101.

116. Ibid., 103.

117. Robert D. McFadden, "Brawley Case: Public's Conflicting Views," *New York Times*, October 29, 1988.

118. William Glaberson, "As Brawley Trial Plods, the Public Shrugs," *New York Times*, May 21, 1998.

119. Ibid.

120. *Outrage's* depictions of the Stewart and Bumpurs killings are interesting. It notes that "[n]eedless to say, the officers [who were accused of strangling Stewart] had been acquitted of any wrongdoing in his death" and says that "of course, the officer who fired the shotgun [that killed Bumpurs] was acquitted of all charges" (McFadden et al., *Outrage*, 33). The matter-of-fact tone for discussion of the fact that police who kill black people are let off the hook by the legal system is striking coming from *New York Times* reporters. This tone was noticeably absent when the paper was actually reporting on the killings of Stewart and Bumpurs. In this context, though, the goal is to set the stage for an explanation of why blacks could be so easily duped by a later hoax, and the claim that racist cops are taken for granted is central to this project. Provisional acceptance of earlier racism makes it easier to dismiss the allegations currently under consideration. (It is also possible that the book is just parroting what it perceived to be the voice of the black community at the time.)

121. McFadden et al., *Outrage*, 33–34.

122. Ibid., 58.

123. A version of this argument was used to explain black support for the

verdict in O. J. Simpson's criminal trial. Many commentators assumed that African Americans had different historically based understandings of the criminal justice system and that their understandings of the past tainted their ability to judge the specific evidence in this trial. Katheryn K. Russell notes that in real numbers, far more whites than blacks believed that Simpson was innocent (60 million whites thought he was not guilty, compared with 22 million blacks), but the media generally decided to report the racial "opinion divide" in terms of percentages rather than raw numbers. (Surveys showed that 70 percent of blacks believed that Simpson was innocent, while 70 percent of whites believed he was guilty.) She argues that "the constant media focus upon those Blacks who thought Simpson was innocent helped create the image that 'The Black Viewpoint' was slightly crazed and fanatical." Russell also notes that the mostly black jury in Simpson's criminal trial has been ridiculed throughout the mass media and that the verdict was seen as irrational. There was even a suggestion in the wake of the trial that jurors should be administered IQ tests before being seated on juries (Russell, *The Color of Crime*, 49–51). Alexander and Cornell, in "Dismissed or Banished?" discuss the jury's verdict at length, considering the various kinds of evidence that the jury had to weigh and the accusations that they simply would not convict Simpson because of his race. The authors conclude that the jury's verdict was, indeed, based upon a reasoned assessment of the available evidence.

124. Bob Herbert, "Protesting Too Much," *New York Times*, December 4, 1997. Another report in the *Times* about the rally made similar points, as it noted that "many people [in Bedford-Stuyvesant] discredited the grand jury report, though few were familiar with the results of that investigation." The implication was that Brawley's supporters felt no need to base their judgments on facts. Instead, the article quoted a "man who identified himself as Allah Forever, a member of the Muslim group, Nations of God and Earth," who "dictated that her story was not a hoax" (Jim Yardley, "10 Years Later, Brawley Saga Stirs Fewer Passions," *New York Times*, December 8, 1997). The facts that the article took the space to mention the man's name and refer to his affiliation at such length and that the *Times* has so consistently taken the position that Brawley's allegations were a hoax suggest that the *Times* sees black (or at least Black Muslim) "common sense" as radically different from its own.

125. Jim Sleeper, "New York Stories: The Racial Wages of Misogyny; Misogyny and the Tawana Brawley Case," *The New Republic*, September 10, 1990. Some commentators made similar speculations about the O. J. Simpson criminal trial, suggesting that some blacks who supported Simpson knew that he was guilty but thought that given the history of lynching, it was appropriate for a black man who murdered a white woman to get away with it.

126. Stanley Diamond, "Reversing Brawley; Tawana Brawley Case," *The Nation*, October 31, 1988.

127. A third possibility for apparent black support for Brawley that is mentioned occasionally is that there is a racial line that people toe out of fear. For

example, *Outrage* consistently refers to the regulars who spend time in a restaurant called Edgar's Food Shop in Brooklyn, where everyone seems to support Brawley. Throughout the book, we are given little hints that one of the regulars, Squire Bradfield, has doubts about Brawley's story but is afraid to express them. Finally, in the last pages of the book, long after the grand jury report has been released, when Brawley's most ardent supporters have left the restaurant, Bradfield "quietly" says, "I hate to go against my friends, but I really don't believe Tawana Brawley." We are told that when the authors asked him if "he'd ever told any of the Edgar's crowd how he felt," his reply was "quiet, almost bemused: 'What would have happened if I had?'" The question is answered for us: "The scorn, the ostracism, didn't have to be spelled out," and, as one of his friends says, "Don't say things like that. . . . believe me, one of them guys could seriously hurt you" (McFadden et al., *Outrage*, 396–97). An article published during Pagones's civil suit furthered the suggestion that there could be violent reprisals for people who expressed their doubts about Brawley's story. The article stated that a former neighbor of Brawley's was "worried about repercussions." The neighbor is quoted as saying having said, "You never know steps people will take. . . . I have four children and I have to protect them" (Nieves, "Our Towns").

128. Quoted in McFadden et al., *Outrage*, 193.

129. Quoted in ibid., 291.

130. Quoted in ibid., 271.

131. Ibid., 331.

132. Hall, "Gramsci's Relevance," 431. Hall follows Gramsci in arguing that "common sense" is socially constructed, though the nature and fact of that construction is generally hidden. It "represents itself as the 'traditional wisdom or truth of the ages,' but in fact, it is deeply a product of history." Hall does not discuss a specifically African American common sense, but he does argue that common sense is "fragmentary and contradictory," and always open to contest (431). The notion of common sense as historical construction resonates with Michel Foucault's idea of the "episteme," which is meant to describe the ways relations of power create categories of perception and validity. Again, the idea is to chart the "taken for granted" and to suggest that this field must be acknowledged in order for new narratives to be recognized or to make sense (Foucault, *Power/Knowledge*, 197). The idea, however, that there may be different epistemes for different groups is a departure from Foucault. See also Stuart Alan Clarke, who argues for the influence that "racial symbols, racial meanings, and racial understandings" have on common sense (Clarke, "Fear of a Black Planet," 37).

133. *Outrage* notes that "as the Brawley case gained prominence, blacks who rarely read the *Amsterdam News* or *The City Sun* found themselves doing so, and a large proportion of New York's blacks came to believe that black news outlets were their most reliable sources of information (McFadden et al. *Outrage*, 318).

134. For example, the *New York Amsterdam News* and the *New York Beacon* staunchly supported Brawley, while the *Los Angeles Sentinel* was generally much more skeptical.

135. This is one explanation given for African American support of Brawley in the *Times* (Glaberson, "The Case That Haunts Sharpton").

136. Walter Smith, "The Brawley Bunch Very Much Together: Pagones and Grady 'On the Run,'" *New York Beacon*, January 7, 1998.

137. James C. McIntosh, "Four Black Doctors Say Abrams' Report on Tawana Brawley Is 'Too Illicit to Fit' the Medical Record," *New York Amsterdam News*, November 2, 1998.

138. Ibid. Critiques of medical authority as racist might have had a particularly strong resonance within the collective memory of people who relied upon the African American press, given the amount of space that papers like the *Amsterdam News* have devoted to the abuses of science in the famous Tuskegee syphilis experiments.

139. James C. McIntosh, "The Medical Evidence: Attorney General Robert Abrams: Dr. Juggle Mr. Hide," *New York Amsterdam News*, January 21, 1998.

140. Ibid.

141. Walter Smith, "Brawley! Maddox! Mason! Sharpton! Victims of an Unsubstantiated Professional Cover-Up," *New York Beacon*, December 17, 1997.

142. Russell notes that "Black-on-White hoaxes make it easier for Whites to dismiss claims of White racism" (*The Color of Crime*, 82). Indeed, the Brawley case has been cited as a precedent to justify such skepticism about charges of racism in higher education. When the president of the Black Caucus at Penn State University received a death threat, David Warren Saxe, an associate professor of education at the university, said that the letter "could be a Tawana Brawley situation." In response to the death threat and a series of other racist incidents on campus, students protested and managed to get the administration to pledge to "establish a $900,000 Africana Studies Research Center and to add four faculty members to the department of African-American studies." Saxe expressed outrage at these concessions, saying that "[i]t was a threat that came in a letter, and we don't even know if it's real. In response, the university essentially gave those students a million dollars. I'm in shock" (Eric Hoover, "Death Threats and a Sit-In Divide Penn State," *Chronicle of Higher Education*, November 5, 2001).

4. The Hill–Thomas Hearings and the Meaning of a "High-Tech Lynching"

1. Davis and Wildman, "The Legacy of Doubt," 1367.

2. Ibid.

3. For the most comprehensive analysis of these changes, see Ross, "Sexual Harassment Law in the Aftermath of the Hill–Thomas Hearings." Perhaps the most notable change is that just a few weeks after the hearings, the Senate

passed the Civil Rights Act of 1991, which allows victims of sexual harassment to sue for monetary damages. Then-president George Herbert Bush had vetoed an earlier, weaker version of the bill and had threatened to veto this one. His unwillingness to carry through with this threat was probably due to a new need to be seen as concerned about sexual harassment.

4. Hill's allegations were certainly not, however, responsible for Thomas's victory. In fact, six senators who had indicated some degree of support for Thomas before Hill's testimony ultimately voted against his confirmation. It was therefore partly because of Hill's testimony that the vote in favor of Thomas's confirmation (52 to 48) represented the "narrowest confirmation victory in this century" (Resnick, "From the Senate Judiciary Committee to the Country Courthouse," 201).

5. As Jane Mayer and Jill Abramson note, Thomas's charge of racism put the Senate Democrats on the defensive and helped to ensure that they would avoid asking tough questions after that. The overnight polls, which showed that public opinion was solidly in Thomas's favor, have been attributed in large measure to Thomas's expression of outrage in general and to his use of the lynching metaphor specifically (Mayer and Abramson, *Strange Justice*, 304). Kimberlé Crenshaw notes that "Thomas's approval ratings in the black community skyrocketed from 54 percent to nearly 80 percent immediately following" the lynching speech (Crenshaw, "Whose Story Is It, Anyway?" 417). The use of the lynching metaphor was an effective method of firmly shifting the terms of both senatorial and media debate to address the question of Thomas's possible victimization rather than Hill's.

6. Thomas's use of the metaphor of lynching is, therefore, perhaps the most powerful illustration in this book of Burke's claim that "language develops by metaphorical extension, in borrowing words from the realm of the corporeal, visible, tangible and applying them by analogy to the realm of the incorporeal, invisible, intangible," since Thomas is borrowing language that was associated with the most tangible forms of physical punishment and applying it to highly abstract forms of legal and media scrutiny (Burke, *On Symbols and Society*, 250).

7. The idea that Thomas is aware of the difference between his own situation and actual lynchings fits well with Hayden White's comment that "[m]etaphor, whatever else it may be, is characterized by the assertion of a similarity between two objects offering themselves to perception as manifestly different. And the statement 'A = B' or 'A is B' signals the apprehension, in the person making it, of *both* a similarity *and* a difference between the two objects represented by the symbols on either side of the copula" (White, *Tropics of Discourse*, 252). The notion of a "high-tech lynching" clearly points simultaneously to similarities and differences between Thomas's plight and that of victims of "low-tech" lynchings.

8. Quoted in Miller, *The Complete Transcripts*, 18.

9. Clarence Thomas, quoted in ibid., 157.

10. However, as Jacqueline Goldsby notes, television *was* present in more than 60 percent of U.S. households when Emmet Till was murdered. Goldsby writes that this was a case where the categories of "high-" and "low-tech" lynchings "converged in a remarkable way. On the one hand, the manner of Till's death was brutal and simple: the boy was beaten, shot, and drowned by his assailants. On the other hand, the manner of publicity accorded to his murder and the trials that followed was decidedly advanced for its time. From August to November 1955, the newest techniques of television broadcasting and photojournalism primed the public's interest in the case, wiring images of the incident across the nation and around the globe" (Goldsby, "The High and Low Tech of It," 248).

11. Ibid.

12. Elizabeth Alexander's analysis of this piece argues that it tells "not simply the overt story of a lynching but the far more troubling story of the complicity of the photographer, who watches but does not witness, who perpetuates, who is then in effect part of the lynch mob." Alexander notes that "Williams invokes collective memory in three ways. She says that 'Life magazine showed this picture,' and then, 'WHO took this picture? Life answers Page 141—no credit.' *Life* magazine has become 'life' itself, underscoring the irony of a refusal to attribute agency or take responsibility for the crime committed. 'Could Hitler show photos of the Holocaust to keep the JEWS in line?' And then, with the line 'Can you be BLACK and look at this?' Williams forces her viewers to confront the idea of memory that would indelibly affect the very way that you see what is before you" (Alexander, "Can You Be BLACK and Look at This?" 110).

13. Brundage, *Lynching in the New South*, 18.

14. Ibid.

15. See, for example the NAACP's compilations of lynching statistics, which list many examples of lynchings where a primary goal was to inflict as much pain and suffering as possible before death. Genital mutilation was only one of many forms of torture that was used to this end (NAACP, *Thirty Years of Lynching*).

16. Foucault, *Discipline and Punish*, 7.

17. Ibid., 14.

18. However, given the amount of aid that local law enforcement officials often gave to lynch mobs (including handing the mob the prison keys) and the general failure to prosecute mob members, it is plausible to suggest that at their peak, lynchings were, de facto if not de jure, not entirely extralegal.

19. Foucault, *Discipline and Punish*, 14. Even so, Page duBois argues that Foucault's basic chronology ("torture" gives way to "punishment," which is in turn replaced by "discipline") is "resoutely Eurocentric" (duBois, *Torture and Truth*, 154). This is true not only because torture is still practiced in many postcolonial societies but also because that torture is, at least partly, often a First

World import (North Americans are responsible, for example, for "the training and funding of torturers" [155] throughout Latin America). Moreover, "it may be that the function of torture today, rather than the production of truth, is still one of spectacle . . . both for local and international consumption." The spectacle of "broken bodies and psyches" serves not only as an instrument of terrorism but also as a method of comforting "American liberals who rest contented in their view that such things could never happen here" (155).

And, of course, torture is not absent from the United States. As Patricia Williams notes, Thomas himself has played a role in attempting to legitimate certain forms of physical punishment that might include torture. Almost immediately upon taking his seat on the Supreme Court, Thomas wrote a dissenting opinion arguing that "a prisoner who was beaten and bloodied and had his teeth loosened by prison guards should have no constitutional claim under the Eighth Amendment proscription against cruel and unusual punishment, even where the violence was undue, wanton, and excessive" unless medical attention was essential. Williams notes that Sandra Day O'Connor wrote the majority opinion in the case, which "chided Thomas's use of this 'substantial injury' test, pointing out that if the cutoff for constitutional claims is whether someone requires medical attention, this sanctions forms of torture that stop just short of leaving marks on the body" (Williams, *The Rooster's Egg*, 134). American prison literature provides ample evidence that some forms of torture are widespread throughout our legal system; see, for example, Davis, *Angela Davis*. Also consider the 1992 class-action lawsuit against Pelican Bay Prison, which alleged that various forms of torture were endemic there, as reported by John Ross in "High-Tech Dungeon: A Class-Action Lawsuit Charges Pelican Bay Prison with Creating Cruel and Dehumanizing Conditions for 'the Worst of the Worst' of California Prisoners," *San Francisco Bay Guardian*, East Bay edition, September 23, 1992.

20. Foucault, *Discipline and Punish*, 34.
21. Ibid., 49.
22. Ibid., 16.
23. Ibid., 13.
24. Ibid., 19.
25. Ibid., 15.
26. Wiegman, *American Anatomies*, 94.
27. Brundage, *Lynching in the New South*, 5.
28. Wiegman, *American Anatomies*, 94.
29. Morrison, "Introduction," xii.
30. Ibid., xiv.
31. Mayer and Ambramson, *Strange Justice*, 20.
32. Ibid., 21.
33. Ibid., 213.
34. Ibid., 29.
35. Ibid., 30.

36. Ibid., 31.

37. Davis and Wildman, "The Legacy of Doubt," 1379.

38. Quoted in Mayer and Abramson, *Strange Justice*, 118.

39. Ibid., 32.

40. In a statement issued to explain its opposition to Thomas's nomination, the NAACP noted that after his confirmation to a second term at Equal Employment Opportunity Commission (EEOC), Thomas's position on affirmative action "was so hostile against the best interest of black people that the NAACP called for Judge Thomas's resignation at that time" (NAACP, "Questions and Answers on the NAACP's Position on Judge Clarence Thomas," 276).

41. Christina Accomando notes that Thomas was attempting "to reconstruct himself as the 'uppity' one, even though the main criticism he had previously faced was precisely that he had kowtowed to the old order of right-wing Reagan/Bush policies" (Accomando, "Representing Truth and Rewriting Womanhood," 272).

42. The edited volume on the Hill–Thomas hearings that was put out by *The Black Scholar* demonstrates that "the black community" was actually full of dissenting opinions and competing voices in regard to affirmative action as well as to the Hill–Thomas hearings themselves *(The Black Scholar, Court of Appeal)*. If my reading of what Thomas means by "kow-tow[ing] to an old order" is accurate, then the irony of viewing the civil rights establishment's position on affirmative action and old-fashioned lynch mobs' positions on white supremacy as equivalents is stunning.

43. Or as Wiegman argues, "[i]n leveling his charge against the proceedings as a 'high-tech lynching,' Thomas placed himself within that history [of lynching] and sought to distance himself from it, simultaneously defining his corporealization within the logic and social organization of white supremacy, while establishing abstraction (to be a justice) as the only route for undoing the history that the lynch metaphor recalled" (Wiegman, *American Anatomies*, 112).

44. Quoted in Phelps and Winternitz, *Capitol Games*, 10.

45. Mayer and Abramson, *Strange Justice*, 17.

46. Quoted in Phelps and Winternitz, *Capitol Games*, 16.

47. Mayer and Abramson, *Strange Justice*, 21.

48. Quoted in ibid., 21. The fact that Biden said nothing to this effect during the hearings is perhaps further evidence of his need to present himself as antiracist during the height of that political spectacle. Still, it is worth speculating about what might have happened if Biden or another Democratic senator had countered Thomas's lynching charge by saying that he was actually an affirmative action nominee.

49. Kimberlé Crenshaw argues that the decision in *Brown* "has been deployed to do the ideological work of legitimating racial hierarchy," since it is seen as marking a moment that constitutes a "fundamental break with white supremacy" (Crenshaw, "Color Blindness, History, and the Law," 281). Crenshaw goes on to argue that some of the most troubling tenets of *Plessy v. Ferguson*

(an earlier Supreme Court decision, which established the "separate but equal" doctrine and which is widely thought to have been displaced by *Brown*) maintain "viability and vitality" in contemporary jurisprudence.

50. There are countless mass media presentations of this evidence, but I think it is more interesting to refer to the collection of essays on the Hill–Thomas hearings edited by Toni Morrison and Claudia Brodsky Lacour: *Race-Ing Justice, En-Gendering Power*. In her introduction to that collection, Morrison writes that Thomas was to fill "a seat vacated by the single Supreme Court Justice who both belonged to and did represent the interests of that race [African-Americans]" (Morrison, "Introduction," xx). Morrison's reference to Marshall as the "single" justice with these concerns shows that she clearly accorded the Court little legitimacy, but Morrison's claim that Marshall represented "the interests of that race" shows that she has accepted some of the most important assumptions of this legitimating discourse. She presents "that race" and "its" interests monolithically. Marshall was, apparently, saying the right things; the only problem was that he was alone. The diversity of black interests is glossed over in this construction, and the assumption that those interests could be adequately represented by a better collection of justices is left unchallenged. That this sense of Marshall's representation of legitimacy is shared by many of the contributors to the collection is particularly interesting given that all of the essays contained in the book work to show the ways in which the hearings betrayed illegitimate uses and abuses of power.

51. Kendall Thomas argues that Clarence Thomas's stance on affirmative action and welfare and criticisms of civil rights leaders means that "the Senate's confirmation of Clarence Thomas must be understood as a decisive repudiation of that part of our constitutional past during which the Supreme Court was thought to be one of the few institutional arenas in this country in which African Americans and other people of color could successfully wage their struggles for racial justice" and that "in symbolic terms the Thomas nomination was a wholesale rejection of the moral legacy of the Civil Rights Movement, and the memory of the suffering and struggle that the story of that movement has come to represent in American political culture" (Thomas, "Strange Fruit," 382). For the most part, I agree with this statement. But the Bush administration's perceived need to appoint a member of a racial minority points to a continuing need to appear to have accepted the civil rights movement's insistence upon formal equality. Tokenism is problematic because of the ways in which it reduces the civil rights movement to a superficial message about racial inclusion and at the same time can be used to repudiate the movement's larger goals.

52. Alexander, "'She's No Lady, She's a Nigger,'" 6.

53. Ibid., 7.

54. Jewell, *From Mammy to Miss America and Beyond*, 37.

55. Ibid., 35.

56. Thomas and his brother were taken away from Pin Point by their grandfather Myers Anderson when Thomas was six years old. They lived in something

approaching a middle-class household, where they had the time to focus on their academic work in a private parochial school, whereas Emma Mae was left behind in Pin Point, where she had to perform difficult manual labor before and after her days in a segregated public school. By the time she was offered a chance to attend a better school, she had already fallen too far behind academically (Mayer and Abramson, *Strange Justice*, 40).

57. Lubiano, "Black Ladies, Welfare Queens, and State Minstrels," 338.

58. Ibid., 363.

59. Ibid., 335.

60. Thomas was, of course, not the first to discover the political advantages of attacking "welfare dependency" or "welfare queens." Lubiano discusses a variety of ways this figure has been invoked since the Moynihan Report came out. Importantly, as increasing numbers of states are slashing welfare benefits, Lubiano notes that "politicians gain credibility for themselves by coming out against the notion of the United States as a welfare state" (ibid.).

61. Senator Joseph Biden, quoted in Miller, *The Complete Transcripts*, 323. Biden is summing up the charges made by Berry, Senator Alan Simpson, and others against Hill; he is not making the allegation that this characterization of Hill is accurate.

62. Phyllis Berry-Myers, quoted in "Law Professor Accuses Thomas of Sexual Harassment in 1980's," *New York Times*, October 7, 1991, national edition. See also Berry's testimony in Miller, *The Complete Transcripts*, 311.

63. Quoted in Mayer and Abramson, *Strange Justice*, 284.

64. Quoted in Miller, *The Complete Transcripts*, 428.

65. Senator Biden was an important exception in this regard. His questions to Doggett were very difficult, and at one point he even stated that Doggett's belief that Hill was fantasizing about him seemed to be "a true leap in faith or ego, one of the two" (quoted in ibid., 433).

66. Quoted in ibid., 62.

67. See Mayer and Abramson, *Strange Justice*, 306–9.

68. William Safire, "The Plot to Savage Thomas," *New York Times*, October 12, 1993, national edition.

69. Ellen Goodman, "Honk If You Believe Anita," *Boston Globe*, October 17, 1991: 17.

70. Quoted in Miller, *The Complete Transcripts*, 331.

71. Wilkins, "Presumed Crazy."

72. Quoted in Fitzgerald, "Science v. Myth."

73. Wilkins, "Presumed Crazy," 1521.

74. Ibid.

75. Usher, *Women's Madness*.

76. American Psychiatric Association, *Diagnostic and Statistical Manual of Mental Disorders*, 297.

77. Fitzgerald, "Science v. Myth," 1408.

78. Mayer and Abramson argue that "[i]n all probability, the leak was really

several leaks that came from a combination of people, all of whom, to varying degrees, had firsthand knowledge of her story," but they go on to note that an investigation ultimately proved that the idea that the FBI report itself had been leaked, in violation of federal law, was a false issue: "[N]o FBI reports on the matter ever did leak, and no FBI documents were ever the basis of any news report" (Mayer and Abramson, *Strange Justice*, 255).

79. Davis and Wildman, "The Legacy of Doubt," 1370.

80. Maureen Dowd, "The Thomas Nomination: 7 Congresswomen March to Senate to Demand Delay in Thomas Vote," *New York Times*, October 9, 1991, national edition.

81. See Resnick, "Hearing Women," 1333.

82. See Chemerinsky, "October Tragedy," 1510. Chemerinsky points out that the mass media virtually ignored the fact that the hearings into Hill's allegations were held at Thomas's request and argues that this omission made it much easier for Thomas's later calls against a "high-tech lynching" to go uncontested, since old-fashioned lynchings were never held at their victim's behest.

83. Representative Nancy Pelosi's argument about the need for a delay provides an interesting rationale for this political pressure. She stated that "[t]hese allegations may not be true. But women in America have to speak up for themselves and say we want to remove all doubt that the person who goes to the Supreme Court has unquestioned support for women" (quoted in R. W. Apple Jr., "A Pause to Reconsider," *New York Times*, October 9, 1991, national edition). Pelosi's sentiment reflects the opinion of many commentators throughout the mass media at the time of the hearings, despite the fact that it came long after Thomas had famously claimed "not to recall" ever having discussed *Roe v. Wade*. Well before Hill took the stand, the hearings were therefore already about memory and women's rights. The suggestion that a hearing of Hill's allegations could remove any doubt that Thomas had "unquestioned support for women" can therefore be read as an attempt to erase earlier parts of the hearings from collective memory. (Aside from the controversy about *Roe v. Wade*, there had been considerable debate over the facts that Thomas had called a right-to-life publication "splendid" and, as I have discussed, had attacked his sister for "welfare dependency.")

84. Apple, "A Pause to Reconsider."

85. Resnick, "Hearing Women," 1334.

86. Apple, "A Pause to Reconsider." Of course, the same could be said of the *Times* itself.

87. Quoted in ibid.

88. Rhode, "Sexual Harassment," 1459.

89. Quoted in "Judge Clarence Thomas: My Name Has Been Harmed," *New York Times*, October 12, 1991, national edition. While Senator Hatch's ignorance about sexual harassment might be attributed to the fact that sexual harassment law is relatively recent, Thomas's apparent ignorance (his response to Hatch's com-

ment was "I agree") is more difficult to account for, given his previous role as the head of the EEOC, the organization in charge of sexual harassment issues.

90. For a good overview of this literature, see Fitzgerald, "Science v. Myth," and Ross, "Sexual Harassment Law."

91. Quoted in Miller, *The Complete Transcripts*, 126.

92. Lawrence, "'The Message of the Verdict,'" 110.

93. See, for example, Wells's account of Mrs. J. C. Underwood in Ohio, who initiated a sexual encounter with a black man and then charged him with rape partly because she was afraid of the repercussions if she were to have a black child. Because this incident happened in Ohio, the accused man, William Offett, was not lynched, but he was sentenced to fifteen years in prison. Wells writes that "[t]here have been many such cases throughout the South, with the difference that the Southern white men in insensate fury wreak their vengeance without intervention of law upon the Negro who consorts with their women" (Wells, *A Red Record*, 60).

94. Davis, *Women, Race, and Class*, 177.

95. Ibid., 179.

96. Ibid., 182.

97. Brown, "Imaging Lynching," 105.

98. Jordan, "The Power of False Racial Memory and the Metaphor of Lynching," 41.

99. Ibid.

100. hooks, *Black Looks*, 81.

101. For example, Eleanor Holmes Norton claimed that "race trumped sex" (Norton, "And the Language Was Race," 44). Adrienne Davis and Stephanie Wildman claim that "these two images, gender oppression and sexuality, were vying for primacy when Justice Thomas reintroduced the symbol of race, which then became the axis around which all subsequent discourse revolved" ("The Legacy of Doubt," 1380).

102. Jordan, "The Power of False Racial Memory," 40.

103. Brown, "Imaging Lynching," 108.

104. Walker, "Advancing Luna—and Ida B. Wells," 93–94.

105. Even so, Walker is unwilling to just accept the mandate for silence, as the narrator sees this as "virtually useless advice to give a writer" (ibid., 94). Of course, there *was* an important white woman in the hearings: Thomas's wife, Virginia Lamp Thomas. Resnick argues that one aspect of the lynching metaphor was that "Thomas dared the senators to 'lynch' him for being married to a white woman" (Resnick, "From the Senate Judiciary Committee," 40). Kendal Thomas notes, however, that "a tacit consensus very quickly emerged that the public discourse would say as little as possible about the obvious fact that the judge's wife was a woman, to use her husband's phrase, of 'the lighter complexion'" (Thomas, "Strange Fruit," 374).

106. Davis, "Clarence Thomas as Lynching Victim," 78.

107. Jordan, *The Power of False Racial Memory*, 40.

108. Hill, "Moon's Paradox," 182.

109. Ibid., 185.

110. Freedman, "The Manipulation of History," 1362–67.

111. Beard, "Of Metaphors and Meaning," 196.

112. Carby, quoted in Harris, *Exorcising Blackness*, 9.

113. Brown, "Imaging Lynching," 111.

114. Ibid., 102.

115. As Michelle Wallace, in *Black Macho and the Myth of the Superwoman*, bell hooks, in *Ain't I a Woman*, and other black feminist theorists have argued, much the same can be said of other antiracist struggles, including the black power and civil rights movements. I am not arguing, however, that the anti-lynching movement was responsible for Hill's plight. Instead, I am reiterating my claim that the movement was far more successful in challenging stereo-types of black men than those of black women, and I am suggesting that this fact has helped to shape the possibilities for, and limitations of, contemporary antiracist struggles.

116. The title of Nell Irvin Painter's short article about the hearings, "Who Was Lynched?" is a provocative way of touching upon this question. Nell Irvin Painter, "Who Was Lynched?" *The Nation*, November 11, 1991, 577.

117. Hill also challenges Thomas's use of the lynching metaphor directly. She notes that Thomas was "accusing the Democratic senators on the commit-tee, in a thinly cloaked fashion, of a peculiar form of racism aimed only at con-servative blacks—a fusion of racial and ideological bias of which Thomas was now the target." She goes on to say that she "could not help but see the irony in his claim of racism. . . . he had always chosen, both publicly and privately, to belittle those who saw racism as an obstacle. . . . Yet, now having met an ob-stacle to his *own* dream, he blamed racism" (Hill, *Speaking Truth to Power*).

118. Ibid., 16.

119. Ibid., 24. Figure 4 shows a postcard of the lynching of Laura Nelson.

120. Ibid.

121. As I noted in the Introduction, this is the Popular Memory Group's phrase (Popular Memory Group, "Popular Memory," 229).

Conclusion

1. Malik Gaines, "Starting Down Hate," *The Advocate*, January 16, 2001.

2. George Santayana, "Reason in Common Sense," in *The Life of Reason*, as quoted in *The Columbia World of Quotations*, as listed on Bartleby.com, http://bartleby.com/66/29/48129.html (accessed November 9, 2003).

3. Roberta Smith, "Critic's Notebook: An Ugly Legacy Lives On, Its Glare Unsoftened by Age," *New York Times*, January 13, 2000.

4. Roane Carey, "Horror Show," *In These Times*, April 17, 2000.

5. *Without Sanctuary* Web site, Forum page, http://www.musarium.com/withoutsanctuary/main.html

6. Zelizer, *Remembering to Forget*, 15.

7. Brent Staples makes a similar point, writing that with "these horrendous pictures loose in the culture, the ultimate effect could easily be to normalize images that are in fact horrible" (Brent Staples, "Editorial Observer; The Perils of Growing Comfortable with Evil," *New York Times*, April 9, 2000).

8. Zelizer, *Remembering to Forget*, 212.

9. Editorial Desk, "Death by Lynching," *New York Times*, March 16, 2000.

10. Denise Gaines-Edmond, *Without Sanctuary* Web site, Forum page, http://www.musarium.com/withoutsanctuary/main.html, December 20, 2000. Some visitors to the Web site use pseudonyms, and others use only partial names, so it is impossible to verify the identities of anyone posting to the logs. In the text that follows, I refer to authors as they have identified themselves.

11. D. Pennick, *Without Sanctuary* Web site, Forum page, http://www.musarium.com/withoutsanctuary/main.html, December 19, 2000.

12. Bob Jennings, *Without Sanctuary* Web site, Forum page, http://www.musarium.com/withoutsanctuary/main.html, December 15, 2001. "Jennings" writes in part that "I very much enjoyed the pictures. I had several friends over, we ordered pizza and looked at your site for hours."

13. Nathan Bedford Forrest, *Without Sanctuary* Web site, Forum page, http://www.musarium.com/withoutsanctuary/main.html, November 20, 2001.

14. Hall, "Notes on Deconstructing 'the Popular,'" 237.

15. Beard, "Of Metaphors and Meaning."

16. *Do the Right Thing* in particular transforms the lynching metaphor in truly original ways, as its mob of black spectators of a lynching works to put white audiences on notice that racist police brutality will no longer be tolerated. Conversely, films like *A Time to Kill* and *Just Cause* work to sever the lynching metaphor from its historical ties and to render the categories not only of lynching but also of racism devoid of any clear logic or meaning.

17. Omi and Winant intended "racial formation" to be a term that was attentive to the historical transformations of racial categories, but they said fairly little about the ways our sense of the past helps to structure our social identities in the present. By examining racial formation and collective memory together, it is possible to provide a richer sense of the ways racial categories and collective identities are constructed over time. As my analysis of the Tawana Brawley case suggests, our historical understandings of race have profound implications for the ways we view our contemporary surroundings.

18. Lubiano, "Black Ladies, Welfare Queens, and State Minstrels," 347.

19. For a discussion of the controversy surrounding Olabisi's *To Protect and Serve*, see Paul Von Blum, "The Black Panther Mural in LA," *Z Magazine*, July–August 1995, http://zena.secureforum.com/Znet/zmag/articles/july95vonblum.htm.

20. Richard A. Serrano, "Judge Restricts McVeigh Penalty Case Testimony," *Los Angeles Times*, June 4, 1997.

21. "Panel Delays Vote on Pickering, GOP Senator Says Opposition on Left is 'Lynching' Jurist," *Boston Globe*, March 8, 2002. Pickering's record on race (he drafted a memo to suggest ways to strengthen Mississippi's ban on interracial marriage, he has worked to undermine Voting Rights Act protections, and he has even opposed the one-person, one-vote standard) is perhaps why Hatch was relatively quick to abandon the lynching metaphor once commentators pointed out that lynching was intended as a method to secure white supremacy.

22. See, for example, Richard Cohen, "Legitimizing Hate," *Washington Post*, October 15, 1998; "A Tool against Terrorism; Georgia Needs Laws to Fight Hate Crimes," editorial, *Atlanta Constitution*, October 19, 1998; and Jack Thomas, "Powerful Cartoon Proved Open to Misinterpretation," *Boston Globe*, November 2, 1998. Cohen's article discusses lynchings of black men as a response to a racist political climate and argues that Shepard's murder should similarly be understood as a response to antigay hate speech. The editorial in the *Atlanta Constitution* argues that lynching, gay-bashing, and other hate crimes are "crimes that use terror to limit the freedoms of people based on their race, religion, national origin or sexual orientation." Thomas's article discusses an editorial cartoon by Dan Wasserman that was intended to "depict Shepard in a martyr-like pose and to suggest a lynching." The cartoon was variously interpreted, either as a powerful critique of heterosexism or as a stunning endorsement of hate, and to the artist's horror, it was enlisted for antigay purposes. As the article notes, "One factory-worker told Wasserman gay bashers had pasted the cartoon to their lunch boxes." Thomas quotes Wasserman as saying that "maybe people are so accustomed to expressions of homophobia that it was conceivable to them that they could find it in a cartoon by me in the *Globe*. When I saw people picketing Shepard's funeral with signs that said, 'God Hates Fags,' it was like a lynch mob. And it makes me realize this is an even bigger problem than I had imagined."

23. References to lynching in the cases of Bork and Pickering tend to be passing one-liners meant to express outrage at partisan intrusions into what are otherwise ostensibly pristine political processes. The federal judge in the Oklahoma City bombing case was referring to mob influence on legal proceedings in cases like that of the Scottsboro Nine, but he was divorcing lynching from any consideration of race. Many of the lynching references to the murder of Matthew Shepard were more sustained and addressed the role of lynching as terrorism, and at the same time, they made explicit parallels between hate crimes based on race and those based on sexual orientation.

24. See note 55 in chapter 2.

25. See Douglas Martin, "About New York: Racial Hatred through Fresh Eyes," *New York Times*, February 15, 1992, for a good summary of the events surrounding Hawkins's murder. In 1989, a young white woman in the neighborhood of Bensonhurst in Brooklyn told a friend that she had invited a group of blacks and Latinos to her birthday party. To prepare for what was seen as an unacceptable breach of turf, her friend organized a group of a dozen men,

armed with baseball bats and at least one gun, to meet the visitors. The woman had never issued the invitations, but four black teenagers were already walking through the neighborhood in order to inspect a car that was for sale. When they passed the mob of white men, they became targets, and one of the black teenagers, Yusef K. Hawkins, was shot dead. In 1991, then-mayor David Dinkins proclaimed the anniversary of the killing "Yusef Hawkins Day," while Hawkins's father, Moses Stewart, announced that "I began to feel Yusef is no longer my son. Yusuf has grown to be a movement for racial justice, for freedom and equality in this country" (quoted in Aldina Vazo, "Yusuf Hawkins Day Proclaimed," *Newsday*, August 23, 1991). Indeed, Hawkins's murder inspired scores of protests and has become one of the most widely recognized examples of contemporary racism. Spike Lee chose to open *Jungle Fever*, his film about interracial romance set in Harlem and Bensonhurst, with a still photograph of Hawkins.

Christopher Wilson, who is black, was vacationing in Florida in 1993 when he was robbed by three white men before being taken to a field, doused with gasoline, and set on fire. One of his assailants said, "You nigger boy, you Black bastard, you have to die. One more to go," and someone left a note saying, "One less nigger. One more to go. KKK." Wilson was seriously burned over more than 40 percent of his body. Local authorities refused to classify the case as a hate crime or a racially motivated assault until the FBI became involved (Larry Rohter, "Trial Begins for 2 Accused of Setting Man Ablaze," *New York Times*, August 23, 1993).

In June 1998, in Jasper, Texas, three white men chained a black man named James Byrd Jr. to the back of a pickup truck and dragged him two miles until he was dead and his body was mutilated. The prosecution noted that one of the murderers, John William King, has a tattoo that depicts the lynching of a black man. The prosecution also argued that the killing was intended as a publicity stunt to gather attention for a white supremacist organization that King was planning to found. All three of the men were convicted of capital murder. King and Russell Brewer were sentenced to death, while Shawn Berry received a life sentence (see Michael Graczyk, "Racist Tatoos Worn by Accused," *London Independent*, February 19, 1999; see also Lauren Wexler, "A Community Divided; after Texas Murder, Town Barely Budges Status Quo," *Atlanta Journal and Constitution*, March 10, 2002).

26. In February 1999 in New York City, police officers fired forty-one bullets at an unarmed West African immigrant named Amadou Diallo. Diallo was hit nineteen times and was killed. In the wake of the shooting, there was a tremendous resurgence of protest, including massive demonstrations and civil disobedience targeting police brutality. While Al Sharpton was a major force behind these protests, the movement was broader than any movement directed against police violence in recent memory. Former New York mayor David Dinkins was among those arrested, and former mayor Ed Koch had planned on being arrested, but ill health prevented him from participating in

civil disobedience. The officers were acquitted in a criminal trial in February 2000. In March 2002, a judge ordered the city to give lawyers for Diallo's family hundreds of pages of documents in preparation for the family's civil suit against the city (Ron Howell, "City Ordered to Provide Diallo Files," *Newsday*, March 16, 2002).

27. One of the only good things to have come out of the September 11 attacks, it has been said, is a sense of national unity. Even a cursory examination of the contemporary social landscape, however, reveals that unity to be fairly superficial. The attacks from abroad have, unfortunately, been paralleled by a rise in anti-Arab hate crimes that should be seen as their own form of domestic terrorism. On November 20, 2001, the American-Arab Anti-Discrimination Committee (ADC) released a fact sheet, "The Condition of Arab Americans Post 9/11" (http://www.adc.org). By that date, only two months after the attacks, the ADC had documented 520 violent incidents directed against Arab Americans "or those perceived to be such" since September 11. These incidents include assault, arson, and at least six murders. Rates of anti-Arab violence have declined in subsequent months, but they remain alarmingly high. Discussions of unity serve to gloss over these murderously violent social divisions.

28. Marita Sturken writes that the "trope of America's losing its innocence at a precise moment is a well-worn one, a concept reiterated with Pearl Harbor, the Vietnam War, the Watergate scandal, the 1995 Oklahoma City bombing, and other events" (Sturken, *Tangled Memories*, 29).

Works Cited

Archival Collections
Association of Southern Women for the Prevention of Lynching (ASWPL) Papers Microfilm.
Commission on Interracial Cooperation (CIC) Papers. Microfilm.
National Association for the Advancement of Colored People (NAACP) Anti-lynching Publicity and Investigative Papers. Microfilm.

U.S. Government Documents
U.S. Congress. *Congressional Record*. 67th Cong., 2d sess., December 1921 and January 1922.
———. House. *Antilynching*. Hearings before a Subcommittee of the Committee on the Judiciary, on H.R. 41, 80th Cong., 2d sess., 1948.
———. House. *Crime of Lynching*. Hearings before the Committee on the Judiciary, on H.R. 259, 4123, and 11873, 66th Cong., 2d sess., January 29, 1920.
———. House. *Crime of Lynching*. Hearings before a Subcommittee of the Committee on the Judiciary, on H.R. 801, 76th Cong., 3d sess., 1940.
———. Senate. *Punishment for the Crime of Lynching*. Hearings before a Subcommittee of the Committee on the Judiciary, on S. 1978, 73rd Cong., 2d sess., February 20–21, 1934.
———. Senate. *To Prevent and Punish the Crime of Lynching*. Hearings before a Subcommittee of the Committee on the Judiciary, on S. 121, 69th Cong., 1st sess., February 16, 1926.

Articles and Books
Accomando, Christina. "Representing Truth and Rewriting Womanhood: Constructions of Race and Gender in Discourses of U.S. Slavery." Ph.D. diss., San Diego: University of California, 1994.
Alexander, Adele Logan. "'She's No Lady, She's a Nigger': Abuses, Stereotypes, and Realities from the Middle Passage to Capitol (and Anita) Hill." In *Race, Gender, and Power in America: The Legacy of the Hill–Thomas Hearings*, edited by Anita Faye Hill and Emma Coleman Jordan, 3–25. New York: Oxford University Press, 1995.
Alexander, Elizabeth. "'Can You be BLACK and Look at This?': Reading the Rodney King Video(s)." In *The Black Male: Representations of Masculinity in Contemporary American Art*, edited by Thelma Golden, 91–110. New York: Whitney Museum of American Art, 1994.
Alexander, Nikol G., and Drucilla Cornell. "Dismissed or Banished? A Testament to the Reasonableness of the Simpson Jury." In *Birth of a Nation 'Hood:*

Gaze, Script, and Spectacle in the O. J. Simpson Case, edited by Toni Morrison and Claudia Brodsky Lacour, 57–96. New York: Pantheon Books, 1997.

Allen, James. *Without Sanctuary: Lynching Photography in America.* Santa Fe, N.M.: Twin Palms, 2000.

Alonso, Ana Maria. "Gender, Power, and Historical Memory: Discourses of *Serrano* Resistance." In *Feminists Theorize the Political,* edited by Judith Butler and Joan Scott, 404–25. New York: Routledge, 1992.

American Psychiatric Association. *Diagnostic and Statistical Manual of Mental Disorders.* 4th ed. Washington, D.C.: American Psychiatric Association, 1994.

Ames, Jessie Daniel. "Editorial Treatment of Lynchings." *The Public Opinion Quarterly,* January 1938: 77–85.

Anderson, Benedict. *Imagined Communities.* New York: Verso, 1991.

Aptheker, Bettina, ed. *Lynching and Rape: An Exchange of Views.* Los Angeles and Berkeley: University of California Press, 1977.

Armour, Jody D. "Race Ipsa Loquitor: Of Reasonable Racists, Intelligent Bayesians, and Involuntary Negrophobes." *Stanford Law Review* 46 (1994): 781.

Atkinson Miller, Kathleen. "The Ladies and the Lynchers: A Look at the Association of Southern Women for the Prevention of Lynching." *Southern Studies,* Fall and Winter 1991: 261–80.

Beard, Linda Susan. "Of Metaphors and Meaning: Language, Ways of Knowing, Memory Holes, and a Politic Recall." In *African American Women Speak Out on Anita Hill–Clarence Thomas,* edited by Geneva Smitherman, 182–200. Detroit: Wayne State University Press, 1995.

Bederman, Gail. *Manliness and Civilization: A Cultural History of Gender and Race in the United States, 1880–1917.* Chicago: University of Chicago Press, 1995.

Benedict, Helen. *Virgin or Vamp: How the Press Covers Sex Crimes.* New York: Oxford University Press, 1992.

Benford, Robert, and Scott Hunt. "Dramaturgy and Social Movements: The Social Construction and Communication of Power." *Sociological Inquiry,* February 1992: 35–55.

Bernadi, Daniel, ed. *The Birth of Whiteness: Race and the Emergence of U.S. Cinema.* New Brunswick, N.J.: Rutgers University Press, 1996.

Bhabha, Homi K. "A Good Judge of Character: Men, Metaphors, and the Common Culture." In *Race-Ing Justice, En-Gendering Power: Essays on Anita Hill, Clarence Thomas, and the Construction of Social Reality,* edited by Toni Morrison, 232–50. New York: Pantheon Books, 1992.

———. "The Other Question: The Stereotype and Colonial Discourse." In *Out There: Marginalization and Contemporary Cultures,* edited by Russell Ferguson, Martha Gever, Trinh T. Minh-ha, and Cornell West, 71–88. Cambridge: MIT Press, 1990.

The Black Scholar, ed. *Court of Appeal: The Black Community Speaks Out on the Racial and Sexual Politics of Thomas vs. Hill.* New York: Ballantine Books, 1992.

Blee, Kathleen M. *Women of the Klan: Racism and Gender in the 1920s.* Berkeley and Los Angeles: University of California Press, 1991.

Bogle, Donald. 1992. *Toms, Coons, Mulattoes, Mammies, and Bucks.* New York: Continuum, 1992.

Bowser, Pearl, and Louise Spence. "Identity and Betrayal: *The Symbol of the Unconquered* and Oscar Micheaux's 'Biographical Legend.'" In *The Birth of Whiteness: Race and the Emergence of U.S. Cinema,* edited by Daniel Bernardi, 56–80. New Brunswick, N.J.: Rutgers University Press, 1996.

———. *Writing Himself into History: Oscar Micheaux, His Silent Films, and His Audiences.* New Brunswick, N.J.: Rutgers University Press, 2000.

Brown, Elsa Barkley. "Imaging Lynching: African American Women, Communities of Struggle, and Collective Memory." In *African American Women Speak Out on Anita Hill–Clarence Thomas,* edited by Geneva Smitherman, 100–134. Detroit: Wayne State University Press, 1995.

Brown, Mary Jane. *Eradicating This Evil: Women in the American Anti-Lynching Movement, 1892–1940.* New York: Garland Publishing, 2000.

Brundage, W. Fitzhugh. "Black Resistance and White Violence in the American South, 1880–1940." In *Under Sentence of Death: Lynching in the South,* edited by W. Fitzhugh Brundage, 271–91. Chapel Hill: University of North Carolina Press, 1997.

———. *Lynching in the New South: Georgia and Virginia, 1880–1930.* Chicago: University of Illinois Press, 1993.

———, ed. *Under Sentence of Death: Lynching in the South.* Chapel Hill: University of North Carolina Press, 1997.

Burke, Kenneth. *On Symbols and Society.* Edited by Joseph R. Gusfield. Chicago: University of Chicago Press, 1989.

Butters, Gerald R., Jr. *Black Manhood on the Silent Screen.* Lawrence: University Press of Kansas, 2002.

Campbell, Christopher P. *Race, Myth, and the News.* Thousand Oaks, Calif.: Sage Publications, 1995.

Carby, Hazel V. "'On the Threshold of Woman's Era': Lynching, Empire, and Sexuality in Black Feminist Theory." In *"Race," Writing, and Difference,* edited by Henry Louis Gates Jr., 301–16. Chicago: University of Chicago Press, 1986.

———. *Reconstructing Womanhood: The Emergence of the Afro-American Woman Novelist.* New York: Oxford University Press, 1987.

Chadbourn, James Harmon. *Lynching and the Law.* Chapel Hill: University of North Carolina Press, 1933.

Chemerinsky, Erwin. "October Tragedy." *Southern California Law Review,* March 1992: 1497–1516.

Clarke, Stuart Alan. "Fear of a Black Planet: Race, Identity Politics, and Common Sense." *Socialist Review* 21, nos. 3–4 (July–December 1991): 37–60.

Cole, David. *No Equal Justice: Race and Class in the American Criminal Justice System.* New York: New Press, 1999.

Crenshaw, Kimberlé Williams. "Color Blindness, History, and the Law." In

The House That Race Built, edited by Wahneema Lubiano, 280–88. New York: Vintage Books, 1998.

———. "Whose Story Is It, Anyway? Feminist and Antiracist Appropriations of Anita Hill." In *Race-Ing Justice, En-Gendering Power: Essays on Anita Hill, Clarence Thomas, and the Construction of Social Reality*, edited by Toni Morrison, 402–40. New York: Pantheon Books, 1992.

Cripps, Thomas. *Black Film as Genre*. Bloomington: Indiana University Press, 1978.

———. "[Black Film as Genre] Definitions." In *Cinemas of the Black Diaspora: Diversity, Dependence, and Oppositionality*, edited by Michael T. Martin, 357–64. Detroit: Wayne State University Press, 1995.

———. "The Making of *The Birth of a Race:* The Emerging Politics of Identity in Silent Movies." In *The Birth of Whiteness: Race and the Emergence of U.S. Cinema*, edited by Daniel Bernardi, 38–55. New Brunswick, N.J.: Rutgers University Press, 1996.

———. "Oscar Micheaux: The Story Continues." In *Black American Cinema*, edited by Manthia Diawara, 71–79. New York: Routledge, 1993.

———. "The Reaction of the Negro to the Motion Picture *Birth of a Nation*." In *Focus on* The Birth of a Nation, edited by Fred Silva, 111–24. Englewood Cliffs, N.J.: Prentice-Hall, 1971.

Dalton, Russell J., Manfred Kuechler, and Wilheim Burklin. "The Challenge of New Movements." In *Challenging the Political Order: New Social Movements and Political Movements in Western Democracies*, edited by Russell J. Dalton, 3–20. London: Oxford University Press, 1990.

Davis, Adrienne D., and Stephanie M. Wildman. "The Legacy of Doubt: Treatment of Sex and Race in the Hill–Thomas Hearings." *Southern California Law Review*, March 1992: 1367–91.

Davis, Angela Y. "Afro Images: Politics, Fashion, and Nostalgia." In *Picturing Us: African American Identity in Photography*, edited by Deborah Willis, 170–79. New York: New Press, 1994.

———. *Angela Davis: An Autobiography*. New York: Bantam, 1974.

———. *Blues Legacies and Black Feminism: Gertrude "Ma" Rainey, Bessie Smith, and Billie Holiday*. New York: Pantheon, 1998.

———. "Clarence Thomas as Lynching Victim: Reflections on Anita Hill's Role in the Thomas Confirmation Hearings." In *African American Women Speak Out on Anita Hill–Clarence Thomas*, edited by Geneva Smitherman, 178–81. Detroit: Wayne State University Press, 1995.

———. "Race and Criminalization: Black Americans and the Punishment Industry." In *The House That Race Built*, edited by Wahneema Lubiano, 264–79. New York: Vintage Books, 1998.

———. *Women, Race, and Class*. New York: Vintage Books, 1981.

Douglass, Frederick. "Lynch Law in the South." *The North American Review*, July 1892: 17–24.

Dray, Phillip. *At the Hands of Persons Unknown: The Lynching of Black America.* New York: Random House, 2002.

DuBois, Page. *Torture and Truth.* New York: Routledge, 1991.

Ducey, Mitchell F. "The Commission on Interracial Cooperation Papers, 1919–1944, and the Association of Southern Women for the Prevention of Lynching Papers, 1930–1942: A Guide to the Microfilm Editions." Ann Arbor, Mich.: University Microfilms International, 1984.

Duggan, Lisa. *Sapphic Slashers: Sex, Violence, and American Modernity.* Durham, N.C.: Duke University Press, 2000.

Eagleton, Terry. *Ideology: An Introduction.* London: Verso, 1991.

———. *Literary Theory: An Introduction.* Minneapolis: University of Minnesota Press, 1983.

Epstein, Steven. "Democratic Science? AIDS Activism and the Contested Construction of Knowledge." *Socialist Review,* April–June 1991.

———. *Impure Science: AIDS, Activism, and the Politics of Knowledge.* Berkeley and Los Angeles: University of California Press, 1996.

Ferrell, Claudine L. *Nightmare and Dream: Antilynching in Congress, 1917–1922.* New York: Garland Publishing, 1986.

Fitzgerald, Louise F. "Science v. Myth: The Failure of Reason in the Clarence Thomas Hearings." *Southern California Law Review,* March 1992: 1399–1409.

Fletcher, George P. *A Crime of Self-Defense: Bernhard Goetz and the Law on Trial.* New York: Free Press, 1988.

Fletcher, Jim, Tanaquil Jones, and Sylvere Lotringer, eds. *Still Black, Still Strong: Survivors of the War against Black Revolutionaries.* New York: Semiotext(e), 1993.

Foucault, Michel. *Discipline and Punish: The Birth of the Prison.* New York: Vintage, 1979.

———. *Power/Knowledge: Selected Interviews and Other Writings, 1972–1977.* Edited by Colin Gordon. New York: Pantheon Books, 1980.

Freedman, Estelle B. "The Manipulation of History at the Clarence Thomas Hearings." *Southern California Law Review,* March 1992: 1362–67.

Gabriel, Teshome H. "Ruin and the Other: Towards a Language of Memory." In *Otherness and the Media,* edited by Hamid Naficy and Teshome H. Gabriel, 211–19. Chur, Switzerland: Harwood Academic Publishers, 1993.

———. "Third Cinema as a Guardian of Popular Memory: Towards a Third Aesthetics." In *Questions of a Third Cinema,* edited by Jim Pines and Paul Willemen, 53–58. London: BFI Publishing, 1989.

———. "Thoughts on Nomadic Aesthetics and Black Independent Cinema: Traces of a Journey." In *Out There: Marginalization and Contemporary Cultures,* edited by Russell Ferguson, Martha Gever, Trinh Minh-ha, and Cornell West, 395–410. New York: New Museum of Contemporary Art, 1992.

Gaines, Jane. *Fire and Desire: Mixed-Race Movies in the Silent Era.* Chicago: University of Chicago Press, 2001.

———. "Fire and Desire: Race, Melodrama, and Oscar Micheaux." In *Black American Cinema*, edited by Manthia Diawara, 49–70. New York: Routledge, 1993.

Garber, Marjorie. "Character Assassination: Shakespeare, Anita Hill, and *JFK*." In *Media Spectacles*, edited by Marjorie Garber, Jann Matlock, and Rebecca L. Walkowitz, 23–40. New York: Routledge, 1993.

Gates, Henry Louis, Jr. "The Naked Republic." *The New Yorker*, August 25, 1997, 114–23.

Geertz, Clifford. *Local Knowledge: Further Essays in Interpretive Anthropology*. New York: Basic Books, 1983.

George, Nelson. *Blackface: Reflections on African-Americans and the Movies*. New York: HarperCollins Publishers, 1994.

Giddings, Paula. "The Last Taboo." In *Race-Ing Justice, En-Gendering Power: Essays on Anita Hill, Clarence Thomas, and the Construction of Social Reality*, edited by Toni Morrison, 441–70. New York: Pantheon Books, 1992.

Goffman, Erving. *Frame Analysis: An Essay on the Organization of Experience*. Boston: Northeastern University Press, 1986.

Goldsby, Jacqueline. "The High and Low Tech of It: The Meaning of Lynching and the Death of Emmett Till." *The Yale Journal of Criticism* 9, no. 2 (1996): 245–82.

Gooding-Williams, Robert, ed. *Reading Rodney King, Reading Urban Uprising*. New York: Routledge, 1993.

Grant, Donald Lee. *The Anti-Lynching Movement, 1883–1932*. San Francisco: R and E Research Associates, 1975.

Gray, Herman. *Watching Race: Television and the Struggle for "Blackness."* Minneapolis: University of Minnesota Press, 1995.

Green, J. Ronald. "'Twoness' in the Style of Oscar Micheaux." *Black American Cinema*, edited by Manthia Diawara, 26–48. New York: Routledge, 1993.

Griffin, Larry J., Paula Clark, and Joanne C. Sandberg. "Narrative and Event: Lynching and Historical Sociology." In *Under Sentence of Death: Lynching in the South*, edited by W. Fitzhugh Brundage, 24–47. Chapel Hill: University of North Carolina Press, 1997.

Grindstaff, L. A. "Double Exposure, Double Erasure: On the Frontline with Anita Hill." *Cultural Critique*, Spring 1994: 29–60.

Guerrero, Ed. *Framing Blackness: The African American Image in Film*. Philadelphia: Temple University Press, 1993.

Gunning, Sandra. *Race, Rape, and Lynching: The Red Record of American Literature, 1890–1912*. New York: Oxford University Press, 1996.

Halberstam, Judith. "Imagined Violence/Queer Violence: Representation, Rage, and Resistance." *Social Text*, Winter 1993: 187–201.

Halbwachs, Maurice. *The Collective Memory*. New York: Harper and Row, 1980.

———. *On Collective Memory*. Chicago: University of Chicago Press, 1992.

Hale, Grace Elizabeth. *Making Whiteness: The Culture of Segregation in the South, 1890–1940*. New York: Pantheon Books, 1998.

Halkias, Alexandra. "From Social Butterfly to Modern-Day Medea: Elizabeth Broderick's Portrayal in the Press." *Critical Studies in Mass Communication* 16, no. 3 (1999): 289–307.

Hall, Jacquelyn Dowd. "'The Mind That Burns in Each Body': Women, Rape, and Racial Violence." In *Powers of Desire: The Politics of Sexuality*, edited by Ann Snitow, Christine Stansell, and Sharon Thompson, 328–49. New York: Monthly Review Press, 1983.

———. *Revolt against Chivalry: Jesse Daniel Ames and the Women's Campaign against Lynching.* New York: Columbia University Press, 1993.

Hall, Stuart. "Gramsci's Relevance for the Study of Race and Ethnicity." In *Stuart Hall: Critical Dialogues in Cultural Studies*, edited by David Morley and Kuan-Hsing Chen, 411–40. New York: Routledge, 1996.

———. "Notes on Deconstructing 'the Popular.'" In *People's History and Socialist Theory*, edited by Raphael Samuel, 227–42. London: Routledge and Kegan Paul, 1981.

———. "The Whites of Their Eyes: Racist Ideologies and the Media." In *Silver Linings*, edited by George Bridges and Rosalind Bruat, 1981. London: Lawrence and Wishart, 1981.

Haraway, Donna J. *Modest_Witness@Second_Millennium. FemaleMan_Meets_Oncomouse: Feminism and Technoscience.* New York: Routledge, 1997.

Harris, Cheryl I. "Whiteness as Property." In *Critical Race Theory: The Key Writings That Shaped the Movement*, edited by Kimberlé Crenshaw, Neil Gotanda, Garry Peller, and Kendall Thomas, 276–91. New York: New Press, 1995.

Harris, Trudier. *Exorcising Blackness: Historical and Literary Lynching and Burning Rituals.* Bloomington: Indiana University Press, 1984.

Hartman, Saidiya V. *Scenes of Subjection: Terror, Slavery, and Self-Making in Nineteenth-Century America.* New York: Oxford University Press, 1997.

Hill, Anita Faye. "Marriage and Patronage in the Empowerment and Disempowerment of African American Women." In *Race, Gender, and Power in America: The Legacy of the Hill–Thomas Hearings*, edited by Anita Faye Hill and Emma Coleman Jordan, 271–92. New York: Oxford University Press, 1995.

———. "Moon's Paradox." In *The Darden Dilemma: 12 Black Writers on Justice, Race, and Conflicting Loyalties*, edited by Ellis Cose, 169–87. New York: Harper Perrenial, 1997.

———. *Speaking Truth to Power.* New York: Doubleday, 1997.

Hill, Anita Faye, and Emma Coleman Jordan, eds. *Race, Gender, and Power in America: The Legacy of the Hill–Thomas Hearings.* New York: Oxford University Press, 1995.

Hodes, Martha. "The Sexualization of Reconstruction Politics: White Women and Black Men in the South after the Civil War." In *American Sexual Politics: Sex, Gender, and Race since the Civil War*, edited by John C. Fout and Maura Shaw Tantillo. Chicago: Chicago University Press, 1993.

hooks, bell. *Ain't I a Woman: Black Women and Feminism*. Boston: South End Press, 1981.

———. *Black Looks: Race and Representation*. Boston: South End Press, 1992.

———. *Outlaw Culture: Resisting Representations*. New York: Routledge, 1994.

———. *Reel to Real: Race, Sex, and Class at the Movies*. New York: Routledge, 1996.

———. *Yearning: Race, Gender, and Cultural Politics*. Boston: South End Press, 1990.

Irwin-Zarecka, Iwona. *Frames of Remembrance: The Dynamics of Collective Memory*. New Brunswick, N.J.: Transaction Publishers, 1994.

———. *Neutralizing Memory: The Jew in Contemporary Poland*. New Brunswick, N.J.: Transaction Publishers, 1989.

Jackson, Phyllis Jeanette. "Re-visioning and Re-viewing Women of African Descent in the American Visual Tradition." Ph.D. diss., Northwestern University, 1996.

JanMohamed, Abdul R., and David Lloyd. "Toward a Theory of Minority Discourse: What Is to Be Done?" In *The Nature and Context of Minority Discourse*, edited by Abdul R. JanMohamed and David Lloyd. Oxford: Oxford University Press, 1990.

Jewell, K. Sue. *From Mammy to Miss America and Beyond: Cultural Images and the Shaping of US Social Policy*. New York: Routledge, 1993.

Johnson, Claudia Durst. *To Kill a Mockingbird: Threatening Boundaries*. New York: Twayne Publishers, 1994.

Johnston, Hank. "A Methodology for Frame Analysis: From Discourse to Cognitive Schemata." In *Social Movements and Culture*, edited by Hank Johnston and Bert Klandermans, 217–46. Minneapolis: University of Minnesota Press, 1995.

Jones, G. William. *Black Cinema Treasures Lost and Found*. Denton: University of North Texas Press, 1991.

Jones, Jacquie. "How Come Nobody Told Me about the Lynching?" In *Picturing Us: African American Identity in Photography*, edited by Deborah Willis, 152–57. New York: New Press, 1994.

Jordan, Emma Coleman. "The Power of False Racial Memory and the Metaphor of Lynching." In *Race, Gender, and Power in America: The Legacy of the Hill–Thomas Hearings*, edited by Anita Faye Hill and Emma Coleman Jordan, 37–55. New York: Oxford University Press, 1995.

Jules-Rosette, Bennetta. *Black Paris: The African Writers' Landscape*. Urbana and Chicago: University of Illinois Press, 1998.

Kennedy, Randall. *Race, Crime, and the Law*. New York: Vintage Books, 1998.

Lakoff, George, and Mark Johnson. *Metaphors We Live By*. Chicago: University of Chicago Press, 1980.

Lang, Kurt. "How the Past Lives On." *Contemporary Sociology* 22, no. 4 (1993): 596–600.

Lang, Robert. "*The Birth of a Nation*: History, Ideology, Narrative Form." In

The Birth of a Nation, edited by Robert Lang, 3–24. New Brunswick, N.J.: Rutgers University Press, 1994.

Lawrence, Charles R., III. "'The Message of the Verdict': A Three-Act Morality Play Starring Clarence Thomas, Willies Smith, and Mike Tyson." In *The Legacy of the Hill–Thomas Hearings: Race, Gender, and Power in America*, edited by Anita Faye Hill and Emma Coleman Jordan, 105–29. New York: Oxford University Press, 1995.

Lee, Cynthia Kwei Yung. "Race and Self Defense: Toward a Normative Conception of Reasonableness." *Minnesota Law Review* 81 (1996): 367.

Lee, Spike, and Lisa Jones. *Do the Right Thing*. New York: Fireside, 1989.

Lipsitz, George. *The Possessive Investment in Whiteness: How White People Profit from Identity Politics*. Philadelphia: Temple University Press, 1998.

———. *Time Passages: Collective Memory and American Popular Culture*. Minneapolis: University of Minnesota Press, 1990.

Litwack, Leon F. *Trouble in Mind: Black Southerners in the Age of Jim Crow*. New York: Alfred A. Knopf, 1998.

Lubiano, Wahneema. "Black Ladies, Welfare Queens, and State Minstrels: Ideological War by Narrative Means." In *Race-Ing Justice, En-Gendering Power: Essays on Anita Hill, Clarence Thomas, and the Construction of Social Reality*, edited by Toni Morrison, 323–63. New York: Pantheon Books, 1992.

———, ed. *The House That Race Built*. New York: Vintage Books, 1997.

MacLean, Nancy. *Behind the Mask of Chivalry: The Making of the Second Ku Klux Klan*. New York: Oxford University Press, 1994.

Malveaux, Julianne. "The Year of the Woman or the Woman of the Year: Was There Really an 'Anita Hill Effect?'" In *African American Women Speak Out on Anita Hill–Clarence Thomas*, edited by Geneva Smitherman, 159–68. Detroit: Wayne State University Press, 1995.

Mamet, David. *The Old Religion*. New York: Free Press, 1997.

Margolick, David. *"Strange Fruit": Billie Holiday, Cafe Society, and an Early Cry for Civil Rights*. Philadelphia: Running Press, 2000.

Martin, Michael T. *Cinemas of the Black Diaspora: Diversity, Dependence, and Oppositionality*. Detroit: Wayne State University Press, 1995.

Massood, Paula J. *Black City Cinema: African American Urban Experiences in Film*. Philadelphia: Temple University Press, 2003.

Mayer, Jane, and Jill Abramson. *Strange Justice: The Selling of Clarence Thomas*. New York: Plume, 1995.

McFadden, Robert, Ralph Blumenthal, M. A. Farber, E. R. Shipp, Charles Strum, and Craig Wolff. *Outrage: The Story behind the Tawana Brawley Hoax*. New York: Bantam Books, 1990.

Messaris, Paul. "The Polarizing Tendency of Mass Media: Press Reviews of *Do the Right Thing*." *Mass Comm Review* 20, no. 3, 4 (1993): 220–28.

Miller, Anita, ed. *The Complete Transcripts of the Clarence Thomas–Anita Hill Hearings: October 11, 12, 13, 1991*. Chicago: Academy Chicago Publishers, 1994.

Mills, Nicolaus. "Howard Beach—Anatomy of a Lynching: New York Racism in the 1980s." *Dissent*, Fall 1987: 469–83.

Morrison, Toni. "Introduction: Friday on the Potomac." In *Race-Ing Justice, En-Gendering Power: Essays on Anita Hill, Clarence Thomas, and the Construction of Social Reality*, edited by Toni Morrison, vii–xxx. New York: Pantheon Books, 1992.

Morrison, Toni, and Claudia Brodsky Lacour, eds. *Birth of a Nation 'Hood: Gaze, Script, and Spectacle in the O. J. Simpson Case*. New York: Pantheon Books, 1997.

National Asociation for the Advancement of Colored People (NAACP). *Thirty Years of Lynching in the United States, 1889–1918*. New York: National Association for the Advancement of Colored People; Ballantine Books, 1919. Reprint, New York: Arno Press and the *New York Times*, 1969. Page references are to the 1969 Arno Press and *New York Times* reprint edition.

———. "Questions and Answers on the NAACP's Position on Judge Clarence Thomas." In *Court of Appeal: The Black Community Speaks Out on the Racial and Sexual Politics of Thomas vs. Hill*, edited by *The Black Scholar*, 275–77. New York: Ballantine Books, 1992.

Norton, Eleanor Holmes. "And the Language Was Race." *Ms.*, January–February 1992: 43–45.

Omi, Michael, and Howard Winant. *Racial Formation in the United States from the 1960s to the 1990s*. 2d ed. New York: Routledge, 1994.

Painter, Nell Irvin. "Hill, Thomas, and the Use of Racial Stereotype." In *Race-Ing Justice, En-Gendering Power: Essays on Anita Hill, Clarence Thomas, and the Construction of Social Reality*, edited by Toni Morrison, 200–214. New York: Pantheon Books, 1992.

———. "Who Was Lynched?" *The Nation*, November 11, 1991, 577.

Park, Marlene. "Lynching and Antilynching: Art and Politics in the 1930s." *Prospects: An Annual of American Cultural Studies* 18 (1993): 311–65.

Patterson, Orlando. *Rituals of Blood: Consequences of Slavery in Two American Centuries*. New York: Basic Cervitas Books, 1998.

People vs. Goetz: The Summations and the Charges to the Jury. Edited by Carol A. Roehrenbeck. Buffalo, N.Y.: William S. Hein Company, 1989.

Phelps, Timothy M., and Helen Winternitz. *Capitol Games: The Inside Story of Clarence Thomas, Anita Hill, and a Supreme Court Nomination*. New York: Harper Perennial, 1993.

Pinchin, Catherine Bryn. "The Misrule of Metaphor." Ph.D. diss., University of Calgary, 1996.

Popular Memory Group. "Popular Memory: Theory, Politics, Method." In *Making Histories: Studies in History-Writing and Politics*, edited by Richard Johnson, Gregor McLennan, Bill Schwartz, and David Sutton, 205–52. London: Hutchinson, 1982.

Raper, Arthur F. *The Tragedy of Lynching*. 1933. Reprint, New York: Dover, 1970.

Reed, John Shelton. "An Evaluation of an Anti-Lynching Organization." *Social Problems* 16 (Fall 1968): 172–82.

Reid, Mark. *Redefining Black Film*. Berkeley and Los Angeles: University of California Press, 1993.

———, ed. *Spike Lee's* Do the Right Thing. New York: Cambridge University Press, 1997.

Resnick, Judith. "From the Senate Judiciary Committee to the Country Court-house: The Relevance of Gender, Race, and Ethnicity to Adjudication." In *Race, Gender, and Power in America: The Legacy of the Hill–Thomas Hearings,* edited by Anita Faye Hill and Emma Coleman Jordan, 177–227. New York: Oxford University Press, 1995.

———. "Hearing Women." *Southern California Law Review,* March 1992: 1333–45.

Rhode, Deborah L. "Sexual Harassment." *Southern California Law Review,* March 1992: 1459–66.

Rosales, Arturo. *¡Pobre Raza! Violence, Justice, and Mobilization among Mexican Lindo Immigrants, 1900–1936*. Austin: University of Texas Press, 1999.

Ross, Susan Deller. "Sexual Harassment Law in the Aftermath of the Hill–Thomas Hearings." In *The Legacy of the Hill–Thomas Hearings: Race, Gender, and Power in America,* edited by Anita Faye Hill and Emma Coleman Jordan, 228–41. New York: Oxford University Press, 1995.

Rubin, Lillian B. *Busing and Backlash: White against White in an Urban School District*. Berkeley and Los Angeles: University of California Press, 1972.

———. *Quiet Rage: Bernie Goetz in a Time of Madness*. New York: Farrar, Straus and Giroux, 1986.

Russell, Katheryn K. *The Color of Crime: Racial Hoaxes, White Fear, Black Protec-tionism, Police Harassment, and Other Macroaggressions*. New York: New York University Press, 1998.

Schechter, Patricia A. *Ida B. Wells-Barnett and American Reform, 1880–1930*. Chapel Hill: University of North Carolina Press, 2001.

———. "Unsettled Business: Ida B. Wells against Lynching; or, How Anti-lynching Got Its Gender." In *Under Sentence of Death: Lynching in the South,* edited by W. Fitzhugh Brundage, 292–317. Chapel Hill: University of North Carolina Press, 1997.

Schudson, Michael. *Watergate in American Memory: How We Remember, Forget, and Reconstruct the Past*. New York: Basic Books, 1992.

Schwartz, Barry. "The Social Context of Commemoration: A Study in Collec-tive Memory." *Social Forces* 61, no. 2 (December 1982): 374–402.

Shohat, Ella, and Robert Stam. *Unthinking Eurocentrism: Multiculturalism and the Media*. New York: Routledge, 1994.

Silva, Fred. "Introduction." In *Focus on* The Birth of a Nation, edited by Fred Silva, 1971. Englewood Cliffs, N.J.: Prentice-Hall, 1971.

Singleton, John. "Rosewood: Like Judgment Day." In *Rosewood: Like Judgment Day*, edited by Michael D'Orso, i–xxxii. New York: Boulevard Books, 1996.

Slotkin, Richard. *Gunfighter Nation: The Myth of the Frontier in Twentieth-Century America*. New York: Atheneum, 1992.

Smith, Valerie. *Not Just Race, Not Just Gender: Black Feminist Readings*. New York: Routledge, 1998.

Snead, James. *White Screens, Black Images: Hollywood from the Dark Side*. New York: Routledge, 1994.

Snow, David A., and Robert D. Benford. "Master Frames and Cycles of Protest." In *Frontiers in Social Movement Theory*, edited by Aldon D. Morris and Carol McClurg Mueller, 1133–55. New Haven: Yale University Press, 1992.

Snow, David A., Robert D. Benford, E. Burke Rochford Jr., and Steven K. Worden. "Frame Alignment Processes, Micromobilization, and Movement Participation." *American Sociological Review* 51 (1986): 464–81.

Spelman, Elizabeth V. *Inessential Woman: Problems of Exclusion in Feminist Thought*. Boston: Beacon Press, 1988.

Spigel, Lynn, and Henry Jenkins. "Same Bat Channel, Different Bat Times: Mass Culture and Popular Memory." In *The Many Lives of the Batman: Critical Approaches to a Superhero and His Media*, edited by Roberta E. Pearson and William Uricchio, 117–48. New York: Routledge, 1991.

Staub, Michael. "The Whitest I: On Reading the Hill–Thomas Transcripts." In *Whiteness: A Critical Reader*, edited by Mike Hill, 47–62. New York: New York University Press, 1997.

Sturken, Marita. "Cultural Memory and Identity Politics: The Vietnam War, AIDS, and Technologies of Memory." Ph. D. diss., University of California, Santa Cruz, 1992.

———. *Tangled Memories: The Vietnam War, the AIDS Epidemic, and the Politics of Remembering*. Berkeley and Los Angeles: University of California Press, 1997.

Taibbi, Mike, and Anna Sims-Phillips. *Unholy Alliances: Working the Tawana Brawley Story*. New York: Harcourt Brace Jovanovich, 1989.

Tannen, Deborah, ed. *Framing in Discourse*. New York: Oxford University Press, 1993.

Taylor, Clyde. "The Re-Birth of the Aesthetic in Cinema." In *The Birth of Whiteness: Race and the Emergence of U.S. Cinema*, edited by Daniel Bernardi, 15–37. New Brunswick, N.J.: Rutgers University Press, 1996.

Thomas, Kendall. "Strange Fruit." In *Race-Ing Justice, En-Gendering Power: Essays on Anita Hill, Clarence Thomas, and the Construction of Social Reality*, edited by Toni Morrison, 364–89. New York: Pantheon Books, 1992.

Tillman, Ben. "The Black Peril." Reprint in *Justice Denied: The Black Man in White America*, edited by William M. Chace and Peter Collier, 182. New York: Harcourt, Brace and World, 1970.

Tolnay, Stewart E., and E. M. Beck. *A Festival of Violence: An Analysis of South-*

ern Lynchings, 1882–1930. Urbana and Chicago: University of Illinois Press, 1992.

———. "When Race Didn't Matter: Black and White Mob Violence against Their Own Color." In *Under Sentence of Death: Lynching in the South*, edited by W. Fitzhugh Brundage, 132–54. Chapel Hill: University of North Carolina Press, 1997.

Turner, Patricia A. *Ceramic Uncles and Celluloid Mammies: Black Images and Their Influence on Culture*. New York: Anchor Books, 1994.

Usher, Jane M. *Women's Madness: Misogyny or Mental Illness?* New York: Harvester Wheatsheaf, 1991.

Vélez-Ibáñez, Carlos G. *Border Visions: Mexican Cultures of the Southwest United States*. Tucson: University of Arizona Press, 1996.

Vendryes, Margaret Rose. "Hanging on Their Walls: An Art Commentary on Lynching, the Forgotten 1935 Art Exhibition." In *Race Consciousness: African-American Studies for the New Century*, edited by Judith Jackson Fossett and Jeffrey A. Tucker, 153–76. New York: New York University Press, 1997.

Waldrep, Christopher. "War of Words: The Controversy over the Definition of Lynching, 1899–1940." *The Journal of Southern History* 66, no. 1 (2000): 75–100.

Walker, Alice. "Advancing Luna—and Ida B. Wells." In *You Can't Keep a Good Woman Down*, Alice Walker, 85–104. New York: Harcourt Brace Jovanovich, 1981.

Wallace, Michelle. *Black Macho and the Myth of the Superwoman*. New York: Verso, 1990.

Weinglass, Leonard. *Race for Justice: Mumia Abu-Jamal's Fight against the Death Penalty*. Monroe, Maine: Common Courage Press, 1995.

Wells, Ida B. *Mob Rule in New Orleans: Robert Charles and His Fight to the Death. The Story of His Life. Burning Human Beings Alive. Other Lynching Statistics*. Chicago, 1900.

———. *On Lynchings:* Southern Horrors, A Red Record, *and* Mob Rule in New Orleans. New York: Arno Press and the *New York Times*, 1969.

———. *A Red Record: Tabulated Statistics and Alleged Causes of Lynchings in the United States, 1892—1893—1894*. Chicago, 1895.

———. *Southern Horrors: Lynch Law in All Its Phases*. New York: New York Age Print, 1892.

White, Hayden. *Metahistory: The Historical Imagination in Nineteenth-Century Europe*. Baltimore: The Johns Hopkins University Press, 1973.

———. *Tropics of Discourse: Essays in Cultural Criticism*. Baltimore: The Johns Hopkins University Press, 1978.

Wiegman, Robyn. *American Anatomies: Theorizing Race and Gender*. Durham, N.C.: Duke University Press, 1995.

———. "The Anatomy of Lynching." *Journal of the History of Sexuality* 3 (1993): 445–67.

Wilkins, David. "Presumed Crazy: The Structure of Argument in the Hill/ Thomas Hearings." *Southern California Law Review,* March 1992: 1517–22.

Williams, Patricia. *The Alchemy of Race and Rights.* Cambridge, Mass.: Harvard University Press, 1991.

———. "A Rare Case of Muleheadedness and Men." In *Race-Ing Justice, En-Gendering Power: Essays on Anita Hill, Clarence Thomas, and the Construction of Social Reality,* edited by Toni Morrison, 159–72. New York: Pantheon Books, 1992.

———. *The Rooster's Egg.* Cambridge, Mass.: Harvard University Press, 1995.

———. "Spirit-Murdering the Messenger: The Discourse of Fingerpointing as the Law's Response to Racism." In the symposium "Excluded Voices: Realities in Law and Law Reform." *University of Miami Law Review* 42 (1987): 1–27.

Wilson, William Julius. *The Declining Significance of Race: Blacks and Changing American Institutions.* Chicago: University of Chicago Press, 1978.

———. *The Truly Disadvantaged: The Inner City, the Underclass, and Public Policy.* Chicago: University of Chicago Press, 1987.

Wright, Richard. *Black Boy.* New York: Harper, 1945. Reprint, New York: HarperCollins, 1993. Page references are to the 1993 reprint edition.

Yearwood, Gladstone, ed. *Black Cinema Aesthetics: Issues in Independent Black Filmmaking.* Athens, Ohio: Center for Afro-American Studies, 1982.

Zangrando, Robert L. *The NAACP Crusade against Lynching, 1909–1950.* Philadelphia: Temple University Press, 1980.

Zelizer, Barbie. *Covering the Body: The Kennedy Assassination, the Media, and the Shaping of Collective Memory.* Chicago: University of Chicago Press, 1992.

———. *Remembering to Forget: Holocaust Memory through the Camera's Eye.* Chicago: University of Chicago Press, 1998.

Zerubavel, Yael. *Recovered Roots: Collective Memory and the Making of Israeli National Traditon.* Chicago: University of Chicago Press, 1995.

Index

Affirmative action: Thomas's stance on, 120–21, 194n51

African American men: false accusations of crime made against, 84–85, 90, 182–83n72; myth of the black rapist, 6, 8–14, 30–31, 33–34, 89, 114; representations of hypersexuality, 3; stereotyped as criminal or dangerous, 3, 74–77, 81–84, 85, 86, 90, 93, 94–98, 108, 180–81n49

African American press: coverage of the subway vigilante case, 79–80; coverage of the Tawana Brawley case, 105–6; on false accusations against black men, 88–89

African American women: conundrum regarding crimes of black men, 131–32; sexual victimization of, 18–19, 30, 39, 64, 68, 122–23; stereotyped as sexually duplicitous and available, 18–19, 100–101, 108, 113, 127, 160n74; victimization not remembered in public discourse, 30–31, 105–6, 107–8, 133–35; as victims of Southern lynchings, 20–22, 24–25, 160n73, 162n84; writers, 20

Alexander, Elizabeth, 191n12

Allen, Barry, 70, 73

Allen, James, xxxi, 138

Alonso, Ana Maria, 150n26

Ames, Jesse Daniel, 6, 13. *See also* ASWPL

Amsterdam News, 79, 89, 105–7

Antebellum South: sexual victimization of black women in, 122–23; slave system, xxiii, 118

Anti-Arab attacks: post-9/11, 146

Antilynching legislation efforts, 155–56n17; Costigan-Wagner Anti-Lynching Bill, 11, 20; Dyer Anti-lynching Bill, xv

Antilynching movement, 3, 4, 6; challenging myth of the black rapist, 12–15, 30–31, 114; discourse of, xvi, xxix–xxx, 1–31; Howard University student protest (1934), 8; impact on collective memory, 142; impact on popular opinion, 27–31; on the racially constructed perceptions of rape, 18–20; white women's role in, 6, 15–18, 29, 156n26, 162–63n96. *See also* ASWPL; CIC; NAACP; Wells, Ida B.

Antirape movement: and the myth of the black rapist, 129–31

Antisexist discourse: vs. antiracist discourse in the Hill–Thomas hearings, 113–14

Armstrong, Paul (character in *Just Cause*), 50–51, 52–53

ASWPL (Association of Southern Women for the Prevention of Lynching), 2, 10, 16–18, 156nn23, 26, 159–60n67; founding of, 6; and white women's role in the antilynching movement, 6, 15–18, 29, 156n26, 162–63n96

Barnett, Albert E., 17–18

Barnett, Ida Wells. *See* Wells, Ida B.

Beacon, 105–6

Bederman, Gail, 162n84

Bell Curve, The, 138

Benford, Robert: and Scott Hunt,
    157n34
Berry-Meyers, Phyllis, 124
Biden, Joseph, 121, 192n48
Birth of a Nation, The, 34, 40, 164n13;
    NAACP opposition to, 36–37, 40
Birth of a Race, The, 37–38
Black fear. *See* Racialized fear
Black men. *See* African American men
Black women. *See* African American
    women
Bowser, Pearl: and Louise Spence,
    166n26, 167n36
Brawley, Tawana. *See* Tawana Brawley
    case
Briggance, Jake (character in *A Time
    to Kill*), 55, 56, 58–59
Brown, Charlotte Hawkins, 16
Brown, Elsa Barkley, 130, 133–34
Brown, Tanny (character in *Just
    Cause*), 51, 52, 53
Brownmiller, Susan, 130
Brown v. Board of Education, 122,
    193–94n49
Brundage, W. Fitzhugh, 9, 27–28,
    151nn32, 40, 42, 152n47, 154n62,
    158n45, 154n62, 191n13, 192n27
Brute, The, 38
Buggin' Out (character in *Do the
    Right Thing*), 42–45
Bumpurs, Eleanor, 147, 177n22
Burke, Kenneth, xviii–xix, 149n10
Burnett, Charles, 168n43
Bush, George H.: administration, 121
Byrd, James, Jr., 145, 201n25

Cabey, Darrell, 70, 73
Call and Post (Cleveland), 88–89
Canty, Troy, 70, 73
Carby, Hazel V., 18, 133, 198n112
Carey, Roane, 138
Carrier, Sylvester, 64–65, 66
Castration: depiction of in *Just Cause*,
    53; and lynching, 48–49, 115,

    153n56, 155n5, 173n76; meta-
    phorical castration in *Do the Right
    Thing*, 44
Chadbourn, James H.: *Lynching and
    the Law*, 6
Chamlee, George W., 9
Chaney, James, 173n82
Chin, Mel: *Night Rap*, 49
Chivalry: gender-race interactions
    involved in Southern code of,
    15–16, 17, 18–19, 22. *See also*
    White women
CIC (Commission on Interracial
    Cooperation), 2, 16, 172–73n74;
    research on lynching, 5–6, 24
Cinema, xxx; adaptation of lynch-
    ing narratives in, 33–36, 45–46,
    67–78, 142, 167n35; race films and
    countermemory, 36, 164–65n14,
    167nn36–38. *See also Birth of a
    Nation, The; Do the Right Thing;
    Ghosts of Mississippi; Just Cause;
    Last Seduction, The*; Lee, Spike;
    Micheaux, Oscar; *Time to Kill, A*
Civil war, xxiii. *See also* Post-
    Reconstruction era
Clark, Larry, 168n43
Cole, David, 180n49
Collective memory, xxi–xxii, xxxi, 63,
    154n64; and common sense, 70;
    contested construction of history,
    xxii, 156n34; countermemory,
    36; and credibility, 70, 91–109;
    as "cultural memory," xxi–xxii,
    150n24, 163n3; and discovery,
    166n26; as a gendered resource for
    antiracist activism, 134–35, 142;
    lynching spectacles intended to
    construct, xvii, xx–xxiii; "memory
    workers," xxii; and racial forma-
    tion, xx–xxi, 70, 102–3. *See also*
    Lynching as a metaphor; Memory
    holes; Racialized fear; Septem-
    ber 11 attacks

Commission on Interracial Cooperation. *See* CIC

Common sense: and credibility, 91–109; Gramsci on, xix, 188n132; racialized fears and, 80–82, 178nn32, 33; racially constructed understandings of, 101–4, 108–9; and "reasonableness" as self defense in the Goetz defense, 80–84; and "reason" in the Tawana Brawley case 101–9. *See also* Lynching; Racial formation

Communication media. *See* Media

Corporeality, 118–19, 120

Costigan-Wagner Anti-Lynching Bill, 11, 20

Credibility: *See* Collective memory

Crenshaw, Kimberlé, 190n5, 193–94n49

Crime: fear of as the basis for subway vigilante's support, 74–76; interracial, 89, 131–32; stereotypes of as criminal black men, 3, 74–77, 81–84, 85, 86, 90, 93, 94–98, 108, 180–81n49

"*criminalblackman*" stereotype, 3, 74–77, 81–84, 85, 86, 90, 93, 94–98, 108, 180–81n49. *See also* Russell, Katheryn K.

Cripps, Thomas, 166nn21, 24

Cynthia (character in *Secrets and Lies*), 33–34

Davis, Angela Y., 130, 132, 169n46, 172n73, 178n32

De La Beckwith, Bryon, 60, 61, 62

DeLaughter, Bobby, 61–62, 63. *See also Ghosts of Mississippi*

Demonstrations, 7, 91, 201–2n26

Diallo, Amadou, 146, 201–2n26

Doggett, John, 124, 125

D'Orso, Michael: *Like Judgment Day*, 64

Do the Right Thing (Spike Lee film),

41–46; critique of racial themes, 48, 49–50; crowd response in, 47–48; hypersmasculinization in, 43; lynching metaphor analyzed, 46–48, 49, 169–70n52, 170n60, 171n66, 199n16

Douglass, Frederick, 12, 161n82

duBois, Page, 191–92n19

Du Bois, W. E. B., 37

Duggan, Lisa, 153n58

Dungeon, The, 38

Dyer Anti-Lynching Bill, 23

Earl (Bobby) (character in *Just Cause*), 50, 52–54

Economic factors related to lynching, xxv, xxviii–xxvix, 27–28

Edwards, Daniel: lynching of, 1–2, 15

Efrem (character in *Within Our Gates*), 38–39

Embodiment, 118–19, 120

Essentialism, 35

Evers, Medgar, 60, 61, 62, 63. *See also Ghosts of Mississippi*

Evers, Myrlie, 61

Fanon, Frantz, 99

Farrakhan, Louis, 105

Fear. *See* Racialized fear

Feminism: antirape movement and the myth of the black rapist, 129–31; Hill–Thomas hearings pitting antisexist discourse against antiracist discourse, 113–14

Films. *See* Cinema

Fletcher, George P., 83, 179–80n38

Flora (character in *Birth of a Nation*), 34

Foucault, Michel: *Discipline and Punish*, 117–18, 188n32, 191n16, 191n19, 192n20

Franklin, Leo: lynching of, 38

Friedman, Myra, 77–78

Frontier justice, 151n37, 167–68n42

Gabriel, Teshome H., xxii, 150n27

Gaines, Jane, 39, 40, 163n1, 165–66n20

Garrett, Finis, xv, xvi

Gender. *See* African American men; African American women; Feminism; Race-gender interactions; White women

Ghosts of Mississippi, 60–63

Giddings, Paula, 160n74

Gilliam, Dorothy, 83

Goetz Anti-crime and Self Defense Act, 72

Goetz, Bernhard: acquittal of, 79–80, 174n3; cross-racial support diminishing over time, 74–76; fear of crime as the basis for his support, 74–76; fear of vigilante justice in wake of, 79–80, 143; his shooting of four black teenagers, 70–71, 73, 176–77nn16–17, 177n20; Judge Wachtler's opinion on "reasonableness," 80–82; legal defense of appealing to racialized fears, 78–79; media handling of the case, 71, 73, 74–78; police handling of the case, 73, 73–74; as a popular hero as a subway vigilante, 71–73; racial motivations, 77–78, 177n22, 179n36, 179–80n38

Goldsby, Jacqueline, 191n10

Goodman, Andrew, 173n82

Gunsaulus Mystery, The, 38

Gramsci, Antonio: on "common sense," xix, 188n132

Griffith, D. W.: *Birth of a Nation*, 34, 40

Griffith, Michael, 145, 170n55

Grimes, Timothy, 170n55

Guardian Angels, 71, 78

Guerrero, Ed, 36, 164–65n14, 168–69n44

Gunning, Sandra, 20, 158–59n50

Gus (character in *Birth of a Nation*), 34, 163n1

Hailey, Karl Lee (character in *A Time to Kill*), 55–57

Hailey, Tonya (character in *A Time to Kill*), 55–56

Halberstam, Judith, 170–71n63

Halbwachs, Maurice: on collective memory, xxi, 150–51n30

Hale, Grace Elizabeth, 152n 47, 153n55, 153n58

Halkias, Alexandra, 182n68

Hall, Jacquelyn Dowd, 5

Hall, Stuart, 141, 188n132

"Hanging signifier": lynching as a, 50, 141–42

Hanson, Marla, 95

Harlem after Midnight, 38

Harris, Cheryl, 83

Harris, Trudier, 153n56, 154n65, 170n59

Hartman, Saidiya, 161n82

Hatch, Orrin, 128

Hawkins, Yusef K., 145, 200–201n25

Herbert, Bob, 103

Herrnstein, Richard, 138

"High-tech lynching": reference by Clarence Thomas, xv, xx, xxx–xxxi, 111, 112, 113, 114–16, 133, 135, 143–45, 149n6, 190nn5, 6, 7, 193n43. *See also* Hill–Thomas hearings

Hill, Anita Faye: as a black woman claiming sexual harassment, xv, xxx, 111, 112–13, 144; challenging Thomas's lynching metaphor, 198n117; efforts to depict her as delusional, 125–27; efforts to reclaim memory of black women's victimization, 134–35, 145; her challenging of a black male problematic, 132–33; "Moon's

Paradox," 132–33, 134; opposition focus on her sexuality, 123–24, 126–27; polygraph examination of, 125; portrayed as manipulated by white feminists, 130–31; *Speaking Truth to Power*, 135

Hill–Thomas hearings, 111–35; antisexist discourse pitted against antiracist discourse during, 113–14, 129–31; black women's victimization forgotten in, 123–24, 129, 131, 133–35; race-gender interactions complicating the lynching metaphor in, 112–14, 129–31, 133, 144–45, 149n6; use of the lynching metaphor in, xv, xx, xxx–xxxi, 111, 112, 113, 114–16, 133, 135, 143–45, 149n6. *See also* Hill, Anita Faye; Thomas, Clarence

Historical amnesia. *See* Memory holes

Hodes, Martha, 149n40

Holiday, Billie, 51

Hollywood. *See* Cinema

Holocaust, 138–39

hooks, bell: on *Do the Right Thing*, 46, 172n71

Howard Beach, Queens, racial incident, 46, 97, 170n55

Hypermasculinization, 43

Ianniello, Matthew, 97

Ice-T, 47

Images of lynching, xx, xxviii, 137, 138–41

Imagined violence, 170–71n63

Interracial rape, 171–72n70

Interracial relationships: labeled as rape, 14–15, 159n60, 173n81, 197n93

Irwin-Zarecka, Iwona: on "memory workers," xxii

Jewell, K. Sue, 123

J.F.K., 41

Johnson, James Weldon, 13–14, 22

Jordan, Emma Coleman, 130, 131, 132

Jungle Fever: rape theme in, 171–72n70, 201n25

Just Cause: lynching theme in, 50–54, 68; themes of innocence and guilt in, 53–54

Kennedy, Randall, 180n48

King, Martin Luther, Jr., 61, 147

King, Ralph: role and portrayal of in the Tawana Brawley case, 93–94

KKK. *See* Ku Klux Klan

Knowledge: contested construction of, xxii, 156n34

Kothe, Charles, 124–25

Kovel, Joel, 99

Ku Klux Klan (KKK), xxiv, 12, 36, 38, 61, 70; *Birth of a Nation* influencing, 164n13; in the film *A Time to Kill*, 57

Language: as metaphorical extension, xviii–xix

Lankford, William C., 11

Last Seduction, The, 33, 34

Latinos, 178–79n34; lynching of Mexicans, 151–52n42

Lawrence, Charles R., III, 129, 149n5, 197n92

Lee, Harper, 164n13. *See also To Kill a Mockingbird*

Lee, Spike, 41, 46, 48, 169–70n52, 170n55. *See also Do the Right Thing; Jungle Fever*

Legal lynchings, 51, 57, 60

Leigh, Mike: *Secrets and Lies*, 33–34

Lipsitz, George: on the contesting of historical memory, xxii; on the possessive element in whiteness, 83–84

Louima, Abner, 138

Lubiano, Wahneema: on racialized

"shortcuts," xvii; on the "welfare queen" stereotype, 123, 195n60

Lynching, xx; of African American women, 20–22, 24–25, 160n73, 162n84; as both a sexual and racial crime, 131; common features of, xxvii–xxviii, 48, 115–16; and common sense, xix–xx; defined, xvii; history of, xvii, xxiii–xxv, 40, 199n7; images and photos of, viii, xx, 137, 138–41; and racial formation, xix–xx; the *Without Sanctuary* exhibit, 137–41. *See also* Rape and lynching

Lynching as a metaphor, xvi–xix, 29–31, 133–34, 142; contemporary resonance of, 90, 108–9, 145–46; as a "hanging signifier," 50, 141–42; "high-tech lynching" reference of Clarence Thomas, xv, xx, xxx–xxxi, 111, 112, 113, 114–16, 133, 135, 143–45, 149n6, 190nn5–7, 193n43; reinforcing the racial order, xvi, 13–14; symbolizing racial oppression, xvii, 30, 138–39, 145. *See also* Spectacle lynchings

Lynching narratives, 2; black women's victimization erased in, 113, 133–35; civilization vs. barbarism in, 24–25, 39

Mackey, John, 119

Maddox, Alton: role and portrayal of in the Tawana Brawley case, 93, 95–97

Mainstream press, 1–2, 143, 176n13; advance notices of lynchings in, 25, 27; antilynching movement confronting, 6–7; coverage of false accusations against black men, 86, 87–88; coverage of the Tawana Brawley case, 91–92,

107–8, 185–86n107; handling of the subway vigilante (Goetz) case, 71, 73, 74–78; handling of the Susan Smith case, 183–84n81; Hill–Thomas hearings as media spectacle, 111, 115

Malcolm X, 61, 147

Mandingo (film), 41

Manhunts, 89

Marshall, Thurgood, 121, 194n50

Martin, Emma Mae, 123

Masculinity: hypermasculinization, 43

Mason, C. Vernon: role and portrayal of in the Tawana Brawley case, 94–97, 104–5

Mass demonstrations. *See* Demonstrations

Masters, William, 179n34

Mayer, Jane: and Jill Abramson, 190n5

McFadden, Robert, et al. *See* Outrage

Media: constructions of "blackness" in, xxx; movements' use of, 155n8; sensationalism of crime, 84. *See also* African American press; Mainstream press

Meeropol, Abel, 51, 172n73

Memory holes, 62, 142; lynching victimization of African American women not remembered, 30–31, 105–6, 107–8, 133–35

"Memory workers," xxii

Metaphor, xvii–xviii, 149n11; metonym, xviii

Micheaux, Oscar, 38, 165n20; *Within Our Gates*, 38–41, 165n20, 166n26, 167n36

Michel, Harriet R., 79–80

Michigan Chronicle, 88

Misogyny, 187n125

Mississippi Burning, 173–74n82

Moon, Felicia and Warren: in Hill's analysis, 132–33, 134

Moore, Gary, 63
Morrison, Toni, 119, 194n50; on Hill–Thomas hearings, 194n50
Movies. *See* Cinema
Mr. Mann (character in *Rosewood*), 66–67
Mulligan, Robert, 164n13. *See also To Kill a Mockingbird*
Murray, Charles, 138
Myth of the black rapist, 6, 8–14, 30–31, 33–34, 89, 114; anti-lynching movement's challenge to the myth, 12–15, 30–31, 114. *See* also African American men; Rape

NAACP (National Association for the Advancement for Colored People): campaign against lynching, 2, 4–7, 13, 152–53n48; discourse against lynching, 25–27; in the film *A Time to Kill*, 57; opposing Thomas nomination, 120; opposition to screening of *Birth of a Nation*, 36–37, 40
National Coalition for Women's Mental Health, 125–26
Native Son, 164n13, 173n80
Neal, Claude: lynching of, xviii, xxv–xxvii, 27, 28, 152–53n48
Negra, La, 166n26
Nelson, Laura: lynching of, 20, 21, 135, 161n82
Nerney, May Childs, 37
New Deal, xxviii, 154n62. *See also* Roosevelt, Franklin D.
New Social Movements, 155
New York Guardian Angels. *See* Guardian Angels
New York Times, 138; on false accusations of black men, 86; on the subway vigilante case, 71, 74–75, 76; on the Tawana Brawley case,

91–92, 107, 185–86n107. *See also* Media
New York Urban League. *See* Urban League
Nunn, Bill, 75

Olabisi, Noni, 143, 144
Omi, Michael, and Howard Winant: on racial formation, xix–xx, 199n17
Organized forgetting. *See* Memory holes
Ossie (character in *Jungle Fever*), 171–72n70
Outrage, 94, 95–96, 184n83, 184–85n89; portrayal of Tawana Brawley in, 100–101, 102

Pagones, Steve: defamation suit against Tawana Brawley, 91, 98, 103
Parker, Alan, 173–74n82
Paul (character in *Just Cause*), 50–51, 52–53
PBS documentary on the Rosewood massacre, 63–64
Pelosi, Nancy, 196n83
People v. Goetz. See Goetz, Bernhard
Plessy v. Ferguson, 193–94n49
Police brutality, 145–46, 169–70n52, 170–71n63, 181n57
Political movements. *See* Social movements
Popular Memory Group, xxii
Post-9/11. *See* September 11 attacks
Post-Reconstruction era, 2; practice of lynching integral to, xxiii–xxiv, 14, 118
Power: and collective memory, xxii; ruling groups' use of ideology, xix
Press. *See* African American press; Mainstream press; Media
Protest. *See* Demonstrations
Public opinion: in Goetz case

racial opinion divides over time, 76–77; racial differences in, 102–4, 108–9; racial differences in perceived credibility of Tawana Brawley, 101–2

"Race films." *See* Cinema

Race-gender interactions: absent in discourse during the Hill–Thomas hearings, 129–30; in constructions of Southern womanhood, 18–19; and the erasure of black women's victimization, 134–35; in the opposition's portrayal of Anita Hill, 126–27; in the Southern code of chivalry, 15–16, 17, 18–19, 22. *See also* African American men; African American women; White women

Race-reversal scenarios, 83, 104; in *A Time to Kill*, 55, 58–60

Racial formation, xix–xx, xxxi, 108–9, 199n17; and collective memory, xx; and common sense, xix–xx

Racial hoaxes: Charles Stuart hoax, xxi, 84, 85–87, 143; false accusations against black men, 84–85, 90, 182–83n72; mainstream media coverage of, 86, 87–88; Susan Smith hoax, xxi, 84–85, 143. *See also* Smith, Susan; Stuart, Charles; Tawana Brawley case

Racialized fear, 187–88n127; appeals to, in defense of the subway vigilante (Goetz), 78–79; black fear of vigilante violence, 79–80, 117–18; Goetz legal defense appealing to, 78–79, 180n46; stereotypes of black male criminality and, 74–76, 81–84, 85, 86, 180–81n49

Racialized violence, 69–109; massacre and film based upon, 64–67; race riots, 45–46; racial terrorism, 2, 3, 14, 38, 82, 145–46

Racially constructed perceptions: antirape movement neglecting analysis of, 129–31; and jury nullification, 173n77, 186–87n123; of rape, 18–20, 122, 129; of Southern womanhood, 18–19; in understandings of "reasonableness" and common sense, 101–4, 108–9

Racial project, xx

Racial protests, 91

Racial spectacles, xx, 69, 111, 112, 142–43

Racism, 48, 50; association of black with dirt and defilement, 99–100; scapegoating, 88

Racism and gender. *See* Race-gender interactions

Radio Raheem (character in *Do the Right Thing*), 42–45, 48, 49, 169n51

Ramseur, James, 70, 73

Rape: antilynching movement's challenge to the myth of the black rapist, 12–15, 30–31, 114; intraracial, 131–32; myth of the black rapist, 6, 8–14, 30–31, 33–34, 89, 114; racially constructed perceptions of, 18–20, 122, 129; voluntary interracial relationships labeled as, 14–15, 159n60

Rape and lynching, xv, xvi, 1–2, 158n45, 158–59n50, 171–72n70; assumed link and challenges to, 8–11, 20–22. *See also* Lynching

Raper, Arthur F.: *The Tragedy of Lynching*, 6

Reagan, Ronald, 72–73

Reasonableness: as a racialized component of self-defense claims, 80–84

Reason and common sense. *See* Common sense

Reconstruction. *See* Post-Reconstruction era

"Red Summer," 40
Reed, John Shelton, 156n26
Reid, Mark, 166n32, 168n43
Reiner, Rob, 60. *See also Ghosts of Mississippi*
Representational politics, 34, 35; antilynching movement concerned with, 3, 6
Resnick, Judith, 128
Reverse racism, 184–85n89
Rhode, Deborah L., 128
Roark, Ellen (character in *A Time to Kill*), 57–58
Roosevelt, Franklin D., 20. *See also* New Deal
Rosales, Arturo, 151n42
Rosewood: film based on race massacre, 60, 63–67
Rosewood massacre, 63–64
Ross, Susan Deller, 189n3
Roth Horowitz Gallery: *Witness* exhibit, 137
Rubin, Lillian B., 77, 176n9, 177nn18, 20
Rural modernization, xxviii–xxix
Russell, Katheryn K., 82, 180n46

Sal (character in *Do the Right Thing*), 41–45
Sandiford, Cedric, 170n55
Santayana, George, 138
Schechter, Patricia, 155nn9, 11, 14
Schudson, Michael, xxii, 150–51n30
Schumacher, Joel, 54, 54–60. *See also Time to Kill*
Schwartz, Barry, xxii, 150–51n30
Schwerner, Micahel, 173n82
Scott, Emmett J. *See Birth of a Race*
Scott, Marie: lynching of, 135
Scottsboro Nine, the, 200n23
Secrets and Lies, 33–34
September 11 attacks: and collective memories of terrorism, 146–47, 202nn27–28

Sexual harassment: as a new social and juridical concept, 111–12, 113, 126, 128–29. *See also* Hill–Thomas hearings
Sharpton, Al: role and portrayal of in the Tawana Brawley case, 93, 97–98, 105, 202n26
Shepard, Matthew: his murder regarded as a lynching, 145, 200n22
Shohat, Ella: and Robert Stam, 35, 163–64nn11–12
Signification: lynching as a "hanging signifier," 50, 141–42
Simpson, O. J.: trial of, 173n77, 186–87n123
Singleton, John, 60, 63, 64. *See also Rosewood*
Sisson, Thomas, xv, xvi, 10–11
Slave system, xxiii, 118
Slotnick, Barry: defense in the Goetz case, 78–79
Smith, Roberta, 138
Smith, Susan: her false story of a black perpetrator, xxi, 84–85, 143
Snow, David A.: and Robert D. Benford, 157n34
Social construction. *See* Racially constructed perceptions
Social movements: concerned with representational politics, 3, 6, 34, 35, 155; contesting collective consciousness, 156n34; New Social Movements, 155. *See also* Antilynching movement; Feminism
Spectacle lynchings, xvii, xx–xxiii; intended to enforce collective memory, xxvi–xxviii; during post-Reconstruction era, 2–3, 22–24; standard sequence of events, xxviii. *See also* Spectacles: racial
Spectacles: media, 111, 115; racial, xx, 69, 111, 112, 142–43
Specter, Arlen, 124, 128
Stacy, Rubin: lynching of, 26

Stereotypes (racial), xxvi; of the
criminal black man, 3, 74–77,
81–84, 85, 86, 90, 93, 94–98, 108,
180–81n49; of the welfare queen,
123, 195n60

"Strange fruit," 51

Stuart, Carol, 84

Stuart, Charles: falsely charging a
black perpetrator, xi, 84, 85–87,
143

Sturken, Marita: on cultural memory,
xxi–xxii, 150n24, 163n3, 202n28

Subway vigilante. *See* Goetz,
Bernhard

Sununu, John, 119

Sylvia Landry (character in *Within
Our Gates*), 38–39, 167n37

Symbol of the Unconquered, The, 38

Tanny (character in *Just Cause*), 51,
52, 53

Tawana Brawley case: accusation
against white males in, 91–93,
189n142; media portrayal of
Tawana Brawley, 98–99, 100–101;
Pagones's defamation suit, 91, 98,
103; perceptions of her credibility differing by race, 101–2, 143;
perspectives on medical evidence
differing by race, 106–7

Taylor, Fannie, 65–66

Terrorism: post-9/11 reconstruction
of, 146–47, 202nn27–28; racial
terrorism, 2, 3, 14, 38, 82, 145–46

Thomas, Clarence, 121, 123, 131,
192n19, 194–95n56; claiming
he was the victim of a "high-
tech lynching," xv, xx, xxx–xxxi,
111, 112, 113, 114–16, 133, 135,
143–45, 149n6, 190nn5, 6, 7,
193n43; focus on his body, 119,
120; his anti–affirmative action
stance, 120–21, 194n51; his race
not an obstacle to his nomina-

tion, 121–22; his repudiation of
his sister's welfare dependency,
123, 195n60; strategic focus on
his biography and character in
the hearing, 119–20, 123, 128–29.
See also Hill–Thomas hearing

Thomas, Kendall, 99

Thunderheart, 173n82

Till, Emmet, 62, 174n86, 191n10

Tillman, Ben, 10, 160n75

Time to Kill, A, 50, 54–55, 56, 68; race
reversal themes in, 55, 58–60;
reversal of the lynching narrative
in, 55–57

To Kill a Mockingbird, 40–41, 51,
164n13

Tolnay, Stewart E., and E. M. Beck:
on the history of Southern lynching, xxiv–xxv, 151n40

Tonya (character in *A Time to Kill*),
55–56

Torture, 116, 117, 191–92n19

Totenberg, Nina, 127

Townsend, Robert, 168n43

Urban League (New York), 79–80

Vélez-Ibáñez, Carlos, 151n42

Vendryes, Margaret, 157n32

Vigilante justice, 56, 79–80; frontier
justice, 151n37; legal and moral
issue of "reasonableness," 80–82;
lynch mobs, 152n47, 200n23;
posses, 152n47

Vigilante Task Force (New York City
Police Department), 70, 72

Violence. *See* Imagined violence;
Lynching; Police brutality;
Racialized violence

Virginian, The, 168n42

Wachtler, Sol: writing decision in the
subway vigilante case, 80–82. *See
also* Common sense; Reasonableness

Waldrep, Christopher, 149n8
Walker, Alice: "Advancing Luna—
    and Ida B. Wells," 131–32,
    197n105
Walker, Lee, 25
Ward, Benjamin, 73–74
"Welfare queen" stereotype, 123,
    195n60
Wells, Ida B.: challenging myth of
    the black rapist, 12–15, 39, 159n52,
    197n93; discourse against lynch-
    ing, 15; on the racially constructed
    perceptions of rape, 18–20; *A Red
    Record*, 1–2, 4, 6, 155n14, 162n86;
    Southern Horrors, 15, 20
Wendy Crow (film character), 33
White, Hayden, 149n10, 190n7
White, Walter, 11–12
White fear. *See* Racialized fear
Whiteness: as a form of property,
    83–84
White supremacy: contemporary,
    140–41; lynching a reinforcement
    of, xvi, 2–3, 46, 115, 199n12
White women: and chivalry, 15;
    complicity in lynching narra-
    tive, 17; role in the antilynching

movement, 6, 15–18, 29, 156n26,
    162–63n96; as victims in lynching
    narratives, 15; white womanhood,
    22. *See also* ASWPL
Wiegman, Robyn: on common
    features of lynching, xxiii–xxiv,
    115, 118; on the Hill–Thomas
    hearings, 193n43; on lynching and
    castration, 48–49, 153n56
Wilkins, David, 125–26
Williams, Patricia, 115, 116, 177n22,
    186n108, 191n12
Wilson, Christopher, 145, 201n25
Wilson, James Q., 180n46
Wilson, Woodrow, 36
Winant, Howard. *See* Omi, Michael,
    and Howard Winant
Winfrey, Oprah, 174n86
Within Our Gates. See Micheaux,
    Oscar
Without Sanctuary exhibit, 137–41
Wright, Richard, 140–41, 153n54

Zangrando, Robert L., 29
Zelizer, Barbie: on collective memory,
    xxi–xxii, 154n62; on remembrance
    of atrocities, 138–39

Jonathan Markovitz is a lecturer in sociology at the University of California, San Diego. He has published articles on race relations in the United States, collective memory, film, gender, and popular culture. His current research involves an investigation of racially based self-defense claims in criminal trials.